An
ENCOUNTER
—— WITH ——
HISTORY

THE 98TH DIVISION (INSTITUTIONAL TRAINING)   THE GLOBAL WAR ON TERRORISM, 2001-2005

Copyright © 2006 Edited by LTC Timothy J. Hansen and SGM Jocene D. Preston.

Published in the United States by Evolution Impressions.

Printed in the United States of America.

Library of Congress Cataloging-in-Publication Data

Main entry under title:

An Encounter with History.
The 98th Division (IT) and the Global War on Terrorism: 2001-2006.

p.   cm.

ISBN 0-16-076157-3

1. United States—History.   2. History, Military.   3. United States Army Reserve

I. Hansen, Timothy J.   II. Preston, Jocene D.   III. Title.

For sale by the Superintendent of Documents
U.S. Government Printing Office, Washington, D.C. 20402
http://bookstore.gpo.gov/

An Encounter with History

The 98th Division
and the
Global War on Terrorism:
2001-2005

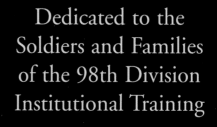

Dedicated to the
Soldiers and Families
of the 98th Division
Institutional Training

CONTENTS

98TH DIVISION (INSTITUTIONAL TRAINING)
FALLEN SOLDIER DEDICATION

On November 11, 2005, this memorial was placed at the
Rochester International Airport in dedication of the
five members of the 98th Division who were killed in action
while serving in support of Operation Iraqi Freedom.

MAY WE FOREVER REMEMBER
THE ULTIMATE SACRIFICE
OF OUR BROTHERS IN ARMS
WHILE FIGHTING FOR DEMOCRACY.

To the Iroquois Division –

On September 3, 2004, the 98th Division received mobilization orders for Operation Iraqi Freedom. This mobilization was the first overseas deployment for the unit since World War II. The mission, known as the Foreign Army Training Assistance Command (FA-TRAC), called for training the new Iraqi Army and Iraqi security forces. An expeditionary force of more than 700 Iroquois warriors were trained and equipped at four sites: Camp Atterbury, Fort Bliss, Fort Hood, and Fort Benning.

Looking back to the World War II era, the 98th Division mobilized in September 1942 at Camp Breckinridge, Kentucky, located 157 miles southwest from Camp Atterbury. For nearly a year, the 98th trained in all aspects of warfighting—from marksmanship to fortification construction—on the expansive 52,000 acres of Camp Breckinridge. It was a trying time for many, but the 98th hardened its warrior soul for the privations of war.

Originally shuffled into the mix for the invasion of Japan (Operation Olympic), the 98th Division, 15,000 soldiers strong, stood ready to deploy from the Hawaiian island of Maui in 1945. Japanese surrender came sooner than expected, but still the division landed on the Japanese shores of Wakayama and set itself up as an occupying force in the prefectures of Osaka, Nara, Wakayama, and Nire. The mission expanded to the demobilization of the Japanese Armed Forces, the seizure and destruction of arms and munitions, and the reallocation of supplies suitable for civilian use. The 98th accomplished all of these tasks and went a step further by building a bridge of trust and friendship with the Japanese populace, marking its place in the ranks of the "Greatest Generation."

Fast-forward to today and behold a lighter and leaner 98th Division reflagged as a training division and trimmed to 3,000 strong, but still ready to serve the needs of the nation. The demands of Operation Iraqi Freedom required an accelerated training schedule which crammed warfighting skills into forty-one days. For the first time in its history, the 98th addressed the realities of the asymmetric battlefield, training in counterinsurgency techniques and preparing to face an enemy that knows no fronts. The 98th made full use of the 33,000 acres at Camp Atterbury and marched everywhere. It was at Camp Atterbury that the Advisory Support Teams (later renamed Military Training Teams), the heart of the FA-TRAC mis-

Warrior of Yesterday and Today

sion, formed in days that began in the dark morning hours and ended well after sunset.

In fall 2004, the 98th Division landed in Baghdad and filled the ranks of the Multinational Security Transition Command-Iraq, the unit charged with assisting the Iraqi government in developing, training, and equipping the new Iraqi Army and Iraqi security forces. Unlike those who served in World War II, this generation of warriors tapped into its vast pool of drill sergeant and instructor expertise and went about the business of training Iraqi soldiers and officers to prescribed standards under the constant threat of insurgent attack and under the most Spartan of conditions. In short order, instruction and support teams spread out across all points in Iraq from Al Kasik in the north to as far south as Umm Qasr. They wasted no time in establishing contact with Iraqi security units and connected with these soldiers with the help of interpreters. These dedicated warriors helped build the six divisions of the new Iraqi Army. They also established officer and noncommissioned officer education schools at the Kirkush Military Training Base. They trained Iraqi police, the Highway Patrol, the Special Police Commandos, and the Iraqi Border Police. As with their forebears of WW II, they built

bridges of trust and friendship along the way.

The service of the 98th did not stop with FA-TRAC. The division fielded soldiers to such other diverse locations as Guantanamo Bay, Cuba, the Horn of Africa, Kuwait, Jordan, and Afghanistan. Even in these remote locations, Iroquois warriors worked and contributed to the success of the mission.

The 98th knows the cost of war. Five soldiers from its ranks died in Iraq's struggle for freedom. Their actions exemplified tremendous bravery, courage, and selflessness. They have become an inspiration to all Americans. They are the best of what American soldiers can be.

When freedom reigns once more in these oppressed lands, we will look back and realize the good that we did. Yes, the 98th was there in the fight and served with honor.

LTC Tony Morales and MSG John Compitello greet soldiers in Kuwait.

HEADQUARTERS, DEPARTMENT OF THE ARMY
98TH DIVISION (INSTITUTIONAL TRAINING)
2035 GOODMAN STREET NORTH
ROCHESTER, NEW YORK 14609-1098

REPLY TO
ATTENTION OF:

AFRC-TNY-CG

17 June 2004

MEMORANDUM FOR 98th Division (IT) Commanders and Command Sergeants Major

SUBJECT: Mobilization Alert

1. The 98th Division (IT) will continue to provide Soldiers for missions in support of our Army and, in the near future, may possibly send Soldiers overseas, within the next 100 days, to provide Foreign Army Training Assistance. That mission would help build Iraqi Armed Forces, as an element of the Office of Security Cooperation, and support the US goal of assisting Iraq re-establish national sovereignty.

2. It is imperative that we accelerate pre-mobilization training with emphasis on warrior ethos, physical fitness, weapons proficiency and MOS competency. Conduct Soldier Readiness Processing (SRP) NOW and ensure families are ready.

3. It is anticipated that the mobilizations will be phased in, over time, and may last up to 18 months. Any questions, requests for interviews, or media requests for comment will be directed to the 98th Division (IT) Headquarters, ATTN: Mr. Todd Arnold, telephone (800) 238-3138 ext. 203.

BRUCE E. ROBINSON
Major General, USAR
Commander

Thoughts from the Command

Major General
Bruce E. Robinson

Originally conceived as a combat division to bolster the American contingent in World War I, the 98th Division has served in many capacities since its inception—from a component of the Organized Reserve in the early 1920s, to an assault force in training during World War II, to an occupying force in Japan following the Second World War, and finally to a training division in the U.S. Army Reserve. Culled primarily from the northeastern United States, members of the 98th have stood ready to serve their nation, in peace and war, for nearly ninety years.

The 98th Division (IT)'s involvement in the Global War on Terrorism commenced immediately after the September 11, 2001 attacks on America, as some of our soldiers were in the vicinity of the World Trade Center and the Pentagon. Others were first responders or aided in rescue and recovery efforts. The Global War on Terrorism is America's first protracted war fought exclusively by an all-volunteer force. The Army Reserve is an integral part of this war effort and has transitioned from a strategic reserve to an operational reserve. Inherent in our capability is the individual training of soldiers. As a result, the 98th Division was tasked to develop the means to export our expertise overseas.

The concept of a Foreign Army Training Assistance Command (FA-TRAC) progressed to an operational mission in the short span of four months with the 98th Division taking the lead role. Elements of the 98th Division were mobilized on September 11, 2004, trained at Fort Bliss, Texas, and Camp Atterbury, Indiana, and deployed to Iraq to perform the FA-TRAC mission. Thus we helped lay the foundation for the building of a new Iraqi Army and security forces. In addition to the FA-TRAC mission in Iraq, our soldiers have been deployed to Afghanistan, Ethiopia, Jordan, Kuwait, and elsewhere.

This book is but a brief chapter in the Global War on Terrorism and a glimpse of the contributions of our valiant Iroquois Warriors during operations Enduring Freedom and Iraqi Freedom. It is dedicated to the magnificent soldiers of America's Army, the Army Reserve, the Iroquois Warriors of the 98th Division, and our families and employers.

We are eternally indebted to and will always remember and honor our Fallen Comrades: SGT Lawrence Roukey, MSG Paul Karpowich, SSG Christopher Dill, LTC Terrence Crowe, and SFC Robert Derenda.

Command Sergeant Major
William A. Grocott

In April 2004, the 98th Division (IT) was tasked to plan and implement a new initiative called the Foreign Army Training Assistance Command (FA-TRAC). It seemed to be the right choice; after all, the 98th is a training division that builds and develops soldiers at all levels, from basic training to officer and noncommissioned officer professional development, and we are good at our jobs.

During predeployment training conducted at Camp Atterbury, Indiana, and Fort Bliss, Texas, the 98th embraced new members who came from other units and the Inactive Ready Reserve. These soldiers trained alongside their brothers and sisters of the Iroquois Warrior Division, laying the foundation for teams that would work together for the next twelve months. After weeks of preparation, the soldiers of the 98th, both new and veteran, were ready to deploy to theater.

As our soldiers began to meet mission requirements in Iraq, Kuwait, and Jordan, several things happened—they enhanced the original mission with their professional job performance, took on greater responsibilities, and put their civilian job skills and knowledge to use in ways not envisioned by the original personnel plans.

In April 2005, Major General Robinson and I visited many of our soldiers in theater. We watched them in action as they trained and mentored Iraqi soldiers and performed the day-to-day tasks of managing the Multi-National Security Command-Iraq, the unit which oversaw the training and equipping of the new Iraqi Army and security forces. We were duly impressed by the hard work and personal courage demonstrated by our soldiers in accomplishing their historic mission.

Unfortunately, the mission in Iraq was not without personal sacrifice and loss. Five of our soldiers were killed in action, and several others were injured or wounded. We will never forget our fallen comrades. Their lives and accomplishments were a tribute to the first three precepts of the Warrior Ethos—*I will always place the mission first; I will never accept defeat; I will never quit.*

My compliments to the outstanding soldiers of the 98th Division—your dedication and performance far exceeded what was initially planned for, and you are all truly professional soldiers with whom I am extremely proud to serve.

Brigadier General
Richard A. Sherlock

The pages that follow contain a brief overview of the accomplishments and the wartime experiences of the soldiers of the 98th Division (Institutional Training) during their historic mission in support of Operation Iraqi Freedom. Our mission (which included support for the Multi-National Force-Iraq, the Multi-National Security Transition Command-Iraq, and the Multi-National Corps-Iraq) was the first large-scale deployment of 98th Division soldiers for combat operations in a war zone in the division's history, and it was the first overseas deployment of 98th Division soldiers since World War II.

We mobilized, trained, and deployed more than 740 Iroquois Warriors to Iraq, including those soldiers who came to the 98th Division from the Individual Ready Reserve and other Army Reserve units. I am extremely proud of the performance and dedication of each and every soldier. Your achievements were outstanding and your record was brilliant. No soldiers or units anywhere in our army could have surpassed your performance as you were mobilized and deployed, on short notice, to support a mission whose requirements changed rapidly. It was an extraordinary privilege for me to have served with you as the senior Iroquois Warrior in Iraq.

Your accomplishments cannot be overstated as each of you contributed directly to the rebuilding of capable and battle-tested Iraqi security forces. Over the course of our deployment, these forces became capable of providing safety and security for their families, their cities, and their nation as they emerged from decades of tyranny under the rule of a despicable regime that killed hundreds of thousands of its own citizens and invaded two of its neighbors.

Five of our fellow soldiers made the ultimate sacrifice during our mission. This book is dedicated in their honor, to their memory, and to the price that was and continues to be paid by their families.

It would be remiss to not recognize the contributions of the entire 98th Division and all of our soldiers who remained in the United States. They supported our forces in Iraq and continued to perform our full slate of institutional training missions while we were gone. We also need to recognize and thank our families and friends, who supported us down range, and also our employers, who supported the nation and our army by looking after us and our families during the deployment. We could not have performed our mission without them.

Brigadier General
Sanford E. Holman

Only time will tell how the history of the Global War on Terrorism is written, but no matter what is recorded, the narrative will undoubtedly include a discussion of the 98th Division's Iroquois Warriors and their deeds in support of Operation Iraqi Freedom.

Between fall 2004 and early 2005, more than 700 soldiers of the 98th Division deployed to Iraq, where they were assigned to the Multi-National Security Transition Command-Iraq (MNSTC-I). MNSTC-I, whose mission was to rebuild, equip, and train Iraq's security forces, had three major elements. First was the Coalition Military Assistance Training Team, which was responsible for organizing, equipping, and advising the Iraqi Armed Forces (IAF). Second was the Joint Headquarters Advisory Support Team, which assisted the Joint Headquarters of the IAF in developing an effective command and control system that enabled Iraqi military leadership to conduct joint operational planning, deployment, and redeployment of the IAF, and provided strategic military advice to the national government. Third was the Civilian Police Assistance Training Team, which was tasked with organizing, training, equipping, and mentoring the Iraqi civilian police and border forces, and with monitoring, advising, and certifying Iraq's Facilities Protection Service.

Midway through the 98th Division's deployment, many Iroquois Warriors were reassigned to Multi-National Corps-Iraq (MNC-I), the tactical unit that was responsible for overall combat operations in Iraq and was partnered with the Iraqi security forces in fighting the insurgency. In other words, Iroquois Warriors along with their cross-leveled and Inactive Ready Reserve comrades in arms were at the tip of the spear, working diligently and courageously with MNC-I and the Iraqi security forces to combat the insurgency.

Although the successful Iraqi elections of January 30, 2005, can be seen as a major highlight of the mission in Iraq, many other great deeds were also accomplished. However, these deeds came at a high cost as five Iroquois Warriors made the ultimate sacrifice. All Iroquois Warriors, their families, and their friends can take great pride in the accomplishment of this historic mission. May God continue to bless the 98th Division and may God bless America.

Colonel
Frank A. Cipolla

I will never forget July 4th, 2004, the day I departed the United States for Iraq along with the FA-TRAC advance team. Lieutenant Colonel Phil McGrath, Captain Ramin Dilfanian, and I made up that contingent. Little did I know how much I would come to respect the sweat, suffering, and sacrifice of not only the soldiers of the 98th Division, but of all soldiers committed to Iraq's struggle for independence and freedom.

We first set up operations at the Presidential Palace in Baghdad. Our primary task was to coordinate reception and integration of the 98th Division's Advisory Support Teams (ASTs) and support personnel due to arrive in the fall. By the time our soldiers arrived, I was working as the director of the Command and Control cell in Taji. Colonel Larry Kelly, Colonel Jody Daniels, Major Ann Pellien, and Master Sergeant Brian Kramer were stellar in assisting me with the numerous staff assignments and in the reception and air movement of our ASTs. Under the cover of darkness, the Chinooks and Black Hawks flew our teams to the remote reaches of the country. My heart was with each of them as I stood and watched them depart into the night.

Once the training mission was fully underway, I returned to the 98th Division Headquarters to work as the division chief of staff in January 2005 and to prepare for the return of our troops later in the year. It was also my good fortune to travel with Major General Robinson at this time to meet and speak with our Iroquois warrior families from Saco, Maine to Paducah, Kentucky. Whenever I informed them of their soldiers' hard work in Iraq, their faces reflected an incredible pride.

At the Veterans Day ceremony held in Rochester, my head sank to my chest when Chaplain Womack prayerfully spoke the names of our five fallen soldiers: Sergeant Larry Roukey, Master Sergeant Paul Karpowich, Staff Sergeant Christopher Dill, Lieutenant Colonel Terrence Crowe, and Sergeant First Class Bob Derenda. May we always honor them in our formations and in our hearts.

In fall 2005, we celebrated the return of our soldiers with Welcome Home Warrior ceremonies. A deep sense of pride and awe overwhelmed me whenever I glanced at our soldiers and their families during these gatherings. At the conclusion of the last ceremony, I realized we are now home.

Colonel
Michael R. Smith

Establishing and maintaining internal security for an entire country is a daunting task even for a fully trained, equipped, and experienced police force. Add to the mix an active insurgency, and the mission becomes something of a Herculean effort. In the case of Iraq, this mission falls upon the Ministry of Interior and its more than 250,000 security, police, and border forces, many of whom are new to the job.

Under the direction of the Multi-National Security Transition Command-Iraq, the Civilian Police Assistance Training Team (CPATT) was tasked to help develop the Ministry of Interior (MOI) and its security services. This includes recruiting, training, equipping, coaching, and sustaining the Iraqi Police Service, Border Police, Special Police Commandos, Facilities Protection Service, Major Crimes Unit, and the National Investigation and Intelligence Agency.

More than forty soldiers from the 98th Division, representing nearly 50 percent of CPATT's assigned strength, formed the backbone of the unit as it stood up in 2004. As the CPATT chief of staff, I am involved in all aspects of the command and its objectives to train and equip the MOI forces. When the soldiers of the 98th first arrived in theater, the Special Police Forces were comprised of about 3,000 members who were loosely organized and poorly trained— they were marginally able to conduct company-level missions with coalition support. Today, the Special Police Forces total more than 22,000 professionals organized as a Commando Division, a Public Order Division and a Mechanized Police Brigade. These forces have come a long way in the past year. They recently deployed as a combined Special Police Brigade task force and successfully planned and executed a complex mission with minimal coalition support. As of November 2005, we trained more than 110,000 police, with the balance of MOI forces to be trained and equipped by early 2007.

98th Division soldiers, LTC George Crowell, COL Mike Smith and
1SG Thomas Pennington.

MOI forces also played an integral role in democratizing Iraq, as demonstrated by their performance in establishing security during the January 2005 elections. Coalition Forces drafted and directed the security plans for the first Iraqi elections in Januray 2005. For both the National Referendum in November and the second National Elections in December 2005, it was the Iraqi MOI that drafted and directed the security plans. The role of Coalition Forces had become one of providing logistical support. On an increasing basis, the MOI has taken the lead in planning and executing security missions through Iraq, a trend that will continue through 2006 and beyond.

In closing, I'd like to thank my fellow Iroquois Warriors of CPATT for the outstanding job they did in Iraq. Every 98th Division soldier left a lasting impression on the country's fledgling democracy. The leadership and determination of our soldiers were an inspiration to not only the Iraqi police but also to the CPATT family.

"It is not the critic who counts: not the man who points out how the strong man stumbles or where the doer of deeds could have done better.

The credit belongs to the man who is actually in the arena, whose face is marred by dust and sweat and blood, who strives valiantly, who errs and comes up short again and again, because there is no effort without error or shortcoming, but who knows the great enthusiasms, the great devotions, who spends himself for a worthy cause;

who at the best, and who at the worst, if he fails, at least he shall never be with those cold and timid souls who knew neither victory nor defeat."

Theodore Roosevelt

Colonel
Robert G. Catalanotti

This past year and a half has been an amazing journey for the 98th Division, and it has been an incredible honor for me to have been a part of it. The adventure began on September 11, 2004, as my wife Karen and I shook hands with many of the deploying soldiers of the 98th as they boarded flights to Camp Atterbury, Indiana, and Fort Bliss, Texas, where they would begin training and processing for deployment to Iraq. After many hugs and handshakes, I boarded a flight the following day and arrived at Camp Atterbury to take on the critical mission of preparing our soldiers

COL Catalanotti introduces GEN Casey in Taji.

emotionally, physically, and academically to enter an active war zone. After three intense months in Indiana, I was selected to go forward to Iraq, and said good-bye to the highly energetic staff at Atterbury, including Major Sherrie Lowther, Sergeant Major Jocene Preston, and Master Sergeant Reneé Leblanc, who had worked tirelessly preparing our soldiers for deployment.

Upon arrival in Baghdad, I was given the incredible opportunity to command Taji, the largest military training base in Iraq, where I was responsible for more than 15,000 Iraqi soldiers, almost 500 Coalition forces and hundreds of private contractors. I was also fortunate as a commander to have the very best leaders assigned to my command, including Lieutenant Colonel Mike Corriveault, Command Sergeant Major Milton Newsome, Major Mike Floru, Lieutenant Colonel Teresa Baginski, Lieutenant Colonel Phil McGrath, and Colonel Bob Lawless. The list goes on of the many outstanding 98th Division leaders assigned to Taji: Chaplain David Pillsbury, Captain Stacey O'Keefe, Master Sergeant Brian Kramer, Captain Adam Davidson, Captain Bob Devito, Captain Scott Demers, First Lieutenant Bill Gritsavage, and many others.

Departing Taji at the end of the tour was an emotional experience. I had become very attached to my soldiers and my Iraqi counterparts, specifically Colonel Abbas, the Iraqi base commander. He and I had developed a strong professional and personal relationship, to the point where I had visited his family several times in Baghdad. He insisted on a regular basis to talk with my wife and children in broken English when I would call home by satellite phone. After leaving Taji, there were many days that I would wonder what the future would hold for Iraqi leaders and their families. Even after several months, many Iraqi leaders continue to e-mail me regularly. On New Year's Day, for example, I received more than fifteen e-mails from many Iraqis wishing my family peace and happiness.

COL Catalanotti and COL Abbas at South Gate, Highway 1, Taji.

My experiences in Iraq will always be a highlight of my life. I am very proud of all the soldiers who deployed to Iraq and the many who were stateside operating our Army Reserve centers and meeting the division's other critical missions. My family and I will eternally memorialize our five fallen comrades who made the ultimate sacrifice for our precious liberties. We will never forget these brave warriors! Seeing all of our soldiers at the welcome home ceremonies made a lasting impression on me and has allowed me to bring some closure to the deployment.

Taji Team with phone cards from home.

Colonel
Bradford J. Parsons

The Iroquois Warriors of the 98th Division (IT) participated in the writing of history as they mobilized, trained, and deployed to Iraq under Operation Iraqi Freedom in fall 2004. The 98th Division, which had not been mobilized since World War II, transformed from an institutional training division geared toward a Cold War combat scenario to a unit capable of operating at the tip of the spear in the Global War on Terrorism. The mission in Iraq was to help train a new Iraqi Army capable of defeating the insurgency and offering greater stability to the Iraqi people. The mission and the challenges it presented were truly daunting, but well suited for the warriors of the 98th.

During the deployment, the 98th Division was tasked to staff the headquarters of the Multi-National Security Transition Command-Iraq, the Coalition Military Assistance Training Team, and the Civilian Police Assistance Training Team, and work as embedded Advisory Support Team trainers with the divisions of the new Iraqi Army. Soldiers of the 98th worked diligently and professionally during the

COL Parsons and interpreter.

year-long deployment, giving the Iroquois Division well-deserved recognition as a mission-capable and professional unit. Among other accomplishments, the division earned this level of recognition by the efforts its soldiers put forth in mentoring the Iraqi Security Forces as they provided security for the successful elections of January 30, 2005. Unfortunately, the 98th Division's respect came with a heavy price, as five of our fellow soldiers made the ultimate sacrifice in the conduct of the mission.

The deployment to Iraq provides a valuable lesson to both current and future Iroquois Warriors of the 98th Division. Every soldier needs to clearly understand his or her responsibilities and maintain an ever-ready state of preparedness. This includes performing warrior tasks, improving mental and physical conditioning, and remaining flexible in accomplishing the mission. Our soldiers, their families, and family support organizations have met the hardships and challenges of this mission. May God continue to bless the Iroquois Warriors of the 98th Division, their families, and the United States of America.

Chaplain (Colonel)
James P. Womack

The first inkling things were afoot for the 98th Division came in late spring 2004 when Major General Robinson asked me to prepare a plan for religious support in locations overseas and in the United States. At the time, I was serving a tour at Fort Dix, New Jersey, supporting mobilization efforts. After witnessing the emotional extremes of heartbreaking departures and joyful reunions of soldiers and families, I resolved to increase the religious support capabilities of the 98th as its deployment became more apparent. The plan decided upon provided for the general's guidance, and by the time mobilization occurred we had three chaplains and four assistants assigned to the mobilization roster.

I deployed from Fort Bliss, Texas, on September 17, 2004, and after the initial few days in Kuwait arrived at Taji, a military base north of Baghdad. At Taji, I went about—and when joined by chaplain assistant Sergeant First Class Neil Hertzler—setting up a chapel and preparing religious-support operations. Significant memories include the chapel and a congregation of U.S. Army, Navy, Marine Corps, and Air Force personnel, a pulpit constructed by Sergeant First Class Hertzler from old ammunition crates, the distri-

bution of Moon Pies sent from Chattanooga, Tennessee, and coffee from Tim Horton's in Buffalo, New York, walking or jogging inside the compound, a trip to the International Zone to participate in a memorial service for Staff Sergeant Todd R. Cornell from Wisconsin, and getting up on the roof of the "Alamo" to see where all the "booms" were coming from. One of my memories is of Captain Charles Green, an active-duty Advisory Support Team (AST) member, suggesting I take a weapon for protection. I tried hard to explain that chaplains were noncombatants and did not carry weapons; he kept protesting my rationale, arguing I was rather "old" to be walking around the place without a weapon. I could not disagree about the "old" part!

After three months in Iraq, I returned stateside to assume rear-detachment religious support. As a result, I attended many family readiness meetings, and was on the phone trying to work issues soldiers had from overseas, offering reassurances that things would be all right in due time. I also had the sad duty to help inform three of our families of the deaths of their sons and, in one case, husband, in actions in Iraq. We arranged religious support for the demobilization activities and set about preparing for marriage-enrichment seminars. In fact, religious support needs continued past demobilization and continue even now as our division's religious-support personnel seek to provide pastoral care and religious support to soldiers and family members who are in the readjustment phase.

It is very difficult to assess the value of many of our efforts. That is as true for chaplains and chaplain assistants as it is for AST members. It is honest to say that our soldiers did their duties as best they could, stateside and overseas, in the midst of difficult circumstances. I will forever be indebted to the absolutely heroic work of Chaplain (Colonel) Gary Howard who traveled all over Iraq to visit virtually every location that had a 98th Division soldier assigned to it, to Master Sergeant Neil Hertzler for his steadfast loyalty as my assistant, to Chaplain (Lieutenant Colonel) David Pillsbury for his preparatory work stateside and his assumption of my work at Taji, to Sergeant Nick Trumble for his work with Chaplain Howard, and to Sergeant Ryan Haggerty, chaplain assistant and convoy team member! I am indebted to our Unit Ministry Team deployed in Qatar: Chaplain (Major)

Walter Steenson and Staff Sergeant Howard Crosby. Chaplain (Major) Robert Searle was available at home and used his experiences from his deployment to Operation Iraqi Freedom (OIF) in 2003-2004. I am grateful to Chaplain (Lieutenant Colonel) William Pihl, Chaplain (Lieutenant Colonel) Simon Feld, and Chaplain (Lieutenant Colonel) Linda Liebhart, OIF veteran, Master Sergeant Margaret Murray, and Sergeant First Class Robert Matthews for their support to families and soldiers at home. All served in a variety of ways, whenever asked or when they saw a need.

I do believe in a creative spirit in this universe that ever works for good. Our prayers at Taji usually began with this line: *New every morning is your love, great God of light, and all day long you are working for good in the world. Stir up in us desire to serve you and to live peacefully with our neighbors.*

Out of such faith grew the selfless service of our religious personnel. I end with two of our favorite sayings from Taji:

"Today ain't yesterday," and

"It's going to be okay."

Pro Deo et patria,

Chaplain (Colonel) James P. Womack

AFRC-TNY-JA   17 July 2004

INFORMATION PAPER

SUBJECT: Department of the Army (DA) Alert Order 549-04 ONE/OEF/OIF

PURPOSE: To provide guidance to members of the 98th Division (IT) concerning Alert order 549-04.

REFERENCES:

    a. Alert Order 549-04 ONE/OEF/OIF
    b. MILPER Message Number: 03-041, "RC Unit Stop Loss Procedures for the Army Reserve"

INFORMATION:

On 16 July 2004, the Department of the Army issued Alert Order 549-04 ONE/OEF/OIF to the 98th Division (IT). At this time, no information is available regarding the specific operation (if any) that the 98th Division (IT) will be assigned.

This alert notification **does not** necessarily mean that Soldiers of the 98th Division (IT) will be mobilized. An alert order **does not** constitute an order to mobilize. Units can be alerted and never called to active duty. Alert Order 549-04 simply means that the 98th Division (IT) must prepare for a **possible** mobilization.

Alert Order 549-04 does mean that Soldiers of the 98th Division (IT) must work to get their personal affairs in order to be ready for any future mobilization. Aside from this preparation, Soldiers of the 98th Division (IT) should continue their normal routines.

As part of Alert Order 549-04, stop-loss is now in effect for the 98th Division (IT). Stop-loss commences upon the issuance of the alert order and continues through the period of mobilization until 90 days after demobilization. Stop-loss does not effect most involuntary separations or mandatory retirements.

CONCLUSION:

Alert Order 549-04 does not automatically mean that Soldiers of the 98th Division (IT) will be mobilized. Alert Orders are issued as part of prudent planning to ensure that a unit is prepared for an actual activation. Soldiers of the 98th Division (IT) should use this time to get their personal affairs in order to be ready for possible future mobilization. Aside from this preparation, Soldiers of the 98th Division (IT) should continue their normal routines.

OSJA/98th Div(IT)/ext.253

Mission Index

Afghanistan

In a country of nearly thirty million and only about the size of Texas, the U.S.-led coalition continues to provide security, train the Afghan National Army and field the startlingly successful Provincial Reconstruction Teams throughout the country. 98th Division soldiers assigned to Operation Enduring Freedom contributed to the mission in the areas of Civil Affairs, training, and logistics.

Cuba

The actual focus of the world on this Caribbean island is the U. S. Naval Base at Guantanamo Bay located on the island's southeastern side. As the site of the detention center for al-Qaeda and Taliban suspects, media interest increased significantly on the handling of these detainees. Under the glare of scrutiny, the 98th Division soldiers with skills in law enforcement and interrogation contributed significantly to this delicate mission.

The Horn of Africa
Eritrea and Ethiopia

The U. S. presence in the Horn of Africa assures continued regional stability. After thirty years of armed conflict, Eritrea emerged from the oppressive grip of Ethiopia as an independent state in 1991. Both countries warred again over a border dispute for two years and ended their fighting in 2000 at a cost of 80,000 lives. The U.N. Mission in Ethiopia and Eritrea maintains the fragile peace and promotes resolution to the differences of each country. The 98th participated in this peacekeeping mission by answering the need for military observers.

ERITREA

★ Asmara

Nile

Addis
Ababa ★

ETHIOPIA

Prov.
Admin.
Line

Iraq

After three years of conflict in Iraq, the U.S. and its coalition allies remain committed to this country's independence and freedom. In the shadow of a brilliantly-executed invasion, coalition forces immediately focused on establishing a democratic country capable of defending itself. Several soldiers from the 98th joined the security and rebuilding efforts in the months following the invasion. The division's presence in Iraq culminated with the training of the fledgling Iraqi Army under the mission of the Foreign Army Training Assistance Command. Amidst the bitter hostilities of a rising insurgency, over seven hundred soldiers from the 98th worked in vital staff and training positions within the Multi-National Security Transition Command-Iraq.

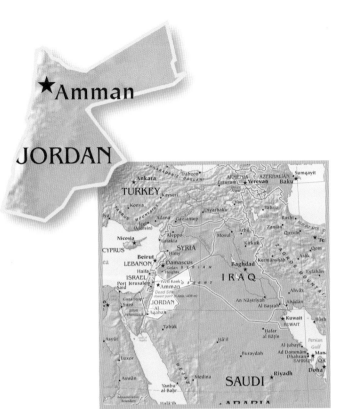

Jordan

Recognizing the importance of stability and security in the Middle East, the Hashemite Kingdom of Jordan quietly assists the coalition effort by providing resources for police training, refurbishing of aircraft and transporting equipment and personnel into Iraq. Because of these increased activities, the 98th answered the coalition's need for a liaison officer to address the details of vendor contracts and payments, visas, and briefing VIPs.

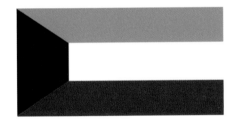

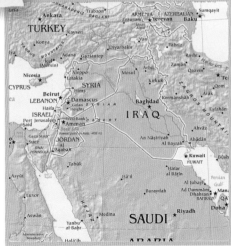

Kuwait

Directly south of Iraq, Kuwait has served as the staging and support platform for much of Operation Iraqi Freedom. The Combined Forces Land Component Command's array of logistical bases sustains the coalition forces in Iraq. A team of support soldiers from the 98th played a key role in coordinating training, transportation and equipment for the FA-TRAC mission.

"Efforts to deter an adversary–
be it an aggressor nation,
terrorist group or criminal organization–
can become the leading edge of crisis response...
Deterrence in crisis generally involves
demonstrating the United States' commitment
to a particular country or interest by enhancing
our warfighting capability in the theater."

A National Security Strategy for a Global Age
December 2000

September 11, 2001
and the
Days Following

In the Morning of 9/11

Had Gregory Hunt of Pittsford been in another part of the Pentagon when the plane struck, he might have died that day.

Nonetheless, he resists thinking of himself as a survivor.

"People who were in the thick of the fire and the explosion, they were the survivors," says Hunt, 56, a brigadier general and assistant division commander of the 98th Division of the Army Reserve on Goodman Street North in Rochester.

But as he describes what happened, it is clear that Hunt was far closer than anyone would ever want to be to the attack that took 189 lives at the Pentagon—125 in the building and 64 on the plane.

Hunt was in a meeting at the Pentagon when he heard of the attacks on the Twin Towers. He and others then stayed where they were rather than take a scheduled break.

At 9:40 a.m., the plane hit near the area where they were supposed to have gone for a break. There was a blast and the building shook. Hunt thought a bomb had gone off.

With others, he headed for an exit — an exit that was stuck, damaged by the blast, until two Marines opened it with the force of their bodies. Hunt emerged from the building to see the smoke, the flames, the strewn airplane parts. "It was horrific," he says.

Photo by Will Yurman

Major General Gregory Hunt

Amid the chaos, people in Rochester who knew that Hunt was at the Pentagon were frantic.

Hunt was in a meeting at the Pentagon when he heard of the attacks on the Twin Towers.

"When the plane hit, my heart sunk," says his daughter, Marilee Taylor, 35, of Victor. "I was worried and hysterical."

Outside the building, Hunt helped people get out of danger.

He thinks now that this activity may have shielded him from the agonies of the morning.

"We were too busy," he says. "We were pretty much occupied with the event. Your training sets in."

Hunt, vice president in charge of operations at Time Warner Cable in Rochester, has returned to the Pentagon four times since September 11. The first time was in December. By then, the rubble had been cleared away.

"It was amazing to see," he says. "Inside the Pentagon there were hundreds and hundreds of

By Jim Memmott
Democrat and Chronicle
Wednesday, September 11, 2002 • Reprinted with permission.

letters and posters written by people around the world."

This kind of concern and support for the military was no surprise to Hunt.

"I happened to walk into a McDonald's a week after September 11," he says. "I was with a gentleman and we were both in uniform. Two families with six or seven kids came up and wanted to shake our hands."

While he has been in a constant military mode since then, Hunt worries that the country may not be thinking enough of September 11 and this country's enemies.

There are times when Hunt is surprised by disturbing memories of September 11, though he doesn't think he has experienced post-traumatic stress.

In talking about his muted reaction, Hunt says he feels a little removed from himself, almost as if he were watching himself in a film.

Nonetheless, he senses he was changed by the experience.

"Not in ways that are obvious," says Hunt, who has three children and three grandchildren. "But I think I spend a lot more time thinking about family issues and grandkids and kids.... . When you've been close to leaving, you tend to look at the big picture. I think I've become a little

more mellow."

Taylor sees the changes, too.

"I see a more sensitive side of him, especially with the grandchildren," she says. "He's very aware of their birthdays, their special events."

Since leaving the 98th Division, Major General Hunt took command of the Kentucky-based 100th Division (Institutional Training) in 2003. With more than 5,000 soldiers in Minnesota, Wisconsin, Michigan, Illinois, Indiana, Ohio, Tennessee, and Kentucky, the 100th Division plays a major role in providing training and education in various military occupational specialties and professional development schools. During the 98th Division's deployment to Iraq, the 100th Division provided additional soldiers to fill critical training and support positions within the Multi-National Security Transition Command-Iraq and its subordinate units.

The Stand Against Terror

There are few who would choose to handle back-to-back missions of a colossal security operation for an international event such as the Olympic Games followed by a highly visible, wartime detainee operation in a remote corner of the world, but Colonel John Perrone, former 98th Division Chief of Staff of Personnel, did just that.

"I received orders to active duty in April 2001," Colonel Perrone recalled matter-of-factly from his director's office at the Homeland Security Management Institute in Rochester, New York. Colonel Perrone worked as the Force Protection Antiterrorism Chief at the 2002 Salt Lake City Winter Olympics. For him, it was the perfect combination of his law enforcement skills from his work in the Monroe County Sheriff's Department and his command-and-staff skills as a senior Army officer.

Assigned to the Joint Task Force Olympics (JTF-O) which fell under the Joint Forces Command, Colonel Perrone worked out of the Utah National Guard Headquarters in Salt Lake City. Responsible for soldiers from active-duty, Guard, and Reserve units, he had the unenviable distinction of reporting to two general officers: Major General Brian L. Tarbet, adjutant general for the state of Utah, and Brigadier General James D. Johnson, commander of JTF-O.

2002 Olympic Venue.

COL John Perrone.

With the naming of this Winter Olympics as a National Special Security Event in 1999, federal law required the Department of Defense to assist with the event's overall security. In those waning summer months of 2001, Colonel Perrone met with other agency directors and integrated military units and equipment into JTF-O. Even with no apparent threat on the horizon, planning and preparation were still necessary for a military force to be available and to handle the unexpected.

When the unexpected happened on September 11th, life in the United States would never be the same. For Salt Lake City, the Winter Olympics hung precariously in the balance. Would the athletes come to compete? Would tourists fill the hotels and dine at its restaurants? Many wondered just what would happen.

"The governor of Utah made the Winter Olympics his top priority," Colonel Perrone commented. Indeed, Utah had invested nearly two billion dollars into the winter games since receiving its designation from the International Olympic Committee in 1995. "All of us were relieved when we heard the president pledge his support to make the games a complete success," he continued. In the eyes of the world, these Olympic Games would come to serve as a test for American resolve and commitment to establish a Homeland Security impervious to the destructive impulses of terrorists and saboteurs.

Almost overnight, the security operation of the games grew exponentially in funding and complexity. By the time the games ended, security costs alone would exceed $300 million. The obscure Utah Olympic Public Safety Command (UOPSC) experienced a similar transformation and now became the focal point for all security operations.

Acting under the guidelines of Presidential Decision Directive 62, the U.S. Secret Service, FBI, and FEMA rolled into town, set up their field headquarters, and worked with the UOPSC. In time, a total of fifteen federal agencies joined the security effort and hooked into the communication lines of this command. This formidable integration of local, state, and federal resources set a benchmark as the first homeland defense operation in the United States. Gradually, the Winter Olympics became more certain in the minds of the media and the public. Utah governor Mike Leavitt recognized this enthusiasm, but mindful of the terrorist threat, commented, "Our efforts can only go to minimize, not eliminate risk."

In the weeks leading up to the Olympics, all military requirements increased from patrols cov-

Black Hawk over Olympic venue.

ering the ninety square miles of Salt Lake City to radar surveillance of air space. Colonel Perrone adjusted his thinking and planning to a theater-level scale and realized the need for more troops. Later in November, Governor Leavitt announced the activation of 2,000 soldiers from the Utah National Guard. According to Major General Tarbet, this was the largest call-up in the history of the state and became part of the first large-scale mobilization under Operation Noble Eagle.

Even with the Utah National Guard call-up, Colonel Perrone had to reach outside the state for another 4,500 soldiers. To preclude any confusion over command and control, Colonel Perrone worked around the clock with a platoon of military lawyers to establish contractual agreements with twenty-seven other states. A daunting task to say the least, but they did it and increased the strength of JTF-O to 6,500.

Next, Colonel Perrone scoured the city and surrounding towns to find housing for his expanded force. Since Army doctrine considers barracks soft targets, he also had to think of security measures such as fencing, guard houses, and closed circuit cameras as force protection and antiterror measures to protect all Department of Defense personnel. JTF-O used everything from shuttered hospitals to defunct car dealerships and abandoned warehouses. The immediate renovations of these existing structures made them into miniature military installations complete with dining facilities, Post Exchange shopettes, barber shops, laundry rooms, and troop medical clinics. Some dubbed their new lodgings the "National Guard Hotel."

To keep patrols and security activities up and running at top speed, JTF-O sought out the 650th Area Support Group, a unit from the locally based 96th Regional Support Command, to provide cooks, mechanics, and drivers for the mission. The resulting "Task Force Log" units occupied eight strategic locations within city limits and serviced the needs of JTF-O.

Remarkably, the pieces for Olympic security continued to lock systematically into place.

> *Even with the Utah National Guard call-up, Colonel Perrone had to reach outside the state for another 4,500 soldiers.*

Confidence levels in the games approached the same heights as before 9/11. In fact, then newly appointed U. S. Homeland Security Director Tom Ridge enthusiastically remarked, "I can say with certainty this will be the most secure sporting event, probably the safest in the world."

With the prospect of facing crowds of up to 70,000 per day, Colonel Perrone ensured all patrol and security teams were trained to standard in such critical tasks as perimeter security, vehicle and personnel screening, and riot control. With single-minded devotion, he worked to keep this behemoth task force transparent to athletes and tourists alike. During those seventeen days in February, 2002, JTF-O patrol teams circulated through the Olympic venues and main thorough-fares, smiled at the crowds, and kept constant vigilance over everything. Security became a key component of the games.

A total of 3,500 athletes safely competed in seventy-eight medal events that year. Except for the slight disturbance at Bud World, tourists moved about the city freely and without fear. Robert Flowers, the UOPSC commander, jubilantly said, "This went down without a hitch…I can't tell you how good that feels."

With the success of JTF-O behind him and the War on Terrorism in full force, Colonel Perrone was called to a part of the world far removed from the fanfare and festivities of Salt Lake City. While Washington tangled with the legal status of captured al-Qaeda and Taliban combatants from the battlefields of Afghanistan, Colonel Perrone quietly assumed responsibility of Camp Delta at Guantanamo Bay Naval Base, Cuba. His responsibilities included command of 1,200 soldiers from active-duty, Guard, and Reserve units, escort operations into and out of Afghanistan, and the overall safeguard of detainees. During his tenure, the detainee population swelled to over 600 as a result of the numerous flights of escort missions from Guantanamo to Afghanistan and back again.

When Colonel Perrone arrived at Guantanamo in April 2002, the searing Caribbean heat and Camp Delta's three missions bore down on him almost simultaneously. Equal priority went to each of the three missions: intelligence collection, detention operations, and criminal investigations. At the heart of these missions, stood the disheveled, pungent, and largely sullen group of enemy combatants originating from over forty-five countries and speaking thirteen languages and multiple dialects. They did not have any of the entitlements of a prisoner of war according to the Geneva Convention and only later were to be legally identified as "enemy combatants." It was a complex situation especially since there was no formal Army doctrine in place to cover this truly unique operation. Colonel Perrone must have thought frequently to himself, "How do we handle this issue?"

COL Perrone patrolling the Guantanamo River.

"I worked with my staff twelve to fourteen hours a day, seven days a week, dealing with everything related to Camp Delta," Colonel Perrone remarked. "But eventually, we were able to improve things and reduce the guard work week down to five and a half days," he added with a smile.

The detainees had just moved from Camp X-Ray into Camp Delta. Camp Delta better reflected United States policy for the humane confinement and treatment of all individuals detained by U.S. Forces. The 816-unit complex consisted of seven smaller facilities contained within a labyrinth of chain-link fence, locked gates, and gravel walkways. Each unit included a bunk welded to the wall, a floor-style flush toilet, a low-slung sink intended for the Muslim cleansing ritual before prayer, and an inscribed arrow pointing toward Mecca. In spite of the austere lifestyle, detainees heard the call to prayer five times a day, ate *halal* (Arabic for permissible) meals for breakfast, lunch, and dinner, and could exercise within fenced courtyards. There was even a library and a literacy program available to them. Sometimes, native foods such as dates, baklava, and tea were served.

"Life was boring but humane," observed Colonel Perrone. "Improvements and privileges increased daily."

Part of his work involved logistical sustainment of the entire operation. In fact, the Camp Delta detainee basic issue consisted of two towels, a washcloth, soap, toothbrush, shower shoes, shirt and trousers, prayer cap and half-inch-thick prayer mat, and a blanket. A camp hospital was established to treat infections and other illnesses. They received medical and dental care, and for many, it was the first time in their lives. Wounds healed and some were fitted with prosthetics. Even their mental health was evaluated, and any suicidal behavior was noted and closely watched. Their health came back to them and each man averaged a weight gain of fourteen to sixteen pounds. For many detainees, life at Camp Delta represented a significant improvement in their standard of living.

No hardened jihadist insurgent ever harbored

> *For many detainees, life at Camp Delta represented a significant improvement in their standard of living.*

the thought that a captor could show such regard and bring light to such a desolate existence. As Major General Geoffrey Miller, the commander of Joint Task Force Guantanamo, aptly noted, "Hope is enormously important in managing a prison population."

Beneath the glare of a critical international media, human rights groups, and concerned citizens, Colonel Perrone worked steadfastly with his staff to ensure the safety and security of detainees, guards, and interrogators. He kept the detention and intelligence operations in balance by establishing a command climate which fostered discipline, focus, and a sense of purpose for a highly sensitive mission. He spoke with the guards at the gate as well as the interrogators on duty, and they listened to him. In short, he built a team capable of handling the most hardened of detainees.

"Handling the likes of a Mohammed al Katan, considered to be the twentieth bomber in the 9/11 attacks, was never easy," said Colonel Perrone. "They are masters of manipulation and you can never let your guard down with any of them." As part of his standing order, no familiarity of any degree between soldier and detainee was allowed, and he constantly reinforced this point.

Though classified, invaluable intelligence was gained at Camp Delta. It is certain that these

> *But more important, history will note the humane treatment of detainees at Guantanamo.*

efforts have preserved life somewhere in the world. But more important, history will note the humane treatment of detainees at Guantanamo. Such actions will no doubt serve to dissolve the vehement intentions of the transnational terrorist groups now confronting us in this war.

Back at the Homeland Security Management Institute, Colonel Perrone sat in his chair and gazed out of his office window as he reflected over the missions at Salt Lake City and later at Guantanamo. He nodded his head and acknowledged, "Yeah, it was quite a period."

Marine stands watch in guard tower overlooking Camp Delta.

Operation Noble Eagle

by CSM Robert Riti, SGM William Hotham, 1SG Vernon Ficcagli, SFC H. Andres Jimenez, and SFC Matthew Smith

Following the tragic events of September 11, 2001, thousands of Individual Ready Reserve (IRR) soldiers were recalled to active duty to serve in the Global War on Terrorism. Many of these soldiers had been out of uniform for years, and required basic and military-occupation-specific refresher training at one of five stateside training posts before they deployed. To support this critical training mission, the 98th Division mobilized several units to the U.S. Army Maneuver Support Center at Fort Leonard Wood, in Missouri. One of these units was 1st Battalion, 385th Regiment (1/385), 1st Brigade, led by Lieutenant Colonel David Showerman and Command Sergeant Major Robert Riti.

Under 1/385's leadership, Echo Company broke several post records...

The original training mission called for a battalion-sized element to mobilize to Fort Leonard Wood to conduct training for 1,725 IRR soldiers. Prior to mobilization, however, the requirement was reduced to two companies of drill sergeants and a headquarters element. Because the number of IRR soldiers that reported for training was considerably less than originally anticipated, the soldiers of 1/385 were tasked out to 2-10, 3-10, and 1-48 Infantry, the Basic Combat Training (BCT) battalions of Fort Leonard Wood's 3rd Basic Combat Training Brigade. Here they would assist their active-duty counterparts with Initial Entry Training (IET).

The drill sergeants of 1/385 eagerly performed their training duties, and were eventually given the opportunity to take an

A soldier negotiates a three rope bridge at Fort Leonard Wood, Missouri.

Command Sergeant Major Riti and First Sergeant Mike Johnson. Every detail of the mission was carefully planned and coordinated to ensure it would meet the Army training standards.

As the weeks passed, each completed training event reflected the commitment and competence of 1/385 assigned to Echo Company. From the drill sergeant to the training sergeant, armorer, and supply sergeant, the training team provided the

entire company of IET soldiers through the entire nine weeks of BCT from Day 1 to graduation. To ensure the mission was a success, the cadre for this unit, Echo Company, 1-48 Infantry, were hand-picked by

98th Division's C Company, 1st Battalion, 390th Regiment at Fort Leonard Wood, Missouri. Committed to training excellence.

BCT at Fort Leonard Wood.

best possible training experience to the IET soldiers. Under 1/385's leadership, Echo Company broke several post records, to include a 98 percent end-of-day qualification rate for basic rifle marksmanship and a 100 percent "go" rate on the end-of-cycle test. Echo Company also excelled in the final Army Physical Fitness Test, and earned streamers for every event related to BCT.

Graduation brought additional recognition for the efforts of 1/385 as Echo Company graduated with one of the highest BCT completion rates in years. In fact, the Fort Leonard Wood command sergeant major and the 3rd BCT Brigade command sergeant major commented on this particular graduation ceremony as the best they had ever attended. The hard work, dedication and professionalism of the drill sergeants and support soldiers of 1/385 resulted in several memorable and notable achievements during the year-long deployment at Fort Leonard Wood.

98th Division's A Company, 2d Battalion, 390th Regiment at Fort Leonard Wood, Missouri. Integrity and teamwork.

The 98th on the Horn of Africa

by SFC Ryan Crissy

Located on the east coast of the African continent, the Horn of Africa has long suffered from seemingly perpetual crises and natural catastrophes. From civil wars in Somalia and Sudan, to drought in Ethiopia, the region and its more than eighty million people have struggled to survive and overcome adversity, both natural and man made.

More recently, the region has become the focus for peacekeeping missions in Ethiopia and Eritrea under the auspices of the United Nations, and for the Combined Joint Task Force-Horn of Africa, headquartered in the nation of Djibouti, whose purpose is to deny Africa as a haven to terrorists. In 2004, Colonel James Elliott of the 98th Division journeyed to Africa to join the UN mission.

Mission with a view: Ethiopian Highlands.

Once part of the ancient kingdom of Aksum, a powerful trading nation in the first century AD, the modern countries of Eritrea and Ethiopia have endured decades of bloody conflict. A guerrilla war fought from 1962 to 1991 resulted in Eritrea's independence from Ethiopia, but currency and trade issues as well as disputes over the border led to renewed conflict from 1998 to 2000. This last conflict, which left more than 70,000 dead and 650,000 displaced, ended when both sides agreed to accept an independent commission's decision on where the border should be.

The ruling, which was issued in April 2002, awarded a disputed town to Eritrea. Although Ethiopia was initially unhappy with the decision, it eventually accepted the judgment "in principle."

Now troops from both countries face each other across a 25-km-wide demilitarized zone that runs for 1,000 km and is patrolled by United Nations troops. Tensions and rhetoric between the two nations have risen since December 2004, when Ethiopia moved as many as 48,000 troops closer to the frontier.

UN Checkpoint on the Ethiopian-Eritrea border.

UN Mi-8 helicopter used by UNMEE staff.

In July 2004, Colonel James Elliott, a 98th Division instructor at the Combined Arms and Services Staff School at Fort Dix, New Jersey, volunteered to serve in the Global War on Terrorism and was assigned to the United States Military Observer Group-Washington. While serving with the group at the Pentagon, Colonel Elliott was asked to join a team of American observers who would travel to the Horn of Africa and serve with the United Nations Mission in Ethiopia and Eritrea. Colonel Elliott jumped at the chance and soon found himself at the John F. Kennedy Special Warfare Center and School at Fort Bragg, North Carolina, where he received whirlwind training in force protection and country orientation.

Later that same month, Colonel Elliott arrived in Eritrea and assumed his position as chief opera-tions officer at the United Nations mission, UNMEE, where he supervised 220 United Nations observers from thirty-eight countries that had contributed troops to the mission.

According to Colonel Elliott, the year he spent in Africa was professionally rewarding and a satisfying experience. "The mission offered insight into the workings of the United Nations and the attitudes and abilities of soldiers from around the world," he said. Colonel Elliott returned back to America in July 2005 and is currently assigned in the Force Development section at the 98th Division Headquarters.

COL James Elliott and fellow United Nations officers.

COL Elliott (left) with UNMEE participants.

5th Battalion Civil Affairs

by CSM(D) William Hotham

It's no secret that Civil Affairs (CA) soldiers are among the most deployed soldiers in the military. Trained to work with foreign governments and civilian agencies and to conduct civil-military operations, including humanitarian assistance, disaster relief, and reconstruction efforts, CA soldiers have been in great demand for many years. Thousands of CA soldiers, more than 95 percent of whom come from the U.S. Army Reserve, have deployed in support of peacekeeping operations in Somalia, Bosnia, and Kosovo, and combat operations in Afghanistan and Iraq. In the wake of increased deployments, plans to expand the civil affairs force have placed greater emphasis on training and retaining qualified CA soldiers.

In August 2004, twenty-two members of Detachment 1, 5th Battalion (Civil Affairs), 3d Brigade, 98th Division, were mobilized to train Civil Affairs soldiers for the U.S. Army Civil Affairs and Psychological Operation Command. Throughout their year-long mission, 5th Battalion trained approximately 1,100 soldiers at Fort Dix, New Jersey; Ft Bragg, North Carolina; and Camp Parks Reserve Forces

Throughout their year-long mission, 5th Battalion trained approximately 1,100 soldiers...

Training Area in California. Among their accomplishments, 5th Battalion was credited with rewriting doctrine materials for the civil affairs reclassification course, basic and advanced noncommissioned officer courses, and the Army's revised civil affairs occupational specialty and reclassification courses, as well as providing a realistic training environment for their students through the use of ranges, equipment, and field exercises. Due in part to the efforts of 5th Battalion, Fort Dix received designation as a center of excellence for all civil affairs reclassification schools.

Presenting the guidon to battalion commander.
From left to right: CSM(D) William Hotham, MAJ Sandra L.E. Forrest, battalion commander, MSG Matthew Osman, and SFC David Pitarri.

The Crossroads of Asia

Afghanistan

A Short Flight Over the Hindu Kush

by LTC Timothy Hansen

"Salaam alaikum!" I exclaimed to the flight crew as I cautiously boarded the Mi-8 transport helicopter at Kabul International Airport one cold and grey January morning. I had worked barely a month at the Logistics Resources section of the Office of Military Cooperation-Afghanistan (OMC-A) before I found myself heading off to the field. I thought of the Afghan Muslim utterance of indifference to fate. *"Inshallah,"* I muttered to myself and took my seat inside the Russian-built aircraft.

Resourcefulness, tact, and an open mind are prerequisite when working in support of U.S. foreign policy objectives. At OMC-A, much of my work centered on contracting services and procuring equipment and supplies for the Afghan National Army (ANA) beneath the veil of Security Assistance, that group of U.S. military aid programs designated for allied nations in the interest of common defense and regional stability. I wondered about the provincial and village leaders whom I would meet in the city of Herat. What were their needs for the National Army Volunteer Centers? What did they think of the emerging ANA? What was their perception of Americans? I heard the whirl of the giant rotors quicken and felt the helicopter pitch forward and lift off the runway.

Above: Roadside warning–a constant reminder of war's bitter legacy. Below: The blue burqha, veil of intrigue and faith.

The Mi-8 leveled off at a cruising altitude of 14,000 feet. An embedded photojournalist sitting next to me attempted to peer out of the yellowed Plexiglas window. The flight mechanic noticed his vain attempts and stumbled over rucksacks toward the aft of the cabin to pop open the rear portals for better views. Aghast at first, I followed his path a few minutes later to glimpse some of the countryside. Squinting against blasts of frigid air, I was held spellbound by the majestic beauty of rock, ice, and blue sky. Clouds scampered past as the wind blew horsetail plumes of snow over the jagged peaks of the Hindu Kush. I read somewhere that these incredible mountains were the foothills of the Himalayas which lay just northeast of the country. I was equally captivated when the helicopter flew evenly with the crests of these imposing summits and ridgelines.

In working with the Afghans, I learned that

the path to cooperation and trust is through the palate. Afghans love to break *naan* (bread) with family, friends, and guests. They take special delight in explaining their many exquisite delicacies. Engrained in their psyche is *melamastia* or hospitality, which is interestingly one of the principal tenets of the Pashtunwali (the Pashtun code of honor). Over mounds of *qabuli* (rice with raisins and grated carrots), lamb kebabs, meat sauces, fruit, and chai, we smiled and attempted small talk with our hosts. At times, I saw in their eyes the lifetime of struggle and sorrow. At other times, I saw a depth of understanding which none of us could ever hope to possess. But above all,

these tribal elders, village chiefs, and businessmen impressed me with their zeal to rebuild and move on with their lives.

The offices of OMC-A are located in downtown Kabul, amid the thick smog and din of the city itself. Not too far from its Hesco walls are the Presidential Palace and the Ministry of Defense. Though composed of many sections, the primary mission of OMC-A in short was to stand up the Afghan National Army. The mission included all aspects from recruiting, to training and educational programs, to developing the army's force structure. The heightened interest in all of our activi-

ties established staff priorities and united all efforts in meeting President Hamid Karzai's goal of a 70,000-strong national army by 2009. It was quite an undertaking in many respects.

Though the urgency to rebuild was at times overwhelming, encouragement came from the world community's torrent of goodwill and generosity to this war-torn nation. The conferences in Bonn, Tokyo, and most recently London, have yielded more than four billion dollars in financial aid. In addition to military assistance, the United States has shipped more than 300,000 metric tons of food to help alleviate the gnawing pains of

Teamwork in the provinces. Promoting commitment and progress.

hunger. Nongovernmental organizations such as the World Bank and the International Monetary Fund have assisted with currency and banking projects. The United States and Germany have worked to establish police academies and counternarcotic training operations. The number and pace of these operations can nearly induce vertigo.

As the economy resurges, so too does the traffic in Afghanistan's cities and towns. In Kabul, the yellow Volga taxis, Technicolor jingle trucks, rickety Indian buses, SUVs, and horse-drawn carts mingle noisily in the confluence of rotaries and come to annoyingly sudden halts. Drivers pay no heed to the traffic signals and pedestrians cross thoroughfares at their own risk. Sidewalk merchants hawk their wares and argue with customers

Three Afghan carpenters begin their day at Pol-e-Charki.

to buy oranges from Kandahar. The shops on Chicken Street have regained their notoriety as the business center of the country, and furniture, computers, DVDs, and myriad distracting tchotchkes from both the East and West fill their display windows.

Yet on the edges of Kabul, the ANA continues to grow and take form. At the Kabul Military Training Center (KMTC) just off Jalalabad Road, raw recruits undergo the rigors of basic training and gain the discipline of a soldier. Pashtun, Hazara, Tajik, and all other ethnicities stand shoulder-to-shoulder in the ranks of the *kandaks* or battalions to form one army. Further down the road is the ANA base at Pol-e-Charki with its expansive motor pools of wheeled and tracked vehicles. From amidst the rusting hulks of T-55 tanks and BMPs of the bygone Soviet era, the mechanized muscle of the army flexes restlessly. The Afghan tricolor of black, red, and green flies resolutely from the flagpole standing in front of Central Corps headquarters. *Nang* and *namoos* (honor and pride) are returning to the army.

After holding *loya jirgas* (grand assemblies), standing firm in the face of saber-rattling warlords, and conducting free elections, Afghanistan is regaining its sovereignty. Though serious issues such as the opium trade still exist, the rule of law has anchored itself among politician, shopkeeper and mullah alike. By UN mandate, NATO established the International Security Assistance Force

(ISAF) with the support of thirty-six countries. Its patrols preserve order on the city streets and keep Kabul International Airport secure. Just recently, ISAF expanded its mission by fielding provincial reconstruction teams to operate in the country-side, undertake reconstruction projects, work with local village leaders, and thereby extend the authority of the central government.

As with all other nations, Afghanistan will need leaders to preserve and defend its freedoms in the years ahead. Perhaps to be remembered as one of America's most enduring contributions is the establishment of the National Military Academy of Afghanistan (NMAA). In 2003, Major General (now Lieutenant General) Karl Eikenberry, then chief of OMC-A, sent a request

Reviewing terms of payment with an Afghan contractor.

to the superintendent of the U.S. Military Academy (USMA) for assistance in starting a four-year military academy in Afghanistan. In rotating tours, the USMA faculty and staff came and worked closely with the plans and design team of OMC-A and the Afghan Ministry of

An ANA artillery battery trains with a D30 122mm Howitzer east of Kabul.

Defense to make the academy a reality. In short order, they drafted a mission statement, developed admission standards, wrote college curricula to meet degree requirements, and culled from the Cadet Leader Development System a military training program to assure commissioning of cadets as competent second lieutenants. They even added a 300-soldier support battalion to the academy's table of organization and equipment. The Ministry of Defense approved designation of buildings, barracks, and grounds at KMTC for the academy. Though modeled after West Point, the spirit of the academy is completely Afghan. The selection process ensures that cadets represent all major ethnic groups from within the country.

Enthusiastic ANA recruits at the Jalalabad National Army Volunteer Center.

sandals to report for duty on "R-day," the academy's reception of new cadets. A month and a half later, 120 cadets graduated from CBT and stood ready to begin academic instruction. A faculty of thirty professors anxiously waited to begin classes in subjects such as mathematics, chemistry, engineering, and history. During the academy's opening ceremony, Abdul Rahim Wardak, Afghanistan's Minister of Defense, spoke eloquently of the academy's mission in producing "loyal, professional, and true leaders for Afghanistan's future without any ethnic, language, or tribal distinction."

With considerable experience in training cadets at the U.S. Military Academy during cadet basic training and intersession phases, the 98th Division readily sent a team forward to assist with the training and transformation of Afghan cadets into leaders of character. Selected from 3d Battalion, 304th Regiment, the contingent of Iroquois warriors consisted

In February 2005, the academy began cadet basic training (CBT) with its first class of cadets. Displaying undaunted determination, some came from distant provinces and trudged through snow wearing only

Unique delivery of supplies in Samangan.

of Lieutenant Colonel Paul Lally, First Sergeant Sean McMullan, Master Sergeant Joseph Conicelli, Master Sergeant Richard Hussey, Sergeant First Class Michael Doughty, and Sergeant First Class Joseph Bradbury. Their arrival into Afghanistan just happened to coincide with the opening of the academy. Overcoming the mind-warping effects of crossing ten time zones, they delved directly into the mission.

They traveled out to the provinces to promote and recruit for the academy. They worked with Indiana National Guard officers and noncommissioned officers (NCOs) also assigned to the academy in drafting training schedules for the weeks ahead. They instructed on marksmanship, range safety, physical training, and land navigation. Before dawn, they were out with the cadets on ten kilometer road marches. They provided to the cadets the substance of the Army leadership training: Be-Know-Do. They helped instill *nang* and *namoos* into the Afghan corps of cadets.

"The NCOs will teach the cadets basic military tasks," remarked First Sergeant McMullen. "They teach periods of instruction on subjects such as how to assemble, disassemble, and maintain the AK-47."

Indeed, the NCO as instructor marked a paradigm shift for the Afghan military, a mirror reflection of the Soviet leadership model in which the officers ran practically everything. Now, it will be the cadets who will experience, appreciate and respect the versatility, organization, and flair of an NCO corps. Most important, they will recognize the Warrior Ethos, the fastidious attention to detail, and the resilient leadership among the NCO ranks.

"PT led by NCOs is one of the hallmarks of the U.S. Army and has been embraced as the standard by the Afghan Ministry of Defense as well," commented Lieutenant Colonel Lally, deputy chief of the Military Academy Implementation Team. "It's a giant leap to move from a completely officer-run training program to an NCO-led program."

The National Academy of Afghanistan symbolizes unity,

The 98th on the ground in Afghanistan. Left to Right: SFC Joseph R. Bradbury, 1SG Sean P. McMullan, SSG Todd Doyle, MSG Joseph Conicelli (98th Division Guidon), LTC Paul P. Lally Jr., MSG Richard H. Hussey, and SFC Michael E. Doughty.

The colors of the Coalition at Camp Phoenix.

strength, and hope for the future. As with West Point, it is "a total institution" in which staff and faculty affect nearly every aspect of a cadet's daily life for the next forty-seven months. The focus is officership. Standards of excellence exist to develop self-discipline, build character, and inspire a lifetime of service to the nation. As these cadets march forward, they live the credo: One Army. One Nation.

In reflecting on the months of planning and building, Colonel James Wilhite, chief of the Military Academy Implementation Team, commented: "History is when a significant event happens at any one time and place…I believe we are on the verge of making such history in the establishment of the NMAA."

For the first time in more than two and a half decades, progress can be seen in Afghanistan. Five corps of the ANA stand as the regional command within the country. Thirty-three National Army Volunteer Centers are now open and produce more than 2,400 recruits a month. As of January 2006, the strength of the ANA stood at 35,000. Provincial Reconstruction Teams continue to fan out across the country and provide needed services to improve the quality of life. Another pile of rubble is removed, and the lights in the neighborhoods of Kabul burn a little longer at night. To the Afghan, all of this is good, but still, life goes on…*Zendagi migzara*.

Operations North of the Panjshir Valley

by LTC Michael Reed

In November 2002, I was activated and deployed to Afghanistan by my unit, the 403d Civil Affairs (CA) Battalion, in Mattydale, New York. I was in charge of a six-soldier Civil Affairs Team Alpha (CAT-A), 450th CA Battalion (Airborne), stationed in the northern city of Mazar-e-Sharif near Uzbekistan. We lived in a house inside a walled residential compound and drove civilian sport utility vehicles. My team's

area of operations (AO) covered five provinces: Balkh, Sar-e-pol, Samangan, Jowzjan, and Faryab. We conducted liaison for the U.S. military with local civil and military officials, community members and leaders, and international and nongovernmental organizations.

Life in Afghanistan was like being transported back in time. Villagers lived in an almost biblical setting, relying upon donkeys, horses, camels, and other animals for their livelihood and transportation. Many of the Afghans we met were extremely hospitable. They often expressed their appreciation to us for leaving families and jobs behind to assist the Afghan people. People usually offered us hot green tea, insisting we stay for a meal. Delicious food, accompanied by very fresh flat loaves of bread was served on a cloth spread on the floor. We sat on cushions, eating with our hands, a few people sharing each dish. This was typically lamb kebabs on metal skewers or *pilau—*

Left: LTC Michael Reed wearing a traditional turban.
Below: The resplendent Tomb of the Exalted in Mazar-e-Sharif. Hazrat Ali, cousin and son-in-law of the Prophet Mohammad, lies entombed within this shrine.

Above: Tantalizing Afghan cuisine.
Right: Afghan tradition - chai and kebabs.

a rice mixture, with raisins, pine nuts, carrots, lamb, or chicken.

My team supported the Islamic Transitional Government of Afghanistan with civil-military, humanitarian assistance, and small infrastructure construction operations. I planned and led missions, which resulted in comprehensive assessments of more than 100 cities and villages for input to the Afghan Information Management System (AIMS) database.

Working in a combat zone hampered our work. There was always the potential for people to try to kill us. We frequently heard the sounds of small-arms fire and explosions. Some of my comrades at other locations were involved in actions in which U.S. military personnel were killed and wounded.

Our CA unit was one of three U.S. Army contingents within our entire AO. We had a signal soldier and fourteen to twenty CA soldiers, comprising two or three CA teams. We also hosted a State Department consular representative in our compound. A Forward Logistics Element (FLE) located near the airport supported an adjacent Jordanian Army hospital. A Special Forces (SF) A-Team lived nearby, as did a three-soldier Psychological Operations (PSYOP) team. The SF soldiers and our CA soldiers provided mutual security for one other.

Our CA teams sometimes performed joint missions with the SF team and the United Nations Assistance Mission in Afghanistan. These were usually missions in which we observed partial disarmament of local militia factions. We also participated in a mission to help

Familiar modes of transport in use since antiquity.

Preparing for a game of buzkashi on the maidan. LTC Reed applies his equestrian skills in northern Afghanistan.

bring peace and stability to local villages in a remote location. We supported UN representatives' efforts to resolve disputes between local commanders' militia factions. The disputes were actually personal in nature, rooted in long-standing familial "blood feuds." We also formed joint security teams with the SF and PSYOP teams for U.S. or Coalition aircraft operations at the airport, VIP visits, and some ceremonial occasions.

My civilian work experience as an acting regional landscape architect with the New York State Department of Transportation contributed to success in the reconstruction of small infrastructure projects, a major part of my job in Afghanistan. My primary civilian job skills directly relate to that type of work. I supervised and worked on identification, submittal, design, specification writing, estimating, bidding, monitoring and final acceptance of forty-nine construction projects valued at $1,687,000. These included

wells, schools, medical and veterinary facilities, small roads, and bridges.

The relationship between my civilian and military careers is a two-way street. Training and experience gained in one realm of activity can be applied in many ways to the other. The organization and management skills I use in the military also benefit my civilian job.

I would like to provide the following advice to other Army Reserve soldiers—maximize the quality time you spend with your family and friends before mobilization and stay in regular contact during deployment. Being apart from my wife and two young children was the worst part of each deployment. During transition periods before and after deploying to Afghanistan, I devoted approximately two-thirds of my time to my family and one-third to the U.S. Army. My family and I stayed in a cabin in Green Lakes State Park before and after the deployment. We also vacationed in Quebec, and made trips to visit relatives living in other states.

Finally, be very careful when you begin living and operating in a hostile environment. Focus on gaining situational awareness as your first priority. It is vital for new soldiers to understand a foreign environment and to seek guidance from those with experience. May God watch over you and keep you safe!

Opposite: View of the Tangi Gharu Gorge looking east toward Jalalabad. (Photo by LTC Timothy Hansen)

Holiday Greetings from Kabul

December 2005

I'd like to thank all for keeping in touch with me and providing an almost monthly supply of tastefully chosen junk food (smile), Beanie Babies (for the orphanage) and toiletry supplies. The troops and I appreciate it, especially the prayers and just for keeping us in your thoughts. Attached is our team picture and some pictures like the Lally family deployment tree that goes with family soldiers sent overseas. It's pretty beat up but means a lot to us.

NMAA was featured in the *Afghanistan Freedom Watch* magazine wherein the academy was cited for conducting the annual admissions day testing on November 8, 2005. The NMAA tested 1,007 candidates with a 200 question written exam. And the academy only admits 270 cadets out of that total, which gave them about a one in four chance to enroll. The "Concord" exam which counts for 80 percent of a candidate's score for admission is like our SAT and was conducted over a three-hour period in the quadrangle in the open. Imagine having to take your SATs on a chair in the sun in the open.

Thank God it did not rain (it did the night before–first time in six months). They had no contingency for that. Some of these young men traveled for days from outlying

provinces such as Kandahar and Herot.

The day before the exam the American mentors (us) conducted the physical agility test which

accounts for the other 20 percent of the candidates' score for admissions. They can't afford sneakers so many ran in their bare feet or socks.

The dean of the academy is actually the same age as I am. The environment and life in general is harsh and so the skin ages quickly and they are in stark contrast to our soft and younger-looking features.

I attached shots of "frisking" to illustrate no

matter the age, Afghans still have the warrior spirit and have weapons on them. The academy staff knows that already and they just do it as a routine.

Inshalla!

Respectfully,

Lieutenant Colonel Paul P. Lally Jr.

Happy Holidays from the entire NMAA Team!

"Through it all, they all had smiles. But for many of them, this was the first time they've ever done anything like push-ups or pull-ups, or sprinted 300 meters. But they're all here because they want to be, not because someone told them to, and that says a lot."

SFC Joseph Bradbury, one of the U.S. advisors from the 98th Division who helped with the event.

Aerial view of KMTC, location of the NMAA.

The Future of Afghanistan

Top Left: Young girl dressed in Afghan blue.
Above: Children of Bagdakhshan.

Recruits practice drill and ceremony at Kabul Military High School.

Ghazni Schoolboys.

Looking at us?

Bound for
Baghdad

Advance Party and Survey Team Depart Fort Bliss, Texas

Every military operation requires an advance party to go forward of the main body and coordinate all of the operational and logistical details of the mission. Before any patrol goes outside the wire or any round is launched down range, this party must work around the clock to set the stage for those to follow. Since a large part of the mission's success rests on this prior coordination, the advance party is perhaps the most demanding phase of the mission.

The 98th Division Foreign Army Training Assistance Command (FA-TRAC) Advance Party consisted of LTC Phil McGrath, CPT Ramin Dilfanian and COL Frank Cipolla. They had the crucial task of reception of the survey team. (July 4, 2004)

Working Inside the Palace

With its commanding views of the Tigris River and trappings of power, Saddam Hussein's Presidential Palace served as an appropriate and convenient location for U.S. Army, joint service, and Coalition commands.

Designed more like a hotel than a seat of government, the palace is a complex of conference rooms, living quarters, kitchens, gardens, and a swimming pool. It usually takes newcomers a few days to find their way among the several offices now set up there.

"Time for staff call!" COL Cipolla breaks for a moment from the rigors of FA-TRAC.

The several portraits of Hussein which once hung in the labyrinth of hallways and foyers have all been removed or covered. Now reconfigured as a headquarters element, the Coalition staff grinds away in preparing PowerPoint briefing slides, firing off e-mail responses, attending the endless rounds of meetings and staff calls, and in following up on all previous coordination.

Setting up shop in the dining hall, COL Cipolla catches up on correspondence with the 98th staff back in Rochester, NY.

Iraqi protesters exercising their freedom to disagree.

Filling the JMD

The survey team canvassed the entire country and assessed the skill levels of several Iraqi Army units. It lined up the assignments for thirty-nine Advisory Support Teams (ASTs). An AST consisted of three officers and seven non-commissioned officers (NCOs).

The survey team also assessed the personnel requirements of the Joint Manning Document (JMD), the force structure of MNSTC-I, and filled 242 critical staff positions with 98th Division soldiers. This strong 98th Division presence in the staff also provided for an effective command and control of all training assistance missions.

CPT Dilfanian inside Baath Party Headquarters, the site of this car bombing. Below: Green Zone cafe following a suicide bombing in October 2004.

The Tip of the Spear

In the Spring 2004, Brigadier General Richard Sherlock and Colonel Frank Cipolla developed the conceptual framework for the Foreign Army Training Assistance Command (FA-TRAC) and delivered their proposed course of action to the highest levels of the Department of the Army and Department of Defense through a series of intense briefings and deliberations. During those whirlwind days at the Pentagon,

> *They paved the way for the 98th to make its mark in history.*

Colonel Cipolla vividly recalled Lieutenant General James Helmly, the chief of the U.S. Army Reserve, leaning over to him and asking, "Are you ready to go?"

After the smoke cleared from the crossfire of questions and rebuttals, Brigadier General Sherlock and Colonel Cipolla stood with approval in hand for the 98th to go forward into Iraq on an unprecedented mission for a U.S.

Group photo of the FA-TRAC Survey Team prior to departure from Fort Bliss on July 19, 2004. Left to right: SFC Edward Stefik, LTC Sean Ryan, BG Richard Sherlock, MSG Brian Kramer, LTC Tony Morales, LTC Lawrence Kelly, LTC Rick Miller, COL William Clegg, LTC Jody Daniels, and MSG John Compitello.

Army Reserve unit. They paved the way for the 98th to make its mark in history.

In June 2004, the division established a 24-hour tactical operations center at its headquarters in Rochester, N.Y. The G1, the division's human resources office, went into hyperdrive as it coordinated with the U.S. Army Reserve Command, First Army, and U.S. Forces Command in preparing mobilization orders and deployment lists. The G4, the logistics section, began to order equipment and supplies for use in a theater of war.

BG Sherlock with an Iraqi Aviation Officer.

In July 2004, Colonel Cipolla, Lieutenant Colonel Phil McGrath, and Captain Ramin Dilfanian embarked to Iraq as the division's advance party. After meeting with Lieutenant General David Petraeus, the commanding general of the Multi-National Security Transition Command-Iraq, they immediately prepared for the arrival of the survey team. The grueling schedule they kept marked the beginning of an incredible mission.

Fort Bliss, Texas: Survey team boards a United Airlines Boeing 747 bound for Kuwait.

COL Jody Daniels continuously gathers intel...

"Check six!"
LTC Rick Miller and COL Larry Kelly prepare for Black Hawk flights.

Sharing the digital workload:
LTC McGrath taps out reports for the FA-TRAC TOC.

BG Sherlock briefs Arab Customs and Culture.

Above: BG Richard Sherlock,
CPT Ramin Dilfanian, and COL William Clegg.

Left: SFC Ed Stefik and MSG Brian Kramer.

Even Santa travels through Kuwait before heading to Baghdad!

Paradigm Shift Hits the 98th

Mobilization is a phased process designed to be concurrent and continuous, rather than sequential. It is designed to rapidly expand and enhance the response capability of the Army in support of a military response to a crisis or natural disaster.

U.S. Army FM 100-17

"During Vietnam, there were no ceremonies...you got drafted, you got on a bus someplace in Buffalo, and you shipped out, and that was it."

MSG Bing Reeves
Headquarters, 98th Division (IT)

Honey, I've just been mobilized...
Mobilized?
But, you're in the Army Reserve!

"One of the biggest changes in the U.S. military in recent years is its growing reliance on Reservists and Soldiers from the National Guard. With over 40% of U.S. Forces in Iraq now drawn from Guard and Reserve units, more and more weekend warriors are being called to active duty."

Melissa Block
National Public Radio

"The original idea of the weekend warrior or the hometown unit, all that has gone by the wayside a long time ago.

We are basically full-time soldiers in a Reserve capacity just waiting for the mission."

Todd Arnold
Chief Executive Officer, 98th Division (IT)

Who We Are and Why We Serve

With a median age hovering somewhere between 34 and 37 years, this group of Iroquois warriors was a mature and diverse lot compared to most mobilized units. Because of the FA-TRAC mission's heavy emphasis on instructors and drill sergeants, the 98th had to tap into other Army Reserve units and even the Inactive Ready Reserve to fill the mission requirements.

Most of those mobilized came from similar situations: married with two to three children; a mortgage and car payments; orthodontist appointments and violin lessons. Some even came from the halls of academia such as the Massachusetts Institute of Technology, the University of Rochester and the University of Vermont.

The degree of skills brought to the table ranged from corporate execs and attorneys, to nurses, book editors, pharmaceutical sales reps,

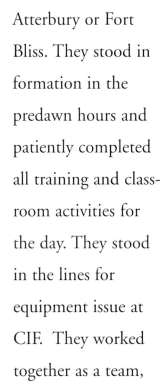

2004/09/16

teachers, bankers and accountants, police officers and advertising directors, and to electricians and carpenters. When they received the call, they grasped the scope and impact of this mission, put their pursuit of the American dream on hold, and prepared their families and employers for the year ahead.

Reeling from the heartache of good-bye, they came and reported for duty at either Camp Atterbury or Fort Bliss. They stood in formation in the predawn hours and patiently completed all training and classroom activities for the day. They stood in the lines for equipment issue at CIF. They worked together as a team, endured the road marches to the ranges, and put up with the chilled autumn rains of Atterbury and searing heat of Fort Bliss. From within the core of their being, came the willingness to serve, to fight and to protect not only those in foreign lands, but those close to the heart.

The Road to Camp Atterbury

On September 8, 2004, the 98th Division mobilized for the mission of training the Iraqi Armed Forces. The plan called for mobilizing and deploying the advance party from Fort Bliss, Texas and four successive groups, M1 through M4, from Camp Atterbury, Indiana. The G1 and G3 sections worked overtime to draft and send orders to all parts of the country, coordinate travel, and set up a 24-hour tactical operations center on the third floor of division headquarters in Rochester, NY.

For some, mobilization started early with the chartered bus waiting in the back parking lot of the Reserve Center. For others, mobilization began with a commercial airline ticket to get them to where they needed to report.

With or without the glare of camera lights, the call to serve a nation in need was answered. Like a slumbering giant, the true character of the U.S. Army Reserve Soldier emerged because this mission rang true; to train and to stand up an army of a nation yearning to be free.

In the six weeks of training at Camp Atterbury, the long hours of training forged the bonds of trust and loyalty needed to survive the chaos of asymmetric warfare.

Camp Atterbury at a Glance

The Indiana Army National Guard and the U.S. Army Reserve presently manage Camp Atterbury. The post's 655-acre cantonment remains open year round to accommodate the training activities of all branches of the Armed Forces as well as federal and local law enforcement agencies. Additionally, a SEAL training camp was established here in 1990. Because of its readily accessible facilities and resources, Camp Atterbury was activated into federal service as a mobilization station for overseas deployment in 2004.

Camp Atterbury's total land mass is currently 33,845 acres. It measures about 12 miles along its north-south axis and just seven miles along its east-west axis. It is located just west of Edinburgh (population: 4,536). Camp Atterbury's sprawling expanse of land and extensive trail network make this post ideal for infantry operations at company, battalion, and brigade levels. Several of the post's ranges are ideal for offensive and defensive tactics.

The U.S. Army spent $38 million in 1942 for the construction of 1,780 buildings and the clearing for ranges at Camp Atterbury. About 275,000 men trained here before heading to Europe, and its hospital treated more than 85,000 patients. After the war, Camp Atterbury assumed a demobilization posture and out-processed 560,595 vets.

Besides serving as a training post, Camp Atterbury also maintained a 60-acre internment camp which held 15,000 German and Italian prisoners of war. In fact, the signature Camp Atterbury rock was carved by an Italian POW by the name of Libero Puccini.

Camp Atterbury reactivated in 1950 to provide training and medical support during the Korean War. The post was relatively dormant during the Vietnam War and did not see any significant activity until the late seventies.

Camp Atterbury has mobilized over 11,000 Guard and Reserve soldiers since its activation in February 2003 and continues to keep pace with the training requirements of Active Component, Guard and Reserve units. Last May, the Department of the Army selected the Camp Atterbury Joint Maneuver Training Center to receive the 2005 Army Chief of Staff's Combined Logistics Deployment Excellence Award for its outstanding troop mobilization efforts in support of the Global War on Terrorism.

Ft. Bliss CONUS Replacement Center

As the designated CONUS Replacement Center for Operation Iraqi Freedom, Fort Bliss has become a state-of-the-art power projection platform. More than 40,000 service members, federal government officials, and defense contractors have deployed and redeployed from Bliss since September 11, 2001.

Team Bliss provides the entire array of services and resources needed for deployment: equipment issue at CIF, weapons qualification and convoy exercises, medical and dental examinations, and administrative and financial support. A total of 293 soldiers from the 98th processed and deployed from here. The stay at Fort Bliss lasted about ten days. The soldiers who deployed from here went on to fill staff positions within the Multi National Security and Transition Command-Iraq.

Foreign Army Training Assistance Command:
Army Reserve Formalizes Assigned Wartime Mission

by LTG James R. Helmly, Chief, Army Reserve

The Army Reserve seeks innovative ways to continue contributing to the performance of training across the Army. To support combatant commanders, the Army Reserve is pursuing the creation of the Foreign Army Training Assistance Command (FA-TRAC), which will conduct foreign army training – a mission that is currently conducted by members of the Army Reserve's 75th Division (Training Support) Advisory Support Teams in Tall Afar, Iraq.

The mission of the FA-TRAC will be to provide foreign armed forces with advice, training, and organizational practices in leadership, Soldier skills, and unit tactics. Army Reserve Soldiers assigned to the FA-TRAC will deploy to the combatant command to live with the host-nation soldiers.

2004/10/18

In Operation Iraqi Freedom, the initial Advisory Support Team has already trained hundreds of Iraqi soldiers as

part of the Coalition Military Assistance Training Team. The 75th Division has led the way as a courageous trailblazer in

this unprecedented Army Reserve mission. It has dedicated itself completely to the establishment of this new army and already has trained nearly 600 Iraqi soldiers who were either new recruits or veterans of the former regime.

"In the first month of training we have put the Iraqis through Military Operations in Urban Terrain training, close quarter combat training, patrolling techniques and formations, tactical checkpoints, and individual movement techniques," said SSG James Mitchell of the 75th Division.

The tactical training was put to use when Iraqi and 75th Division Soldiers conducted patrols with the 2nd Infantry Division Stryker Brigade Combat Team. To ensure training progress, the 75th Soldiers have also accompanied Iraqi soldiers

Helmly with husband and wife, CPT Michael Threlfall and MSG Renee LeBlanc.

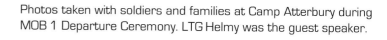
Photos taken with soldiers and families at Camp Atterbury during MOB 1 Departure Ceremony. LTG Helmy was the guest speaker.

Joint Manning Document for the Coalition Military Assistance Training Team (CMATT), and supporting expanded MOS training and mission essential task list development for the Iraqi Army. The FA-TRAC assumed the mission from CMATT in November 2004.

The Army Reserve will continue to maintain its other training capabilities in the seven Institutional Training Divisions and five Training Support Divisions as currently organized.

on both day and night patrols in the local village and terrain around Fort Tallafar.

The 75th Division, headquartered in Houston, Texas has been mobilized since January 2003. The unit's primary stateside mission is to provide training observer controllers and to mobilize the Army's Reserve Components.

The FA-TRAC will be built from the existing structure of the 98th Army Reserve Division (Institutional Training). FA-TRAC will provide several advantages, which include providing "plug and play" training teams to the Combatant Commander, providing Soldiers to fill the current

Year of the Red Sox
and the Importance of a Good Coach

With the Boston Red Sox down three games to none to the New York Yankees in the 2004 American League Championship Series, there was still tension in the air. Maybe "the bridesmaids" would somehow turn things around. Maybe some solid coaching would come through, and 2004 would be their year.

In like manner, would this be the year for the 98th? Would the FA-TRAC mission be its moment of truth? Would its coaching come through?

As with baseball, training an Army does not have a formulaic set of rules and techniques. Victory is attained by its soldiers. The soldiers are trained by seasoned leaders well versed not only with rules but in advising and assessing character.

Colonel Robert Catalanotti bore the burden of preparing the bulk of this division for war. A daunting responsibility with lives at stake, he took command of this mission, worked his staff hard and established vital bonds of trust and friendship with the command and staff of Camp Atterbury, Indiana. By his sin-

cerity and tact, he gained the confidence of Colonel Ken Newlin, the post commander of Camp Atterbury, Lieutenant Colonel Larry Muncie, the deputy post commander and Command Sergeant Major Gary Hildebrand, the post command sergeant major. He also garnered the support of Colonel Gus Stafford, commander of the 85th Training Support Division. At the same time he recognized by name the hard work of the Atterbury team: Lieutenant Colonel Ron Morris, Major Felicia Brokaw, Chief Warrant Renee Romack and her staff, and Chaplain (Lieutenant Colonel) James Cotter.

As the commander of troops, Colonel Catalanotti took the time to speak to his soldiers

COL Catalanotti advises M4 leadership: LTC James Pippert and 1SG Gerard Guilbeault.

in formation, out on the range, and in the dining facility. He listened, counseled, and mentored. His words always encouraged and instilled confidence through the challenges of mobilization.

Colonel Catalanotti adhered to his training schedule with great tenacity. Still, he recognized the needs of his soldiers. He was the first commander at Camp Atterbury to initiate shuttle runs to Edinburgh for soldiers to attend worship services not available on post. As the mobilization groups approached the end of their training, he set up shuttle runs to Wal-Mart for soldiers to buy additional items they would need for their year in Iraq.

Like a good coach, Colonel Catalanotti constantly assessed both training and participants. He made note of those able to handle a higher pitch count and withstand the heat. Through his many observations and conversations, he matched the right personalities on the training teams.

Even with a hectic training pace, Colonel Catalanotti accommodated unique requests for deserving soldiers. Though brief and to the point, two wedding ceremonies were held at Camp Atterbury. First Sergeant Robert Johnson and Sergeant First Class Dale McMahon married

Chrissy and Rob Johnson.

their fiancées right before their departures to Iraq.

The Red Sox broke the curse of the Bambino in 2004, and the

Joan and Dale McMahon with COL C.

98th deployed for a year of historic and incredible milestones in training the Iraqi Army. For both teams, the coaching made the difference.

"We are the most visible mission in the Army right now. Generals come out to visit us every week…

'Let me see your training schedule!' they demand.

We need to make our training more rigorous. You'll get rigorous training [here] with the M16 and 9MM ranges, land nav and language study. From this training, we will derive a synergy [from all of our parts] by the time it is ready to go.

There is no need for vehicles out here because we march everywhere we need to go. Plus, it will help get your feet in shape for the walking and marching you will have to do in Iraq.

As for Atterbury…well, there is great laundry service and you will receive it wrapped in a plastic bag with a prayer card."

COL Robert Catalanotti
FA-TRAC Commander of Troops
Camp Atterbury

COL Catalanotti briefs to MOB 2 on the weeks ahead at Atterbury.

Training for Validation

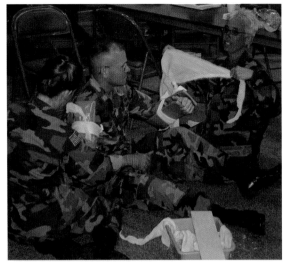

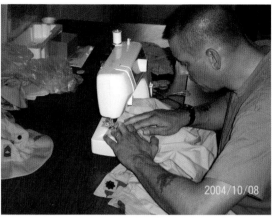

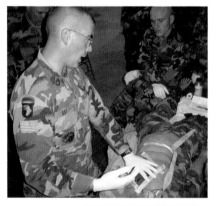

Common Task • Combat Life Saver
Theater Specific • Arabic Language

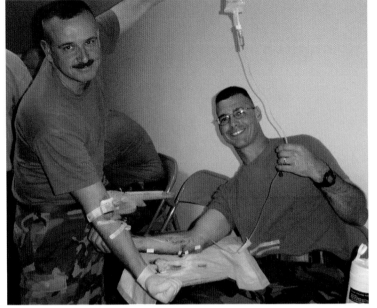

Departures from Indy Airport

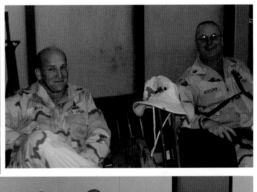

Farewell Ceremonies

Training the
Iraqi Army

The mobilization of the 98th Division was unique in the history of the U.S. Army Reserve. Within the continental United States, the Division massed its troops under the banner of Foreign Army Training Assistance Command (FA-TRAC). The primary objective of the mission was to field thirty-nine Advisory Support Teams (ASTs) to mentor, coach, and advise units of the Iraqi Regular Army and the Iraqi Intervention Force.

The mission also required staff personnel to provide command, control and support of the ASTs. Upon arrival in Baghdad, the teams and support staff filled the ranks of the Multi National Security and Transition Command-Iraq. From Baghdad, the ASTs fanned out across the country and began the work of shaping the Iraqi Army. It was a mission actually suited for Special Operations, but incredibly, the Soldiers of the 98th put their hearts and minds into it, and a year became like a day.

Iroquois Warriors
Quiet Heroes on the World Stage

"It is something great and greatening to cherish an ideal; to act in the light of truth that is far away and far above; to set aside the near advantage, the momentary pleasure…and to act for remote ends, for higher good, and for interests other than our own."

Brigadier General Joshua L. Chamberlain

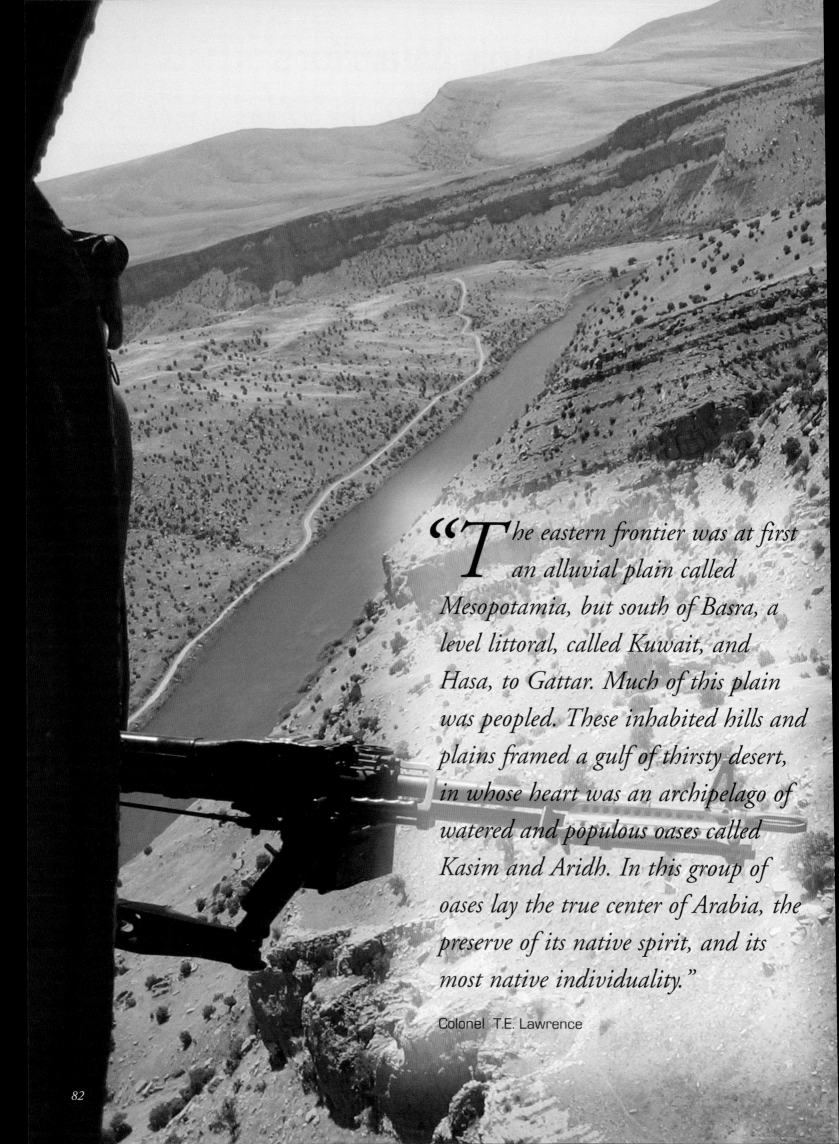

"*The eastern frontier was at first an alluvial plain called Mesopotamia, but south of Basra, a level littoral, called Kuwait, and Hasa, to Gattar. Much of this plain was peopled. These inhabited hills and plains framed a gulf of thirsty desert, in whose heart was an archipelago of watered and populous oases called Kasim and Aridh. In this group of oases lay the true center of Arabia, the preserve of its native spirit, and its most native individuality.*"

Colonel T.E. Lawrence

Profile in Leadership

by SFC Ryan Crissy

Lieutenant General
David Petraeus

Success in Iraq depends heavily on the ability of Iraq's security forces to take charge in the battle against terrorism and the insurgency, and perhaps no one understood this more than Lieutenant General David Petraeus, the first commander of the Multi-National Security Transition Command-Iraq and commander of the 101st Airborne Division during the first year in Iraq. Selected by Washington to help build Iraq's military and police forces from the ground up, Petraeus and his staff used a combination of careful planning, tough resolve, and diplomacy to raise Iraq's security forces, like the mythical phoenix, from the ashes of war.

Known for his intelligence, ability to "think outside the box," and attention to detail, Lieutenant General Petraeus realized that standing up effective Iraqi army and police forces would require several key ingredients: significant financial investment, good training, good equipment, a strong political environment, and, perhaps most

It is units with cohesion, with organization, with a chain of command, with structure and fairly robust combat power that are needed to stand up against something as brutal as the insurgents in Iraq.

important, competent leadership. According to Petraeus, "It is units with cohesion, with organization, with a chain of command, with structure and fairly robust combat power that are needed to stand up against something as brutal as the insurgents in Iraq."

Under Petraeus's command, MNSTC-I, staffed and operated largely by members of the 98th Division, helped the Iraqi government to rebuild hundreds of military bases, border forts, police stations, forward operating bases, police and military academies, and branch and professional development schools. In addition to providing combat and professional training at the battalion, brigade, division, and higher levels, the unit fielded much-needed equipment to the Iraqis, from uniforms, Kevlar helmets, and body armor, to pistols, rifles, radios, and ammunition. Cultivating effective leadership also was a priority, and much effort was spent in assisting the Iraqi ministries in identifying and placing competent Iraqi commanders in positions of authority.

In Lieutenant General Petraeus's more than fifteen months as commander of MNSTC-I, more than 200,000 Iraqi security forces—and some 120 combat battalions—were trained and equipped for the momentous task of helping stabilize Iraq and beat back the insurgency. Reaching this level was no small feat, something Lieutenant General Petraeus would often say was akin to building the world's largest aircraft while in flight—and while being shot at.

He also described the effort, on occasion, as "The Mesopotamian Stampede," in which the effort was to help strengthen the herd, help it gather momentum, keep it headed in the right direction, and sustain it in the face of constant attacks and over the toughest of terrain. If Petraeus and the Iraqi military and police leaders were the range bosses in this "cattle drive," then

Promotion Ceremony for SFC Ryan Crissy with MG Bruce Robinson and LTG David Petraeus.

the 98th Division training and support teams, their other coalition teammates, and their Iraqi counterparts were the cowboys, working steadily to move the new security force units toward self-sustainment and independent operation.

Kuwait
Army Logistics • Don't Leave Home Without It

Among the critical functions of any army operation is logistics—the science of planning and carrying out the movement and maintenance of troops, supplies, and equipment. It is an unceasing activity which integrates itself seamlessly into such familiar forms as the dining facility, the ammunition supply point, and the warehouse.

When the 98th received the order to go forward to Iraq, it also had to respond to the demand for qualified logistics officers and non-commissioned officers. In fact, nearly 80 percent of the MNSTC-I J4 consisted of 98th Division soldiers. They did everything from property book transactions to managing critical classes of supply. They networked critical logistic nodes, convoyed to forward operating bases, and built up reserves of essential stock items. They proved flexible and mobile in support of any requirements from the training teams, other units of the Coalition, and the emerging Iraqi Army.

Noncommissioned officers such as Master Sergeant A. J. Tugaoen jumped into the planning of support activities for the Iraqi Army. They helped to establish and staff three central issue facilities, the company store of sorts which provides uniforms, boots,

Above: MAJ Dave Conner at "home" in Tent City.
Right: MSG A.J. Tugaoen smiles as he prepares to transport supplies.

LTC Rick Miller with KMTB Team.

Doing the impossible.

Quayle rolled up their sleeves and went to work. They off-loaded, inventoried, and issued 550 up-armored Humvees. They learned all the components of the Single Channel Ground and Airborne Radio System (SINCGARS) in record time. They added high-tech items such as the Blue Force Tracker, personal communications devices, and thermal sights to the inventory. Even under the threat of ambush, they ventured to remote forward operating bases, completed a 100 percent invento-

and other personal equipment needed for the rigors of training and combat. When Iraq's Ministry of Defense (MOD) established its national warehouse, 98th Division soldiers assisted with its set up and operation. They tapped into the supply chain and optimized the existing distribution system. In the end, they delivered more than fifty thousand tons of equipment to Iraqi Army and police units throughout the country. They also shipped more than thirty million rounds of ammunition along with eighty thousand weapons. Aligned with joint and Coalition forces, their efforts resulted in sustaining twenty-seven Iraqi battalions, ten major police units, and twenty military training facilities.

At the same time, support of the American warfighters assigned to the training teams and other missions needed due care and consideration. At Taji, just outside of Baghdad, Sergeant First Class Dean Chilton and Staff Sergeant Jennifer

SSG Jennifer Quayle arranges transportation.

ry, and pieced together a property book worth $100 million. Chief Warrant Officer Michael Wade completed property transfers from the stateside 98th Division rear detachment by utilizing a Web-based program. This transaction marked the emerging use of digital technology for logistics applications in the U.S. Army Reserve.

"Rust Never Sleeps"

01.25.2005

In the area of training, MNSTC-I partnered with the Iraqi Army, and the Ministry of Defense (MOD) to develop a logistics co-op program for increasing the technical skills of Iraqi Army officers. Classes focused on the finer details of maintenance, warehousing, procurement, and accounting. According to Lieutenant Colonel George Crowell, an MOD liaison officer for MNSTC-I J4, the program enabled Coalition logisticians to assess the capabilities of the Iraqis and to gauge instruction accordingly.

"Now we work as equals," remarked one Iraqi colonel in the program. "We share information to make one plan."

In this merciless race against time, the Iroquois Warrior relentlessly pushed supplies forward to meet mission requirements. This race

stretched sinew and bone. At the finish, stood a stronger Iraqi Army.

Operating out of Camp Afrifjan, Kuwait, Lieutenant Colonel Tony Morales and Master Sergeant John Compitello worked as the liaison/operations team between MNSTC-I and the Coalition Forces Land Component Command (CFLCC). CFLCC is the service and support activity in Kuwait that coordinates the combined efforts of all land forces in the Iraq theater of operations. Working this part of the mission offered little rest and brought to mind the words of the Neil Young hard-rock classic, "Rust Never Sleeps."

As a team, Morales and Compitello coordinated, cajoled, and ensured billeting, transportation,

meals, and training for the division's 730 soldiers who made up the main body of the mobilization. This influx of personnel extended from September to December 2004. They constantly contended with the issues of vehicle and weapons maintenance and accountability, range scheduling, and safety briefings. In addition to all of their coordination with CFLCC, they received vehicles, ammunition, and other vital equipment for the training teams and shipped them north to Iraq. Their long days blurred into one, and when one contingent of troops was trained and on its way to Baghdad, they had to gear up for the next arrival.

At the neighboring post of Camp Virginia, the team of Lieutenant Colonel Todd Falk, First Sergeant Dennis Martinson, Staff Sergeant Andrew Forneris, and Staff Sergeant Jennifer Quayle handled all of the transportation, food, and billeting requirements of inbound 98th Division personnel. They worked the mission known as Reception, Staging, Onward Movement, and Integration or simply RSOI.

After the last of the main body arrived and shipped to Baghdad, Morales and Compitello received orders to set up shop for the Iraqi

Assistance Group, a Multi-National Corps-Iraq element tasked with the expanded mission of matching incoming military advisors from different branches of the U.S. armed forces with Iraqi security forces. At Camp Buehring, Kuwait, they established a team to handle RSOI requirements and train Active, Reserve, and Guard soldiers, as well as marines and airmen. Major Denise Golliday, First Sergeant Jimmy DeJesus, Sergeant First Class John Wilson, Sergeant First Class Patricia Uyechi, Staff Sergeant Ralph Trenchard, Staff Sergeant Denise Davis, and Sergeant Samuel Askins were part of this team. By July 2005, they had processed more than 400 advisors from all branches of the armed forces.

As with many other units, the 98th Division used the American posts in Kuwait as the stepping-stones into Iraq. The brief time spent in Kuwait was the introduction to the intense heat of the blazing desert sun and the intrigue of the Arab world.

A Team Approach to Teaching Logistics

In addition to setting up service and support activities, 98th Division soldiers moved out to run issuing facilities and instruct on the mechanics of sustaining an army. They spent countless hours one-on-one with their Iraqi counterparts inventorying, securing, and ordering from the various classes of supply. The following command teams handled the actual training missions at the three central issue facilities.

Al Kasik OIC:	MAJ Matthew Rousseau
NCOIC:	1SG John Hollenbeck
KMTB OIC:	CPT James Smith
NCOIC:	MSG Jeff Sims
An Numaniyah OIC:	MAJ Rexall Griggs
NCOIC:	SFC Anthony Scaringi

Training the Iraqi Security Forces

by MAJ James Dirisio

In fall 2004 Brigadier General James Schwitters, commanding general (CG) of the Coalition Military Assistance Training Team (CMATT), was looking for an executive officer (XO) to assist with the burgeoning operational and administrative tasks his command was experiencing. CMATT was going through an unprecedented period of growth at this time, evolving from a ten-person staff with less than 150 embedded trainers to a joint training and operational headquarters that would eventually

MAJ Jim Dirisio.

include a staff of more than forty and more than 500 embedded trainers working as Advisory Support Teams (ASTs), officer and noncommissioned officer (NCO) academy trainers, basic training mentors, and a variety of other roles. Members of the 98th Division filled the vast majority of these slots, bringing the strength of CMATT to nearly 100 percent before Christmas.

I interviewed with Brigadier General Schwitters, who had previously been the commander, 1st Special Operations Detachment-Delta (Airborne), and he selected me to be his XO. Like many members of the 98th, I ended up working in a position that was not a perfect match based on my military occupational specialty, but one for which working in a training assignment had prepared me. In my case, the XO slot was coded as an active-duty combat arms officer, and although I was neither, I was immersed in the mission to train the Iraqi Security Forces (ISF) from day one.

Working on the personal staff of the CG was demanding. Perhaps three days out of each week (sometimes more), I would travel as a member of his personal staff to assess the training of the ISF or to meetings with senior Iraqi and Coalition officers. This was the best part of the job, as I was able to see training and employment of ISF at the tactical level and was also aware of the "big picture." During my year in Iraq, I traveled to Samarra, An Numaniyah, Ar Rustamiyah, Kirkush, Al Kasik, Tall Afar, Mosul, Fallujah, Habbaniyah, Taji, Zakho, Tallil, Tikrit, and Hammam Al Allil, among other locations.

My impressions of the Iraqi soldiers are those of an outsider who was not embedded with any particular unit, as the ASTs were. From what I saw and heard, the soldiers were generally motivated, often fearless, somewhat ambivalent about the dangers and hazards of being in the ISF, committed to a better nation, and able to learn the individual and collective tasks required to fight the insurgency. As we stood up units in fall 2004, and they became operational, the ISF experienced some setbacks due to desertions, but there never seemed to be a shortage of new recruits. By the time the elections rolled around in January 2005, most of the desertion problems in the 1st, 3d, and 5th Divisions of the Iraqi Army had worked themselves out, and the Iraqi soldiers who remained could be counted on to stay and fight.

Along with Brigadier General Schwitters, I visited units from each of the three divisions, to include every brigade and nearly every battalion. I also had the honor to visit many times with the 1st Iraqi Mechanized Brigade and the 1st and 2d Motor Transport Regiments, as well as the military academies at Ar Rustamiyah and Zakho, the Iraqi Training Battalion (later Brigade) at Kirkush, each of the ten training bases where we had Base Support Unit personnel, and several Iraqi Air Force installations. Of all the units we visited, the 1st Brigade of the 1st Division (Iraqi Intervention Force) and the Mechanized Brigade struck me as the most impressive. The 1st Brigade had fought in every major action from Najaf in spring 2004, to Sadr

> *As we stood up units in fall 2004, and they became operational, the ISF experienced some setbacks due to desertions, but there never seemed to be a shortage of new recruits.*

City, Fallujah, Tall Afar, Mosul, and at the time I left, in various locations throughout the contentious and volatile Al Anbar province. The 1st Brigade leaders had a bond with their ASTs (to include a number of 98th Division officers and NCOs) that was unlike any other I witnessed. I believe it was because they had been through so much together. The first ASTs to be wounded (not from the 98th Division) and the first AST to be killed in action (again, not from the 98th) belonged to this brigade. Iraqi casualties of 1st Brigade were among the highest of any unit, but its esprit de corps was magnificent. These men—Iraqis and ASTs alike—were true warriors who consistently took on more than they should have been asked and achieved incredible results.

Similar to the 1st Brigade, 1st Division, the 1st Iraqi Mechanized Brigade was an organization that exhibited a certain élan and warrior mentality that was inspiring. This was an organization that none of the initial plans (appropriately dubbed "Grand Schemes" by their Australian authors in CMATT) had envisioned, but one which played a key role in securing nine major traffic control points in Baghdad during the January 2005 elections. I believe that the Mechanized Brigade's success came from the fact that it was an organization that the Iraqis wanted, not one that the Coalition told them they needed. With the ISF, everything worked better if it was an

SFC Walt Serra, AST.

Iraqi idea. Brigadier General Schwitters used to say that if there was to be a choice between a plan that one of our ASTs had developed and a plan that the Iraqis had developed, the Iraqi plan was usually the best option. This was abundantly evident in the Mechanized Brigade, which beat every manning, equipping, and training milestone developed for it, and which adapted its tactics to fight the insurgency despite the preponderance of its officers having been trained for, and veterans of, large-scale battles on open terrain.

The success of higher headquarters—from division level to the Ministry of Defense (MOD)—was somewhat more elusive during my year in Iraq. Brigadier General Schwitters often spoke of building the Iraqi Army from the bottom up and from the top down, and I believe the most frustrating half of that model was that which

SSG Fabian Rivera, Personal Security Detail.

With the ISF, everything worked better if it was an Iraqi idea.

depended on the staff functions of the MOD. Throughout my experience, the collective might of the CMATT and Multi-National Security Transition Command-Iraq staffs worked with, encouraged, and coerced senior Iraqi officials to perform the functions that our more than 200-year-old army takes for granted: paying soldiers, promoting them, and ensuring that they are fed, equipped, and led by the best available officers and NCOs. These were concepts that did not come easy to Iraqi officers, and it invariably was a more difficult concept to introduce as rank increased.

There were, however, notable exceptions, such as Lieutenant General Nasier Abadi. As the deputy chief of staff, Iraqi Joint Forces, he understood the importance of the administrative and logistical tasks in making the Iraqi Army credible and self-sufficient. He worked tirelessly to realize these things and it is to his great credit that the Iraqi Army achieved as much as it did in the short year in which I observed it. Abadi's boss, General Babekir Zebari, chief of staff, Iraqi Joint Forces, likewise served well and was unafraid to go to the front lines of fighting with us several times to congratulate his soldiers and demonstrate his support.

My overall impression of the 98th Division

personnel deployed to Iraq is extremely positive. We filled key vacancies in several joint staffs, provided the majority of CMATT's ten-man ASTs, staffed key training institutions with highly competent trainers, and reacted to numerous changes throughout the mobilization, deployment, and operational phases of the mission. We did all of this in an extremely ambiguous environment, with little or no doctrine or manuals to tell us how to train a foreign army and without the benefit of an extended ramp up.

We left for our successors, the 80th Division (IT), a wealth of knowledge, volumes of standard operating procedures, and lessons learned, and the validation that a training division could adapt itself to perform the number-one mission of our army, and perhaps of our nation.

AST Members at Camp Anaconda.

The Sisterhood of War

American women have served this nation since the Revolutionary War. They have proved decisive and tenacious in the most dire of circumstances. Even before the presidential rescinding of the risk rule in 1994, women worked close to the front lines of battle and often crossed into combat zones. Many paid the ultimate sacrifice in the defense of our freedoms, but above all, their call to duty was noble and true— and continues to be so to this day.

More than 200,000 women now serve in the ranks of U. S. armed forces, which have a total strength of just over two million. Within the 98th Division, more than 100 women warriors have answered the call to serve at home and abroad in the Global War on Terror. As women they have supported each other through the darkest hours of deployments. As soldiers, they live by the same Army Values and Warrior Ethos that define the actions of all who wear the uniform.

Left to right: SGT Mladenka Fangiullos, CPT Traci St. Denis, MAJ Ann Pellien, MSG Patricia Goodrich, COL Michele Altieri, SFC Marlene Taylor; Front: MSG Donna Harting.

With the recent mobilization to Iraq, several women soldiers of the 98th Division made significant contributions to the mission of training the new Iraqi security forces. From the initial phases to the return home of our troops, they committed themselves to the mission's success.

At the same time, the division remained faithful to its training commitments in the United States. To meet those goals, Major Sandra Forrest, commander of 5th Battalion, 3d Brigade, mobilized along with her instructors and set up operations at Fort Dix, New Jersey, to train and graduate Civil Affairs soldiers. Many of these graduates immediately mobilized to Iraq and Afghanistan and helped to fill a critical shortage within the U. S. Army.

Soldiers who processed through Camp Atterbury, Indiana, will never forget the organizational and regulatory mastery of Sergeant Major Jocene Preston. As the command sergeant major of troops, she kept the priorities straight for Soldier Readiness Processing, the next day's training requirements, and preparation of the battle update briefs. Even after the mission at Camp Atterbury ended, soldiers in Iraq contacted Sergeant Major Preston for information and assistance, ranging from news on newborn children to the status of promotion packets. True to form, she answered them all. Her actions embodied that universal Army maxim we all know so well— "Soldiers first, mission always."

In Baghdad, a small band of women from the 98th filled critical staff positions within the Multi-National Security Transition Command-Iraq (MNSTC-I) and set a standard of excellence. In the legal field, Colonel Michele Altieri worked as the Deputy Staff Judge Advocate and handled Uniform Code of Military Justice actions, Status

COL Jody Daniels.

Flight delay for MOB 4 leads to a game of Pigs.
Left to right: SFC Rick Jean, SFC David Catani,
SGM Jocene Preston, and 1SG Bruce Diamond.

of Forces Agreement issues, and the training of the Iraqi Army's Staff Judge Advocate Corps. She also helped establish an exchange program of Iraqi Army attorneys with the Judge Advocate General's Legal Center and School at Charlottesville, Virginia.

In addition to handling the personnel issues of a joint command in the J1 section, Major Ann Pellien also tracked the location and status of all 98th Division soldiers within Iraq. She was instrumental in providing accurate headcounts to the 98th Division G1 back in Rochester, New York. Her deft processing of efficiency reports and awards throughout the mission benefited many soldiers of the 98th.

Over in the intelligence section or J2, Colonel Jody Daniels assumed directorship in February 2005 and continued to establish the section's reputation as an accurate and timely source of infor-

Soldier recognized by Iraqi army

By Staff Sgt. Engels Tejeda
Staff Writer

When Maj. Norma Vargus learned she would be working with the Iraqi Army, she learned an old lesson: "Never judge a book by its cover."

Vargus, a member of the 98th Institutional Training Division, was mobilized to Iraq nearly a year ago to serve with the Coalition Military Assistance Team of the Multi-National Security Transition Command – Iraq. At first, she was a military liaison at an American base. Then last spring she was told she would be moving to the An Numanyah, an Iraqi-run base in eastern Iraq.

"Being a female in an all male Iraqi army, I feared I would be looked down upon," Vargus said, recounting her feelings when she arrived at the Iraqi training base. "But it has been the opposite. Once you show them you are competent, you are a Soldier."

The mission gave her the opportunity to prove her competency. She was tasked with helping the Iraqis build a training base from scratch. She helped them construct an Iraqi infantry training battalion and to build the only Iraqi military police school within the Iraqi army. Her role was primarily that of a mentor, and she said that it was tough to resist the temptation to try and turn the Iraqi army into a clone of the American forces.

"It's a whole new concept, a whole new process for them," she said of the new Iraqi army. "But as advisers, we don't do the training. They have to do it. Some things they'll take from us, but some

Photo by Staff Sgt. Engels Tejeda

Maj. Norma Vargus reminisces about her mission at An Numaniyah with other U.S. advisers and Iraqi soldiers serving there. Vargus helped set up an Iraqi MP school.

things they won't and you have to be patient."

She said she was concerned with assuring that everything she did as an adviser did not interfere with the Iraqi's ownership of their military. For example, whenever safety was concerned she or another U.S. adviser stepped in. But when non-threatening conditions were at issue, like styles of marching, she stepped back and let them handle it independently.

"It has to be their military," she noted.

In addition to institutional differences,

one of the biggest challenges was the remoteness of the camp, Vargus said.

"There was basically nothing here," Vargus said of the now functioning camp. "The closest American base is 45 minutes away," she said, noting that travel outside the compound was difficult.

Though not alone, she was one of only two females on the whole base, where approximately 400 American troops and over 4,300 Iraqi male soldiers reside.

"It's like a family here. If we are lacking resources, we help each other out.

There is camaraderie," she said.

Vargus also lucked out, she said. Her husband, Lt. Col. Richard Vargus, was mobilized to the same location a few weeks after she arrived.

"Sometimes I feel that it's unfair because so many people here have their family back home," she said.

Having her husband nearby was a mixed blessing, not only because their missions were so different that they got little time together, but also because they were constantly worried about anything happening to one another.

Still, she said the deployment became one of her most rewarding military experiences. Both of her main projects have been successful. The training battalion has been graduating enlistees through its basic training course and the MP school just graduated its second class and is expected to graduate another eight classes within the next six months.

A Reservist of 20 years, she said that working with the MP school was particularly rewarding because she is a part-time police officer in Cornwall, N.Y. She also works for the Social Security Administration there.

As her deployment ended, she said she relearned one of the golden rules.

"You come here with a pre-conceived notion of how bad it will be," she said during an award ceremony held in her honor by an Iraqi commander. "When you look at news programs back home, it's completely different than what you see here. People here are very receptive. . . You shouldn't judge people until you actually have a chance to know them."

Vargus is expected to return home before the 2005 holiday season.

Published in *The Ananconda Times*, November 13, 2005.

mation and analysis. Working with Multi-National Force-Iraq, she helped support the development of intelligence courses for the Iraqi Army and directed the establishment of a military intelligence school at Taji, Iraq. In addition, she supervised the plans for structuring and equipping the new Iraqi Army's military intelligence units. Her tireless efforts to professionalize the Iraqi military's intelligence corps will be long remembered.

At An Numaniyah, Major Norma Vargus worked with other advisors and trainers in the set up of an infantry training battalion. To her credit,

she overcame cultural barriers and mentored and molded many Iraqi noncommissioned officers and soldiers into leaders. Major Vargus even tapped into her police background when called to help establish the Iraqi Army military police school. In all aspects of her work, she maintained selflessness. She advised and shared her insights, but then stood back to allow the Iraqis to build their army.

At the Civilian Police Assistance Training Team Command (CPATT), Sergeant First Class

SFC Marlene Taylor,
MAJ Bob Sile, MAJ Joann Kartes.

Marlene Taylor worked with Major Robert Sile and Major Joann Kartes in wiring CPATT's head-quarters at Adnon Palace in Baghdad with Internet and e-mail capabilities. She handled network communication, satellite connectivity, and user account issues. Given the constant demand for communications, her seven-day work week was standard.

Between the forward operating bases and Baghdad, lines of support had to be maintained. Lieutenant Colonel Theresa Baginski managed convoy operations and lined up trucks, drivers, fuel, and security to meet delivery deadlines. Versatility is the dynamic in logistics, and Baginski did not miss a step in pushing supplies out to the remote reaches of the country.

LTC Theresa Baginski and
MAJ Karen Davies.

At Forward Operating Base (FOB) Shield, near the headquarters of the Iraqi government's Interior Ministry in downtown Baghdad, Major Shauna Hauser kept close hold over the welfare of troops, security, and facility maintenance. As "mayor" of the FOB, her days were filled with training, guard schedules, food service, and base expansion issues. A military police officer in the 98th Division, and a lawyer in the civilian world, Major Hauser seemed the natural choice for running a base that supported soldiers working with the Iraqi police and Interior Ministry.

MAJ Shauna Hauser.

At Taji, Colonel Cheryl Adams, Major Catherine Nadal, Major Karen Davies, and Major Patricia Collins developed combat life saving courses and wrote detailed programs of instruction (POIs) on how to stop bleeding, dress a wound, splint broken limbs, and start an IV. These POIs were quickly translated into

MAJ Catherine Nadal.

Arabic to help meet the huge demand for medics from the Iraqi Army units in the field.

Like all other warriors, they have faced the same exposure to enemy fire and endured the many discomforts, frustrations, and the loneliness borne of fatigue and of being so far from home. But most importantly, they pulled their weight and shared their expertise in support of the war effort. It is entirely fitting that they are a part of the team and are able to add to its diversity. It is this diversity which reflects the strength and greatness of the United States.

Baghdad
Serving Soldiers • Life in the MNSTC-I J1

by MAJ Ann Pellien

The Multi-National Security Transition Command-Iraq (MNSTC-I) staff and headquarters became a working reality when the first group of 98th Division soldiers arrived in Baghdad in September 2004. Beginning with a roster of 124 personnel, MNSTC-I grew to more than 1,400 troops by late 2005. The responsibility for providing personnel and administrative services to these troops, as well as to Iraq's Ministry of Defense (MOD), fell to the MNSTC-I J1, or Personnel Directorate.

Staffed by twenty-one service members from all branches of the U.S. military, representing both the active and reserve components, the J1 consisted of two distinct sections: the Iraqi Cell, which trained and mentored the MOD personnel office, or M1, and the Coalition Cell, which supported MNSTC-I's Coalition elements with personnel administration and strength management. Working in a joint environment was one of the most challenging aspects of the mission, and learning new regulations and standards for each service proved to be both interesting and enlightening.

Among its many duties, the J1 supported the

MNSTC-I staff and headquarters and Coalition Military Assistance Training Team (CMATT) and Civilian Police Assistance Training Team (CPATT) personnel by developing and implementing procedures and policies for emergency leave, rest and recuperation leave, promotions, award submissions and approval, officer and noncommissioned officer evaluation reports, casualty reporting, and other personnel guidelines and procedures. Over the course of the year-long deployment, thousands of personnel actions were completed by the troops of the J1.

The J1 also oversaw development of the Joint Manning Document, which established the personnel requirements for current and future missions of the MNSTC-I headquarters, CMATT, and CPATT. This project included close coordination with the U.S. Central Command and numerous briefings to Lieutenant General David Petraeus, the MNSTC-I commander, and General George Casey, commander of Multi-National Force-Iraq. We also worked closely with the

Coalition countries to assist them in filling their vacancies and acquiring soldiers to support the MNSTC-I mission.

A great deal of effort was put into requesting and acquiring additional Advisory Support Teams and Police Training Teams to support the constantly changing and increasing requirements of the CMATT and CPATT training missions. As the Iraqi military and police forces continued to grow, so did the requirement to support and train their forces, to include the development of new combat support and combat service support units and the Coalition forces to train them.

The J1 also was also heavily involved in training and mentoring the Iraqi M1 to develop similar policies for the Iraqi Armed Forces. Policies such as promotion, pay, centralized identification cards, and especially accountability were virtually nonexistent in the Iraqi military in the past. These policies and procedures were introduced and implemented to the Iraqi Armed forces during the deployment. The J1 also acted as linguist coordinators, providing translators and interpreters throughout the theater of operations.

In addition, the J1 also wrote and submitted the recommendation for MNSTC-I's Joint Meritorious Unit Award (JMUA), an award given by the Department of Defense to joint units that have distinguished themselves "by exceptionally meritorious achievement in pursuit of joint military operations of great significance." The JMUA was awarded on September 8, 2005, and is authorized for wear by troops who were assigned to the MNSTC-I headquarters from July 1, 2004, to March 31, 2005.

Working with the MNSTC-I headquarters staff can only be described as both enlightening and exhausting. The MNSTC-I commander, Lieutenant General David Petraeus, and chief of staff, Colonel James Laufenburg, expected excellence from their soldiers, sailors, airmen, and marines. Anything other than complete success was not an option. Overall the mission was extremely challenging and a great learning experience. Each and every service member who participated should be very proud of his or her tireless efforts to train, equip, and mentor the Iraqi Armed Forces.

J1 during sandstorm, July 14, 2005.

Always Out Front
the MNSTC-I J2 • Intelligence Directorate

by SFC Ryan Crissy

In early September 2004, the 98th Division mobilized the first of several groups of soldiers it would send to Iraq to augment the staff and headquarters of the Multi-National Security Transition Command-Iraq (MNSTC-I). After less than two weeks of deployment preparation and training at Fort Bliss, Texas, and Camp Virginia, Kuwait, this initial group of sixty-one soldiers arrived in Baghdad on September 24, 2004. They came from various backgrounds and professions, such as teachers, police officers, lawyers, and truck drivers, and a variety of military specialties, including logistics, personnel, engineers, and legal affairs. Three of these soldiers, Major Peter Mangerian, Master Sergeant Joel Wright, and Sergeant First Class Ryan Crissy, were assigned to the MNSTC-I J2 or Intelligence Directorate.

At the time of their arrival, the J2 had been staffed by only two service members, Colonel Danelle Scotka of the U.S. Army Reserve and Chief Petty Officer Jeffery Pollard of the U.S. Navy. As director of the J2, Colonel Scotka welcomed the newly arrived soldiers of the 98th and assigned them to positions within the directorate. Major Mangerian, a civil affairs officer who had previous experience in military intelligence, was assigned as the J2 liaison to the Iraqi Ministry of Defense. Master Sergeant Wright, a combat engineer and twenty six-year veteran of the Army Reserve, was made the directorate's noncommissioned officer in charge (NCOIC). Sergeant First Class Crissy, an experienced counterintelligence agent, was appointed the J2's counterintelligence/human intelligence (CI/HUMINT) coordinator. Because MNSTC-I was still a new organization, and these positions had never before been filled, Colonel Scotka provided basic guidance on her expectations for the positions, but otherwise gave the three soldiers the freedom to develop their own duties and responsibilities. This strategy proved extremely successful as each soldier used his civilian skills and military knowledge and experience to meet the directorate's mission of providing the MNSTC-I command, staff, and subordinate units with timely and accurate intelligence support.

Over the next few months, the J2 began to grow as new service members arrived to augment MNSTC-Is staff directorates. In early October 2004, Senior Airman Kandice Saunders of the U.S. Air Force joined the J2 as the section's clerk. Soon after, Staff Sergeant Dennit Goodwin, a counterintelligence agent and instructor with the

98th Division, arrived and was assigned as the section's second CI/HUMINT coordinator. Additional arrivals included Sergeant First Class Robin Fahey, 98th Division intelligence analyst who was later outsourced to the MNSTC-I J3, or Operations Directorate, and Captain David Peterson, a U.S. Army Reserve intelligence officer who was assigned as the J2's liaison to the Civilian Police Assistance Training Team.

As the number of J2 staff increased, so too did the section's responsibilities. From preparing the commanding general's daily intelligence updates, updating attack databases and route analyses, interacting with senior Iraqi intelligence officers, and interviewing walk-in sources, to helping to develop and provide logistical support to the Iraqi Army's reconnaissance and surveillance course, the J2's mission seemed to expand on a daily basis. Other significant accomplishments during those early days included providing route analyses for troop movements in anticipation of the battle for Fallujah in November 2004, tracking significant events and Iraqi military and police casualties during Iraq's free elections in January 2005, and coordinating and planning construction of the MNSTC-I Secure Compartmented Information Facility.

Significant accomplishments included providing route analyses for troop movements in anticipation of the battle for Fallujah.

After a successful nine-month tenure as director of the J2, Colonel Scotka redeployed in February 2005, and leadership of the section passed to Colonel Jody Daniels. Colonel Daniels, an intelligence officer with the 98th Division, had been in Iraq since July 2004, serving as the chief of plans and integration with the Coalition Military Assistance Training Team. Under Colonel Daniels' direction, the section refocused its efforts on providing intelligence training support to the Iraqi military and police forces. She was aided in this by an additional and somewhat unexpected influx of eleven active-duty intelligence professionals to the J2 in March 2005.

To accommodate the new personnel and ensure the commanding general's intent for the J2 was met, the directorate was reorganized into two sections: intelligence support and current intelligence. The intelligence support section was tasked with developing organizational charts and tables of organization and equipment for the new Iraqi military intelligence units, supporting Iraqi intelligence courses, and with planning and developing the new Iraqi intelligence school at Taji, a military base approximately twenty kilometers north of Baghdad. Arrangements were also made to have several J2 personnel join Mobile Training Teams and teach intelligence courses around the country. Even the NCOIC, Master Sergeant Wright, who is a computer programmer in his civilian career, got directly involved in the training mission by developing an intelligence database for the Iraqi military. The current intelligence section, meanwhile, continued to provide intelligence support to MNSTC-I commanding general, staff, and subordinate units, to include daily briefings, attack analyses, CI/HUMINT reporting summaries and threat warnings, security clearance and access badging, and special intelligence products. The efforts of all service members assigned to the J2 resulted in

Under Colonel Daniels' direction, the section refocused its efforts on providing intelligence training support to the Iraqi military and police forces.

successful accomplishment of the directorate's mission, and this was recognized by the highest levels of the command and even the Department of Defense.

Following her selection to the U.S. Army War College, Colonel Daniels left MNSTC-I in June 2005. In August 2005, the J2 experienced an almost 100 percent turnover of personnel, as both the active-duty and 98th Division staff began redeploying and demobilizing. They were replaced by soldiers of the U.S. Army Reserve's 80th Division, who faced the incredible standards set by their predecessors.

Back Row: LtCol Douglas Seagraves (USAF), unidentified Fijian guard, SFC Ryan Crissy (98th DIV), MAJ Timothy Miller (USA), MSG Joel Wright (98th DIV), COL Jody Daniels (98th DIV), SSG Dennit Goodwin (98th DIV), TSgt Wesley Evans (USAF)
Front Row: MAJ Joseph Heim (USAR), Maj John Sirotniak (USMC), CPT Mark Liu (USA), MAJ Peter Mangerian (98th DIV), SrA Kellie Herman (USAF), SFC Nena Crabbs (USAR), SSgt Christopher Morgan (USAF), MAJ Samuel Waller (USA).

The Coordination Hub
Life in the MNSTC-I J3
by MAJ Bob Sile

For the first group of 98th Division soldiers arriving in Baghdad in September 2004, assignment to the Multi-National Security Transition Command-Iraq (MNSTC-I) J3, or Operations Directorate, meant stepping into a bus traveling at full speed. A highly visible, high-stress environment that operated twenty-four hours a day, seven days a week, the J3 provided day-to-day command and control of MNSTC-I and oversaw the development, justification, prioritization, and implementation of projects to train, equip, and mentor the new Iraqi security forces.

It was a highly visible, high stress environment with little room for error.

Working within the MNSTC-I operations center, the J3 generated operations orders and ensured that MNSTC-I's plans and projects were aligned with Multi-National Force-Iraq and the commanding general's intent. These projects usually included close coordination with the U.S. Central Command and numerous briefings to MNSTC-I staff, Lieutenant General David Petraeus (the MNSTC-I commander), and the Department of State.

In addition to providing command and control, the directorate also served as the MNSTC-I coordination hub, generating plans, issuing orders, assessing the current status of operations and tasks, and collecting and publishing feedback on what went well and what did not. The J3 supported internal MNSTC-I staff processes, tracked each staff section's taskings, and coordinated with Multi-National Corp-Iraq and the Coalition Military Assistance Training Team and Civilian Police Assistance Training Team operations staffs.

Each morning began with a MNSTC-I staff briefing, and the J3 published hun-

MAJ George Adams, Mayor of Al Kut, stands with new graduates of the police academy.

dreds of daily, weekly, and monthly operational summaries collected from all staff sections. Numerous briefings were given daily to command personnel and visitors, such as the Secretary of Defense, on problems, project and plan statuses, issues, and draft plan reviews.

Staffed by more than forty service members from all branches of the U.S. military and Coalition partners, both active and reserve, the J3 had to work through several cultural challenges in building a cohesive team from so many different services and nationalities. Other challenges included working in a nonmature environment, for which the J3 had to develop its own procedures and processes to tackle challenging and fluid

missions.

Over the course of the year-long deployment, the J3 mission grew and more personnel were added to the directorate's staff. Despite this influx, the pace of operations remained demanding. Some of the directorate's accomplishments include planning and conducting the expansion of the MNSTC-I headquarters staff, the introduction of Special Police Training Teams, and the replacement of all 98th Division personnel with those from the 80th Division (IT). To meet demanding and diverse mission requirements, the directorate also fielded its own convoy teams, the Rough Riders, to provide security for MNSTC-I personnel traveling throughout Iraq. J3 staff personnel also traveled to remote locations around the country, spending significant periods of time conducting training, attending meetings, and troubleshooting problems. Overall the J3 mission was extremely challenging and was a tremendous learning experience. Every service member who served in the J3 should be proud of his or her efforts to help build, train, and equip Iraq's security forces.

LTG Petraeus receives briefing from SFC David MacMullen, MSG Andrew Krom and MAJ George Adams.

Riding Rough
in the Land of the Two Rivers

by 1LT Chris Henderson

The streets and alleyways of Iraq's cities and villages are some of the most dangerous places on earth. Danger lurks around every corner—piles of trash, apparently harmless, could provide cover for hidden explosives; a parked car, badly damaged and abandoned, could be a vehicle bomb ready to detonate; the man working on the roof of a building overlooking the street could be a spotter for an ambush. Threats, both hidden and not so hidden, made driving through many Iraqi cities a life-and-death gamble that few would take willingly.

American War, as well as a nod to the demands of their job, these modern-day Rough Riders were responsible for conducting a variety of security missions throughout Iraq, from convoy security and escort to area overwatch and protection. Their area of operation stretched from An Numaniyah in the south, to Al Kasik in the north; from Kirkush in the east, to Ramadi and Habbaniyah in the west. Operating in the so-called Sunni Triangle (Baghdad, Samarra, Tikrit, and Fallujah), wasn't uncommon.

Above: Waiting to CM at Martyrs Monument;
Center: SGT "X" Xavier; Right: SSG Rodriguez manning the .50 cal.

In the roughly twelve months that the soldiers of the 98th Division were in Iraq, perhaps no one faced more danger, more often, than the troops assigned to the Rough Riders of the Multinational Security Transition Command. Named for the famous volunteer cavalry regiment of the Spanish-

Comprised mostly of soldiers of the 98th Division, including those who were cross-leveled from other divisions such as the 95th, 100th, 104th, and 84th USAR-RTC, the two twenty-man platoons of the Rough Riders hit the streets of Baghdad and other cities

SFC Semo, lead gunner for convoy team's 2d platoon.

Tight trip to National Bank, downtown Baghdad.

in their up-armored Humvees on an almost daily basis. Although many of the Rough Riders were infantry, others were medics, engineers, personnel specialists, and even chaplain assistants. Other service branches were represented as well—soldiers, sailors, and marines worked side by side to ensure that people and equipment made it safely to their destinations.

During the course of the deployment, the Rough Riders conducted more than 2,000 security missions without losing a single soldier from within their ranks, a record any combat unit would be proud of. Contact with the enemy, however, was inevitable and unfortunately common, as several Rough Riders were injured in firefights and explosive ambushes. Several Riders were decorated for deeds, but many would agree that making it home alive was one of their greatest accomplishments.

2d Platoon just before redeploying.

Digital Warriors
Communications and the MNSTC-I J6

by MAJ Bob Sile

Communication and automation systems are key components of the modern battlefield. An effective and reliable communications network can make the difference in how well commanders can exercise command and control of their forces, increasing their chances of success. During the mission to rebuild Iraq's security forces (ISF), the responsibility for providing communications and automation services to the ISF, as well as the Multi-National Security Transition Command-Iraq (MNSTC-I), fell to the MNSTC-I J6, or Communications Directorate.

The J6 supported the MNSTC-I staff and headquarters and Coalition Military Assistance Training Team (CMATT) and Civilian Police Assistance Training Team (CPATT) personnel by designing solutions to requirements, purchasing, and implementing radio and computer-based systems for Iraqi Ministry of Defense (MOD) and Ministry of Interior (MOI) use nationwide. The J6 supported internal MNSTC-I use of communications and automation systems and the integration of those systems with the other Coalition secure and nonsecure systems. Over the course of the year-long deployment, tens of thousands of handheld and vehicle radios were delivered to Iraqi security forces, hundreds of communications systems and thousands networked computers were installed, and thousands of MOD and MOI users and communications personnel were trained by the troops of the J6.

Staffed by about thirty service members from all branches of the U.S. military, representing both the active and reserve components, the J6 consisted of two distinct sections: the CMATT Cell, which trained and mentored the MOD communications office; and the CPATT C6 Cell, which supported MNSTC-I's CPATT command and was dedicated to training and mentoring the (MOI) communications and automation offices. Working in a nonmature environment for communications systems was the most challenging aspect of the J6 mission. No operable radio or computer systems existed for either the MOD or MOI when the 98th Division soldiers arrived in fall 2004. Power was often unreliable, and the physical environment, with its high heat and dust, would take its toll on systems,

> *Over the course of the year-long deployment, tens of thousands of handheld and vehicle radios were delivered to Iraqi security forces…*

resulting in several crashes. In addition, every Iraqi who would operate or support communications systems in the MOI and MOD needed to be trained.

The J6 also oversaw the development and deployment of the C4I architecture documents, which established the voice communications, networking, and automation requirements for current and future missions of the MNSTC-I headquarters, the Iraqi MOI, and the Iraqi MOD. This project included close coordination with the U.S. Central Command and numerous briefings to Lieutenant General David Petraeus, the MNSTC-I commander, and the Department of State. The C4I architecture was used as the basis for equipping Iraqi Security Forces and then tying those communications systems into both national and tactical networks to provide redundant voice and data support. The J6 played a critical role in creating secure voice and data communications between the Iraqi national government headquarters and those of the ministries' operations command centers to support the two Iraqi national elections and the national referendum.

Left to right: 1LT Andrew Radano, SSG Paul Eastman, SFC Marlene Taylor, MAJ Bob Sile, MAJ Joann Kartes, 1LT Amy Stahler (USAF), TSGT Kevin Washington (USAF), CPT Thomas Guthrie (USMC).

Making friends during our travels.

The J6 worked closely with those Coalition countries that supported specific provinces within Iraq to integrate existing and planned voice and data systems to support the Iraqi security forces' mission. A great deal of effort was put into providing additional communications equipment to support Military Transition Teams and Police Transition Teams to meet the constantly changing and increasing requirements of CMATT and CPATTs training missions. As the Iraqi military and police forces continued to grow, so did the requirement to equip, support, and train their forces, to include the development of new MOD signal support units and the Coalition forces to train them.

The J6 was heavily involved in training and mentoring the Iraqi MOD and MOI signal and communications staffs to develop appropriate policies and procedures for the Iraqi security forces. Policies such as securing systems, standardized operating procedures, and especially account-ability were virtually nonexistent within the Iraqi security forces of the past. These policies and procedures were introduced at the same time as new technologies were implemented to the Iraqi security forces during the deployment. The J6 also coordinated with Coalition and Department of State organizations to provide standardized solutions and integrate systems and data fielded throughout the theater of operations.

J6 personnel spent significant time traveling to locations throughout Iraq to conduct training and site surveys, install equipment, repair systems, train and mentor Iraqi personnel, and troubleshoot problems. Anything other than complete success was not an option as data showed a significant drop in Iraqi security force personnel survivability when reliable communications systems were not present at MOI or MOD locations.

Overall the mission was extremely challenging and a tremendous learning experience. Every member of the J6 should be proud of his or her tireless efforts to train, equip, and mentor the Iraqi security forces.

SFC Marlene Taylor checks communications equipment on roof.

Fallujah

Descent into an Inferno

Spearheaded by two regimental combat teams (RCTs) of the U.S. Marine Corps, with additional support from the U.S. and Iraqi armies, the second battle of Fallujah was launched in November 2004. Initially named Operation Phantom Fury, but later renamed Operation Al Fajr (Dawn) by the Iraqi Ministry of Defense, the objective was to regain control of the city in advance of the national elections in January 2005. While the historical impact of this battle will reverberate in think tanks and university lecture halls in the months and years ahead, mention is in order of the soldiers of the 98th Division who had a hand in the success of this pivotal mission.

Swift and furious, the battle itself was executed in a series of bold and decisive steps. First, the U.S. Army sealed off the city with an impenetra-

ble cordon of military police and infantry battalions. Next, a feint of rapidly moving armored vehicles skirted the southern edge of the city with an accompanying artillery barrage on selected

targets. However, it was the leveling force of an estimated 10,000 American and 2,000 Iraqi soldiers who crossed the railroad embankment just north of the city that decided the outcome of this brilliant assault.

Arrayed in six parallel columns, soldiers and marines moved in deliberate steps from door to door and from neighborhood to neighborhood in search of insurgents and their weapon caches. Day became night, but there was no time for rest.

Though resistance was scattered, platoons were exposed to the constant threats of indirect fire, improvised explosive devices (IEDs), and vehicle-borne improvised explosive devices (VBIEDs). Characterized by emotional extremes ranging from the heights of adrenaline-induced elation to

the dark abyss of fear, military operations in city streets are the most exhausting maneuvers for any soldier—no matter how well trained.

When the insurgency did raise its menacing head, the crackle of Kalashnikov rifles and the woosh of rocket-propelled grenades ensued.

Before the Americans could return fire, the insurgents would melt into the shadows of winding alleyways and narrow streets. Pursuit was often maddeningly frustrating. American intelligence estimated the insurgent strength as somewhere between 1,000 to 3,000 fighters. The electronic eyes of aerial drones buzzing overhead spotted insurgents communicating by cell phones and adjusting mortar tubes as they targeted American positions. At other times, they were seen waving black flags from rooftops to mass their remaining troops, a technique dating back to the days of Napoleon.

Though resourceful and determined, the insurgents felt the choking grasp of the assault, and by midweek the RCTs

"To be sure, the terrorists and insurgents are out to shake our will. But they will not succeed. The Iraqi people, enabled by the military and civilian members of the coalition will succeed."

General George Casey
Multi-National Force-Iraq Commander, June 2005

had reached Highway 10, the road which divides the city of Fallujah in half. They regrouped there—all the while maintaining their vital logistical lines of support into and out of the city. The assault permeated the neighborhoods of Resala, Nazal, and Jebail. Within a week, the American forces defeated the last rebel stronghold. Tanks and armored vehicles pushed through the cluttered streets with troops following on foot. In the end, the insurgency loosed its hold on the city as 1,200 insurgents lay dead and scores of caches were uncovered. In this city of mosques, weapon caches were discovered in sixty of them.

Though the assault ended, the need

for security and order continued. In late November, Colonel Brad Parsons, senior U.S. advisor to the Iraqi Army's 5th Division, met with Colonel Michael Schupp, commander of RCT-1, to augment the security posture of Fallujah with his Advisory Support Teams (ASTs) and Iraqi battalions. Parsons also had to plan for a relief in place for Schupp's battle-weary units. In the midst of intermittent small arms fire, mortar attacks, and IEDs, Parsons and his Iraqi counterpart surveyed the city for placement of their units.

Some AST members, such as Majors John Curwen and Dean Swartwood, arrived earlier and immediately went into patrol mode with their teams and Iraqi units. Master Sergeant Jason Jaskula and Staff Sergeant Christopher Dill partnered with marines in patrolling various sections of Fallujah in pursuit of Abu Musab al-Zarqawi, head thug of al-Qaeda in Iraq. Sergeant First Class Christopher Balch was seriously wounded during a mortar attack while standing guard at a traffic control point not more than a hundred yards away from the Abu Ghurayb prison.

Other teams arrived in December. Major Scott Ward and his team followed their assigned Iraqi Intervention Force unit as it patrolled the north-

ern section of Fallujah. When Major Matt Jones and his team arrived, they immediately attached themselves to 3d Battalion, 1st Marines of RCT-1. Their area of responsibility was framed by a wedge of rough neighborhoods and souks to the

north known as the "Pizza Slice," Route Henry to the east, and the Euphrates River to the west. They kept a 24/7 schedule of patrols and support right up to the day they left Fallujah in late August 2004.

In a remarkable display of Iroquois team spirit, Sergeant Major Cedric Green and Sergeant First Class Dale Fair, both from Jones's team,

collaborated with marines and Iraqi soldiers to uncover one of the largest caches on record. It took three two-and-a-half-ton trucks to remove everything they found. The training teams worked hand-in-hand with their assigned Iraqi units and the marines, and survived numerous ambushes, IEDs, and VBIEDs. Even when the city's electric pump stations failed and the Euphrates flooded much of the area, they continued their missions.

"The Iraqi soldiers are great emulators," Parsons would later comment. "They see, and then do." In the setting of Fallujah, these Iraqi soldiers learned and remembered their lessons quickly. The city was the perfect classroom for their instruction.

According to Parsons, the Iraqi soldiers were able to derive relevant intelligence from local citizens. Though the country suffers from a low literacy rate, the Iraqis possess a notable street savviness per- haps born out of the need to survive the ordeals

of shifting tribal, religious, and political bound- aries. They are also sensitive to the social dynam-

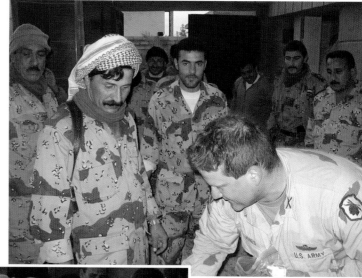

ics of countrymen and foreigners alike, and are astute in the subtleties of body language. Indeed, the words of guerrilla-warfare expert and British Army Colonel C. E. Callwell support these facts when he commented a century ago that local populations "are far more observant than the dwellers in civilized lands."

Even Parsons' staff of fifteen officers and non-commissioned officers (NCOs) kept a seven-day work schedule during their time in Fallujah. They assisted the MTTs in developing mission essential task lists and tables of manning and equipment. NCOs such as Sergeant First Class James Lantvet trained Iraqi soldiers on the use of computer software for personnel actions, helped manage Iraqi interpreters, and advised Iraqi NCOs in coordinating divisional conferences for their nascent army.

A total of seven Iraqi units participated in the battle for Fallujah. Six more Iraqi units, four of which were advised by 98th Division training teams, participated in numerous patrols through the city's restive streets in the weeks after the assault. In the heart of the Sunni triangle, Iroquois warriors taught and mentored the Iraqis on leadership, tactics, and teamwork–lessons that would serve them well in the coming year.

COL Parsons and team investigate a car bombing.

Building Bonds of Trust...

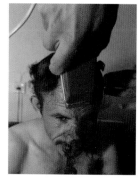
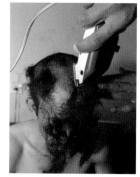

Giving a Sense of Hope

2005/02/17

Taji
Command Sergeant Major View
by CSM Milt Newsome

The mission of the 98th Division was to train the Iraqi soldiers to protect their own country.

I was very fortunate to have served as the 98th Division's senior noncommissioned officer in Iraq. Selected for the position by Major General Bruce Robinson and Command Sergeant Major William Grocott, I had the honor to serve as command sergeant major for the Command and Control Cell, Coalition Military Assistance Training Team (CMATT); Iraqi Assistance Group; and Taji Military Base (TMB).

In September 2004 Taji Military Base (Iraqi side) had

MG Bruce Robinson, CSM Milt Newsome and CSM Bill Grocott.

approximately 1,500 Iraqi soldiers and 100 Coalition soldiers. During the next few months of base reconstruction, under the guidance of Colonel Robert Catalanotti's Base Support Unit staff, the base grew to 600 Coalition soldiers and approximately 15,000 Iraqi soldiers.

Called the Star of Iraq, TMB was the largest Iraqi military base. TMB was also the training center for such units and activities as the Civilian Police Assistance Training Team, CMATT, and the Iraqi National Guard's Basic Combat Training.

I served with outstanding soldiers from the 98th Division and cross-leveled units such as Colonel Catalanotti, Colonel Frank Cipolla, Chaplain (LTC) David Pillsbury, Lieutenant

COL Abbas and LTC Corriveault attend an Iraqi Army graduation ceremony.

COL Robert Catalanotti at South Gate.

COL Robert Lawless and
LTC Andrew Lyons.

Colonel Michael Corriveault, Sergeant Major Christopher Robb, Sergeant Major Ed Saxon, and Master Sergeant Gino Banks.

I would like to personally acknowledge the initial Taji J4 unit members (September 2004): Sergeant First Class Kathleen Menard, Staff Sergeant Deborah Austin, Staff Sergeant Christina Rowe, Sergeant First Class Wilmer Quarles, and SFC Dale Burgdoff for their contribution to the mission.

They did an awesome job with the logistics and

CPT Stacy O'Keefe,
Transportation Advisor.

distribution of materials throughout Iraq. The convoys during the day and the Chinook night missions kept our soldiers supplied with the essential critical equipment they needed.

Of the 760 soldiers from the 98th Division who supported the FA-TRAC mission, five made the ultimate sacrifice: Master Sergeant Paul Karpowich, Staff Sergeant Christopher Dill, Sergeant First Class Robert Derenda, Sergeant

Lawrence Roukey, and Lieutenant Colonel Terrence Crowe. They will be truly missed and never forgotten.

The contributions of all the 98th Division soldiers were second to none and will forever have an effect on Iraq and the freedom of its people.

I am proud to be an American soldier serving in the United States Army as a member of the 98th Division. I will continue to serve my country with pride and dignity in support of the Global War on Terrorism. I thank God for his daily blessings; my family for their sacrifice, support, and understanding; my friends/co-workers for their prayers and the support of my employer. They all played an integral part in my success as a soldier.

BG Richard Sherlock receives plaque from COL Abbas, Iraqi Commander of Camp Taji.

98th Division OES Instructors.

LTC Andrew Lyons, 1SG Dean Chilton, SSG Jennifer Quayle and SSG Michael Richards.

christmas in Iraq

Email from MAJ Bob Sile

Monday, December 6, 2004 • 12:38 pm

Hello to all from this side of the world. My apologies for tardiness in sending out email but have been overwhelmed with work and digging out does not appear likely before the Iraqis elections are held. Doing fine, though.

Have added two people to my group and lost one at the end of the week. The good news is the two newbies are both Army so they will be here for a year. I and my entire crew would like to thank all of you for your generosity in shipping all of the boxes and packets of stuff! We all greatly appreciate all the food, items, and kind words sent by all.

Work for me is a blur of trying to find all the items that are "supposed to be" located somewhere and trying to bring some planning and organization to chaos. My predecessor wasn't one for structure, planning, documentation, or organization so this is causing me problems plus driving me crazy. Still I have a good group and it's amazing the amount of stuff that does get accomplished when you look back each week.

Thought I'd provide some insights into daily life here. Iraq is known here as "the Land of the Not Quite Right." Toilets overflow, there are no street lights, traffic doesn't stay to one side or the other (always exciting!), electric lines just end (no ending in a box for example, they just leave the exposed ends out), food is not all together. For example, I had lunch the other day and had noodles, and meat sauce. Then I ask for Italian spaghetti sauce and told "you have ketchup." Things like that occur constantly. Street signs read "Parking No" or "Way One." Time is "Iraqi-ish" so that when you schedule a delivery for 9am it happens sometime within a couple of hours of that.

We now eat at our palace from a caterer. Food is not bad. But Iraqis have tomatoes and cucumbers but no lettuce for salad. Meats are good; fish is suspect. There is always candy out now and a fast way to get in a fight is to grab someone's diet soda because Iraqis don't make diet ANYTHING! We live in trailers (see attached pictures) and some folks have taken trailer living to new lows! The guy across from me has several pink plastic flamingos. There are Santas, football team logos, plus flower pots, a couple with fake "yards" and someone who had his wife send him dirt and grass seed and planted a yard (don't do me this kind of favor). He likes to walk to feel grass between his toes but there are WAY too many dogs loose for that.

First thing on everyone's minds is safety so each morning we inspect our vehicles before getting in. When anyone gets a package we immediately strip off the return addresses off everything so none of you get some nasty mail.

We work in the palace which has just been turned over to the Iraqis so any work now takes three times as long to get permission for. Iraqi decision-making is VERY centralized and if the top guy is out all decisions wait. They seem to be having difficulty with the concept that they have to make things work. We buy stuff (say a generator) and when it runs out of fuel they expect us to pay for fuel. When we politely decline they posture and do nothing for a while. If you give in you're assured it will happen again shortly. They are used to government giving them things, so the idea that US forces will buy them something but make them pay to run it is new.

We hear car bombs go off (and you see them on news shortly thereafter). Sometimes it's a boom, other times just the smoke plume. The latest bombing near the green zone really rattled the palace here but we all just stopped a second, saw nothing falling, and went back to work. Can't do anything, so we just forge ahead.

Sense amongst troops here is things will become more and more violent up to and just after the elections but violence is focused on Iraqis (police and National Guard) and less and less at Americans. Insurgency is seeing large drops in popularity because of violence against Iraqis so their aim now seems to disrupt voting. After the taking of Fallujah, insurgency seems to be becoming more desperate as they have no secure base from which to operate. Frequencies of attacks, the number of car bombs, etc. all show big drops as insurgents must now move and do not have places in which to build or store bombs, weapons, etc.

Thanksgiving was fine, but it was mostly a work day. Some got off, but after you've done the laundry, slept in, and worked out, you do have much to do, so you might as well work because you know your email is just pages and pages long. But did have turkey.

Christmas trees are already up here. Some are organizing Christmas parties (sorry holiday gatherings) and caroling sessions. I'll have guys all over Iraq those weeks so I'm not doing any of it this year.

Well, gotta run. Again thanks to all for packages, cards, and emails!

Freedom Isn't Free

by MAJ Brian Adelson

February 4, 2005, 12:03 pm

I am not sure if many understand this as much as the Iraqi people do today. For the first time in history they had a free election and I was lucky enough to have a front row seat. (Some may argue that this wasn't the first free election that Iraq has had, but I researched this with several Iraqi people and in their opinion it was).

I was kidding with my Iraqi counterparts explaining that in America a front row seat to an event like this would cost you big money…and I guess leaving my family, friends, and job in the States is big money. Well, as usual I tried to make the best of it, and all I can say is, "Unbelievable."

Many have asked what my duties would be during the elections and for security reasons I could not tell, but now that it is all over, I would like to try and share some of my experiences. The Iraqi unit that I advise had the mission of securing several polling locations to make it safe for the Iraqis to vote. To minimize danger, the planning for this was very close hold and nobody, well except a few of us, even knew the locations until around 3:00 pm on Saturday. They also attempted

to keep the minimum number of sites to make security easier. That is important to know, and you will understand why in a minute.

During the weekend I kept thinking about how much different our voting experience is in America. On Election Day in America, I would imagine many of you conducted business as usual. Going to work, caring for family, possibly on vacation, but life was just routine, with maybe the occasional, "Who are you going to vote for?" conversation.

To compare that to here…On Thursday evening the roads closed. Basically,

ELECTION DAY
January 30, 2005
Convoys Leaving Camp Taji
Enroute to Vote.

people were told to stay home or risk being shot at, and I can attest to the fact that vehicles moving after the "No Roll Policy" went into effect truly risked being shot at. On Friday, the military descended on many villages and set up security. Armed soldiers were patrolling the streets to keep the polling locations safe. Merchants were not able to open their shops. Although, in the village we were in, we made an exception for the bakery. He was a smart entrepreneur, giving us freshly baked bread, before asking us to pull a few strings for him. I also coordinated to have the local drug store remain open for a few hours on Election Day, because working in retail I understand what it means to have competitive hours. A curfew was

enacted and anyone caught out after dark was arrested and held until after the elections.

On Election Day, just to get

the opportunity to vote, most people had to go through at least two searches and sometimes three just to get the chance to stand in line. We don't

even like to get searched when we board a plane.

As different as I found it, I was actually surprised how well people took it. I mean we were telling them that they could not work, go to school, drive, or run any errands for their wife. All they had to do was get up and watch TV for a few days and not feel guilty about being lazy... not

a bad deal. I am sure they also understood how dangerous this weekend could be, and many may have looked upon us as saviors.

For us, it was great to walk around the city and talk with some of the locals. You could sense that some people liked Americans, but then there

were those that didn't. We were talking with the kids and passing out candy and taking pictures with them. Some of the adults would come over and make their kids stay away from us.

We truly understood and just continued to talk with people and tried to gain their trust. By the end of the weekend you could almost sense a change. We basically had free movement around the town. I am sure that being heavily armed helped us a little.

As many of you know, I enjoy meeting new people. I was trying to get them excited about the election, asking everyone if they were going to vote. On Election Day I would make them show me their finger to ensure that they had gone to the polls. I think that my

interpreter thought I was crazy, as many of you will agree to…but many would eagerly hold up their hand to prove that they had voted.

I was having a discussion with an Iraqi colonel that I work with and he said many people will not come out to vote, because there are too many terrorists in this town. All I could think was that I was out walking around all day and talking with people, and there is no way they are terrorists. A

few minutes later the soldiers started to bring in several detainees that were arrested. We had intelligence on many people in the village that were planning to try and sabotage the elections and our unit conducted raids throughout the night and arrested many people. I believe this was the reason that we did not have any incidents in our area.

As I said earlier, we limited the number of polling sites so that we could secure them better. Well, the local politicians did not think that was fair to all of the villages in the area. How can we have a free election if we do not provide access to polling sites in all villages? Since people could not drive how would they get to polling locations that were in other villages? The locals requested a meeting with the Iraqi general and said that they would provide their own security for the sites; they just needed an election official and ballots. I thought this was amazing. The dangers were very

real to each person and place that had voting going on. They wanted their right to vote and they were not going to let the terrorists stop that.

At the end of the day more than 30,000 people in our area were able to vote. The turnout was overwhelming and more than anyone expected. There are only around 50,000 voting-age citizens in this area.

We were sitting around watching the news at the end of the day and you could feel the emotions. One of the interviews that we saw was of an older woman, and she was saying that she was sick but would not miss this opportunity. I could see tears in the eyes of some of the officers' faces. They had dedicated their lives to this, and many of them went without sleep to make sure that it was successful. To know that their efforts were worth it was very rewarding. Making some new friends. They are all future voters.

I was having a discussion with the village mayor and another local politician and he was telling me what life was like under Saddam. He was forced to leave his home and live in another area while Saddam was in power. He

At the end of the day more than 30,000 people in our area were able to vote… There are only around 50,000 voting-age citizens in this area.

only returned after the Americans came in. He said to me, "Allah paved the way for the USA to come in and rid Iraq of Saddam"…he didn't want to give us all the credit. Saddam was in power for 35 years and they could not stop him. Many are thankful for what we did.

On this day in Iraq, the news was very positive. I am sure that in a few days the focus will be on the challenges that Iraq faces in establishing a new government, but for a few hours the people could feel a sense of relief and accomplishment…It was a great day for the future of Iraq. Well, that was my adventure during the elections. I felt blessed throughout the day to be a part of it all.

Dust Storms

"Dust storms in three shapes.

The whirl.

The column.

The sheet.

In the first,
the horizon is lost.

In the second,
your are surrounded by
'waltzing Ginns.'

The third, the sheet,
is copper-tinted.

Nature seems to be on fire."

Michael Ondaatje

Photos submitted by mobilized soldiers April 26, 2005

OPERATION SAVE ALI

Upon completion of Operation Al Jafr, the re-taking of the city of Fallujah, the 1st Battalion, 1st Brigade, 5th Division Iraqi Army (IA), re-deployed to an Iraqi camp, near Baghdad, in order to assist in the base defense. Not long after their arrival, the battalion Advisor Support Trainers (AST) from the 98th Division, were able to convince the base defense unit, 4-1 FA, Ft. Riley Kansas, to cut the IA battalion a slice of the American Area of Operation (AO). Seeing the high level of readiness and training at which the battalion was performing, the BDOC Commander quickly realized the positive effects he could gain by deploying over 250 IA soldiers, at any time, inside his AO. The 1/1/5 began operations in their own AO on March 12, 2005.

On March 20th, 2005, the 1/1/5 was on a routine combat patrol in order to conduct a raid of three suspected Anti-Iraqi Forces (AIF) cell members in a hostile village, south of the base. After the successful apprehension of the three suspects, the unit continued combat operations with a follow on Intelligence Surveillance Reconnaissance (ISR) mission. While patrolling

He observed that he had a blue tint to his skin, was short of breath, and his extremities were abnormally distended.

the village, the IA company commander made contact with the Sheik and had a brief discussion with him inside his home about the status of the village.

While observing the security around the sheik's home two of the AST members spotted a man with his small child coming towards them. The AST members allowed the Iraqi man to approach with his child. A brief discussion ensued and the AST members were able to discern that the man's 9-year old son, Ali, had a very serious medical condition and immediately brought up their team medic to conduct a more thorough examination.

Once the team medic came on site, he immediately diagnosed that the boy had a serious circulatory problem. He observed that he had a blue tint to his skin, was short of breath, and his extremities were abnormally distended. The boy was also very small for his age, stood about 3.5 feet tall, and weighed approximately 45-50 lbs. The team medic spoke to the father through an interpreter and examined the paperwork the man presented to the medic.

The father had several documents. The first was a letter of confirmation from the Iraqi

Ministry of Health stating that there was no treatment available for the boy's condition in Iraq. We believed this letter allowed him to seek help outside the country, which he did, but the costs were too prohibitive. The other documents were in English from an American Physician Assistant (PA) who had seen the little boy in November 2004. The PA's initial diagnosis was Transposition of the Great Vessels. The father told us that since he only speaks Arabic, he was unable to complete the forms the PA had given him. Both of these documents, however, provided enough information for the team to start formulating a plan to address the boy's critical medical condition.

Upon mission completion, the entire advisor team immediately agreed to figure out a way to help Ali. We decided to expand our mission to one of a humanitarian effort that would support the ongoing military mission with the 1st Battalion IA. This humanitarian mission would hopefully win the hearts and minds of this hostile village, preventing further coalition losses.

The first step was to confirm the diagnosis. Fortunately, one of the Troop Medical Clinic (TMC) commanders was a pediatric cardiologist in civilian life and volunteered his time to conduct the examination. The second step was to arrange for a basic echocardiogram machine to be present at the Iraqi medical clinic where we would bring the boy. Lastly, we needed to arrange a patrol to go out and secure the boy and his father.

The following Sunday, Easter, was the perfect opportunity to conduct the mission. The entire team volunteered to go, and everyone was needed in order to ensure security for the patrol. The team moved out in the early morning, arrived at the village, convinced the father to come with us, secured the father and son, and moved back to the medical clinic.

The medical officer was able to conduct a complete examination of Ali while at the medical clinic and confirmed the diagnosis, Transposition of the Great Arteries. Essentially, the arteries between his heart and lungs where reversed. Only through the miracle of the human body, was the boy able to compensate for this defect. However his diagnosis was grim, his life expectancy was very short. In fact, most children with this type of medical condition do not live past the age of five. With his blood oxygen saturation levels hovering at about 68%, the prognosis was death for the boy within 12-18 months. Time was not on our side.

To save this boy we needed to find a surgeon who would perform this complex procedure. Luckily, one of the team members has a co-worker

> *This humanitarian mission would hopefully win the hearts and minds of this hostile village, preventing further coalition losses.*

whose friend is a Pediatric Cardiovascular Surgeon. He graciously agreed to donate his time and services to take the case and, eventually, conduct the procedure.

This generous American would provide his services and expertise free of charge. However, the hospitalization expenses would almost exceed $150,000. This momentary set back was viewed as a new challenge for the 1/1/5 advisor team. Once again, the team's growing army of family and friends at home sprang into action.

Seemingly overnight, a charity website was set up and several fund raising efforts where underway. One of the team member's family involved with a dance studio, managed to raise $15,000, through donations and a black tie event. Another team member used contacts to tap into contributions from Major League Baseball teams and rose almost $20,000, through player donations and an

SSG Chuck Cutler checking Ali's blood oxygen level.

eBay memorabilia auction. Within a couple of weeks, the team was able to raise over $40,000. Sadly, it was still not enough.

Through several other patrols the team medic was able to keep continuous observation on Ali's declining medical condition. His blood oxygen saturation levels had dropped into the low 60's and he was experiencing increased instances of prolonged shortness of breath. The team needed to figure out a way to raise more money or find another solution, and we needed to do it quickly.

Miraculously, one of the team member's civilian co-workers was able to solicit the support of an acute care center. The hospital was willing to donate not only the surgical costs, but through the local community and their Gift of Life Program, they were prepared to cover the entire cost of treatment for Ali. This was truly an unbelievably generous gesture. This friend was also able to coordinate the housing of Ali and his father at the Ronald McDonald House, adjacent to the hospital. Now, the only remaining task was to secure their visas and transportation to the United States.

Once again, the team could not have done it without the support from home. This same friend contacted the local office of a U.S. Senator to secure their support and guidance in order to get Ali and his dad to the United States as quickly as possible. Their help and support was outstanding. The Senator's office was able to outline every step we needed to take as well as every document needed to include pictures and passport requirements.

Within a few weeks, all their paperwork was ready and flights secured. After four months, the dream was coming true. Ali and his dad would depart for Jordan. After securing their visas, they would continue on to the United States to begin life saving steps and treatment for Ali.

Ali and his dad arrived in the United States a couple of weeks after they departed Iraq. Once there, this 9-year-old boy from Iraq began a series of tests and examinations that would change his life forever. Following several days of consultations, it was determined that he was a good candidate for surgery and the procedure was set for August 20th. An intense several hours long procedure reversed his arteries and "little Ali" came out of the operating room, breathing normally with the prognosis of living a full and healthy life.

A few hours later, the 1/1/5 AST team was notified via email of the successful operation. The team was very satisfied with their accomplishment. They managed, with the help of a great team of American citizens, to give the greatest gift of all to an Iraqi boy, the gift of life. Operation Save Ali was mission complete.

> *An intense several hours long procedure… "little Ali" came out of the operating room, breathing normally with the prognosis of living a full and healthy life.*

It must be noted that the entire 98th 1st BN, 1st BDE, 5th DIV, AST Team was involved with Operation Save Ali from start to finish. The patrols were all voluntary and the security that was provided by the team on over 12 combat patrols inside a hostile village was invaluable for the success of the overall mission. The team members performed their jobs in a professional manner and were honored and proud of their accomplishment.

Secondly, since the successful military and humanitarian efforts in this village, any and all hostile action against coalition forces and the base ceased to exist. The village has become a model village and several civil affairs projects have started. We cannot forget to give a special thanks to all of the great Americans that supported Operation Ali.

Finally, a very special thanks to the professionalism and patriotism of the members of the 1st BN, 1st BDE, 5th DIV, Advisor Support Team, "Ali's friends" …the Rogue Team. ✚

Ali's Friends

The
Rogue Team

Top Row: SSG Chuck Cutler; Second Row: CPT Johann Gomez, SSG Ronald Mercier, SFC Joseph Taylor, SFC Andrew Brown; Bottom Row: MAJ Larry Bradley, SFC Benjamin Lowery, SFC Mark Faulkner, SFC William Goguen.

Operations North of the 35th Parallel

In July 2004, the refurbished Al Kasik Military Base became the Iraqi Army's permanent presence in northern Iraq. Located twenty miles northwest of Mosul, this post now provides eight-week basic training courses and an NCO Academy. It also houses up to 6,000 soldiers. Because of its proximity to Iraq's borders with Turkey, Syria and Iran, Al Kasik is strategically positioned to provide security and to help rebuild infrastructure.

The MTTs from the 98th arrived at Al Kasik in the fall of 2004. They immediately went to work with their counterparts from the 3d Iraqi Army Division. Overcoming initial inconveniences of scant supplies and testy radio equipment, these teams set up operations, learned to use the logistical network to their advantage, and

Staging point for patrol

established better lines of communication with their higher headquarters in Baghdad. With daring audacity, they resolved their transportation needs by driving their issue of Humvees from support bases in Kuwait and following other supply convoys, Stryker patrols and even civilian fuel truck convoys across barren stretches of the Mesopotamian desert to Al Kasik.

In addition, these teams fanned out across the Iraqi highland to Tall Afar, Mosul, Sulaimaniya and Kirkuk. They patrolled along the border towns from Zakho to Rabiya. They worked continuously with elements from the 3d and 11th

Armored Cavalry Regiments in denying enemy safe haven in any town or village. They partnered with the Iraqi Security Forces, repelled hit-and-run attacks and aggressively pursued a brutal enemy. In the process, they earned the respect and trust of Iraqi soldiers.

They listened to the Kurds, Iraq's largest minority, talk about their concern for autonomy in the emerging federal government, the Iraqi Kurdish parliament in Irbil and their dream of independence. Former members of the peshmerga even recounted their exploits in bitter battles against Saddam Hussein's army.

...Unfortunately, I am still in Samarra. We are in contact with the enemy daily. I have encountered IED's, Small Arms Attacks, RPG's and numerous other incidents. Luckily, there have been no American injuries only minor vehicle damage. We have sustained some Iraqi casualties and KIA's though. It is sad to see them get wounded and killed. I mean we are working right along side of them and you start to rely on them to cover you in the heat of stuff.

Well, please tell everyone hello there and tell them I miss them. Believe me that Camp Atterbury is like a palace or resort compared to this God forsaken place. Just please remember us in your prayers and pray that we all make it home safely. Take care and God Bless.

v/r

CPT V

The war in this part of Iraq claimed three of this division's warriors: MSG Paul Karpowich at the forward operating base in Mosul on December 21, 2004; LTC Terrance Crowe just outside of Tall Afar on June 7, 2005; SFC Bob Derenda by VBIED on a highway leading from Al Kasik on August 5, 2005.

Back at Al Kasik, Iraqi Army instructors now handle the demands of basic training and mentoring at the NCO Academy. After the several long weeks spent with the MTTs of the 98th, these instructors now train to standard, project a warrior ethos and foster a deep pride in being a soldier.

COL(P) Holman and CSM Riti prepare for
BFV ride to Tall Afar, Iraq.

Right: Memorial for SFC Brett Walden and SFC Robert Derenda;
Below: MAJ Mike Manni and team.

Order of the Spur

"Brave rifles! Veterans! You have been baptized in fire and blood and come out steel!" exclaimed General Winfield Scott to the soldiers of the 3d Mounted Rifles Regiment after a stunning assault on Mexico's Chapultepec castle in September 1847. Scott's salutation captured the fighting spirit of the U.S. Army Cavalry and later became the cavalry's standing motto. The cavalry held fast to those words through victory and defeat and evolved into the lethal force that it is today.

COL(P) Holman, COL H.R. McMaster (Cdr, 3d ACR) and BG Hassan (Cdr, 3d Bde, 3d Iraqi Army Div) observe operations during liberation of Avgani, Iraq. 14 JUL 2005.

During the course of the 98th Division's deployment to Iraq, some warriors of the 98th, such as Lieutenant Colonel Keith Donahoe, had the good fortune to be assigned to such units as the 3d Armored Cavalry Regiment (ACR) in northern Iraq. In addition to training and advising Iraqi soldiers, these soldiers of the 98th learned the ways of the cavalry, from the relentless door-to-door probing of its scouts to the "thunder runs" of its armored vehicles. Along the way, they caught the élan and audacity of the cavalry trooper. With no cavalry doctrine written into any 98th Division program of instruction,

and with little or no prior cavalry training, it is remarkable how such warriors as First Lieutenant Christopher Henderson and the Rough Riders performed and established their credibility as warfighters and advisors.

Their "Spur Ride" was patrolling the hardscrabble streets of towns such as Fallujah, Ramadi, Irbil, and Mosul and repulsing the inevitable ambushes, car bombs and mortar attacks. The U.S. Army's Warrior Ethos surged forth from deep within their hearts. They trusted one another, stood their ground, and fought. It was during these decisive moments that all the years of sweat and toil on the trails of Fort Leonard Wood and Fort Knox would prove their worth. In the chaos of battle, they lived the Army Values and the Soldier's Creed: I am an American Soldier...I will always place the mission first...I will never accept defeat...I will never quit...I will never leave a fallen comrade. Even in the absence of direction, they remained resilient in training, advising and leading their assigned Iraqi soldiers from the front.

Right to left: LTC Keith Donahoe and COL(P) Sanford Holman during visit to Al Kasik with Iraqi Minister of Defense, Dr. Delorme and LTG Babiker, Cdr. Iraqi Joint Forces.

In recognition of their dedication, undiminished enthusiasm, and the excellence of their work, COL H. R. McMaster, commander of the 3d ACR, inducted these warriors into the Order of the Spur. In a tradition which derives from the investiture of knights during the Middle Ages, warriors of the 98th received their spurs, and as the cavalry's red and white guidon flapped in the Iraqi wind, they stood with a fierce pride.

Other soldiers of the 98th were attached to U. S. Special Forces, U. S. Marines, and similar elite units of the Coalition, and they too demonstrated the same degree of dedication and resolve. Those attached to Special Forces, such as Master Sergeant Stephen Vanson , worked closely with Kurdish Peshmerga units on numerous security missions in western Iraq and garnered the privilege to wear the Special Forces' arrowhead insignia on their right sleeves.

Even warriors working administrative and support missions displayed their mettle at the most

3d Brigade, Al Kasik.

DEPARTMENT OF THE ARMY
HEADQUARTERS, 3d ARMORED CAVALRY REGIMENT
CAMP SYKES, IRAQ
APO, AE 09379

REPLY TO
ATTENTION OF:

PERMANENT ORDERS 123-001   15 JUNE 2005

1. Brave Rifles… Veterans… You have been baptized in fire and blood, and have come out steel. Those words spoken by General Winfield Scott are appropriate today as the 3d U.S. Cavalry Regiment executes combat missions in Iraq during OPERATION IRAQI FREEDOM. To recognize the dedication to duty and the sacrifices made while on this deployment, the Troopers that are assigned, attached or OPCON to the Regiment are hereby authorized to wear the 'Brave Rifles' shoulder sleeve insignia on the right shoulder of their uniform. This order is effective immediately.

2. Announcement is made for the deployed Soldiers of the 98th Training Division attached to the 3d Armored Cavalry Regiment during OPERATION IRAQI FREEDOM.

Award: 3d U.S. Cavalry Regiment Shoulder Sleeve Insignia for Former Wartime Service
Date(S) or Period of Service: From 07 March 2005 to a date to be determined.
Authority: HQDA Message 011853Z Feb 02 and AR 670-1 paragraph 28-17
Reason: Participation in OPERATION ENDURING FREEDOM/OPERATION IRAQI FREEDOM
Format: 320

3. Brave Rifles!

H.R. MCMASTER
COL, AR
71st Colonel of the Regiment

critical times. Whether attacked on a convoy supply run or out on a forward operating base, they defended their positions and returned fire. Many received the Combat Action Badge.

Such honors affirm the courage, honor, and devotion of our soldiers. They serve to validate our relevance as determined warfighters. More important, these honors speak to the Warrior Ethos which dwells so strongly amidst our ranks and to the potential we possess to fight and operate at levels we never imagined.

MAJ Gooden and MSG Brooks assist Iraqi Army conducting house to house searches in Tall Afar.

OFFICE OF THE MAYOR

CITY OF TALL 'AFAR

In the Name of God the Compassionate and Merciful

To the Courageous Men and Women of the 3d Armored Cavalry Regiment, who have changed the city of Tall' Afar from a ghost town, in which terrorists spread death and destruction, to a secure city flourishing with life.

To the lion-hearts who liberated our city from the grasp of terrorists who were beheading men, women and children in the streets for many months.

To those who spread smiles on the faces of our children, and gave us restored hope, through their personal sacrifice and brave fighting, and gave new life to the city after hopelessness darkened our days, and stole our confidence in our ability to reestablish our city.

Our city was the main base of operations for Abu Mousab Al Zarqawi. The city was completely held hostage in the hands of his henchmen. Our schools, governmental services, businesses and offices were closed. Our streets were silent, and no one dared to walk them. Our people were barricaded in their homes out of fear; death awaited them around every corner. Terrorists occupied and controlled the only hospital in the city. Their savagery reached such a level that they stuffed the corpses of children with explosives and tossed them into the streets in order to kill grieving parents attempting to retrieve the bodies of their young. This was the situation of our city until God prepared and delivered unto them the courageous soldiers of the 3d Armored Cavalry Regiment, who liberated this city, ridding it of Zarqawi's followers after harsh fighting, killing many terrorists, and forcing the remaining butchers to flee the city like rats to the surrounding areas, where the bravery of other 3d ACR soldiers in Sinjar, Rabiah, Zumar and Avgani finally destroyed them.

I have met many soldiers of the 3d Armored Cavalry Regiment; they are not only courageous men and women, but avenging angels sent by The God Himself to fight the evil of terrorism.

The leaders of this Regiment; COL McMaster, COL Armstrong, LTC Hickey, LTC Gibson, and LTC Reilly embody courage, strength, vision and wisdom. Officers and soldiers alike bristle with the confidence and character of knights in a bygone era. The mission they have accomplished, by means of a unique military operation, stands among the finest military feats to date in Operation Iraqi Freedom, and truly deserves to be studied in military science. This military operation was clean, with little collateral damage, despite the ferocity of the enemy. With the skill and precision of surgeons they dealt with the terrorist cancers in the city without causing unnecessary damage.

God bless this brave Regiment; God bless the families who dedicated these brave men and women. From the bottom of our hearts we thank the families. They have given us something we will never forget. To the families of those who have given their holy blood for our land, we all bow to you in reverence and to the souls of your loved ones. Their sacrifice was not in vain. They are not dead, but alive, and their souls hovering around us every second of every minute. They will never be forgotten for giving their precious lives. They have sacrificed that which is most valuable. We see them in the smile of every child, and in every flower growing in this land. Let America, their families, and the world be proud of their sacrifice for humanity and life.

Finally, no matter how much I write or speak about this brave Regiment, I haven't the words to describe the courage of its officers and soldiers. I pray to God to grant happiness and health to these legendary heroes and their brave families.

NAJIM ABDULLAH ABID AL-JIBOURI

Mayor of Tall 'Afar, Ninewa, Iraq

Appointment in Amman

In addition to the training of the Iraqi Army, the 98th found itself grappling with the training and fielding issues for an Iraqi Air Force (IAF). Iraq was in desperate need of aircraft for reconnaissance, defense, and logistics operations. A host of basic issues waited to be addressed. Where was the best location to train? What aircraft would be needed? Who would be there to follow up on these issues?

West of Iraq lies the Hashemite Kingdom of Jordan, a country considered "lower middle income" by World Bank standards. Though a small country of limited natural resources, the indigenous Hashemite legacy of generosity, diplomacy, and leadership is well known and regarded throughout the Arab world. With a keen appreciation for the balance of geopolitical power in the Middle East, King Abdallah II strengthened his national security goals by aggressively pursuing alliances and partnerships with adjacent nations, multinational corporations, and coalitions. He was openly supportive to the Coalition effort in Iraq from the start. Possessing a sound military infrastructure, Jordan beckoned as logical solution for the training of the Iraqi Air Force in aircraft maintenance operations as well as other related military activities.

In Iraq, the Multi-National Security Transition Command-Iraq searched high and low for someone to work the liaison mission in Jordan. Classes needed to be scheduled with the Royal Jordanian Air Force; aircraft deliveries from the United States to Jordan needed to be tracked; meetings with contractors needed coordination. Enter Lieutenant Colonel Jim Pippert, a lanky Iowan just cross-leveled into the 98th for the Foreign Army Training Assistance Command mission. A successful farmer as a civilian, Lieutenant Colonel Pippert led a life of rising early and working independently. He fully knew the mind-set of suppli-

> *…Multi-National Security Transition Command-Iraq searched high and low for someone to work the liaison mission in Jordan.*

ers and the priority of the bottom line for business.

Lieutenant Colonel Pippert worked the rest of his mission in Amman, an ancient city of 1.4 million originally built on seven hills. He shuttled from embassies to military

LTC Pippert with Iraqi Air Force Huey.

headquarters and contractor offices every day. He quickly became expert in negotiating the many narrow streets and major thoroughfares of the city. Traffic was frequently heavy since Amman is the hub of all the country's highways.

He received the Iraqi Air Force ground and maintenance crews and sent them to Marka Air Base on the northeast side of Amman for their training. He arranged travel and forwarded Iraqi pilots to Army and Air Force flight schools in the U.S. He

handled payroll for the Iraqi students and frequently received an ensuing bevy of complaints over the disparity of pay with rank. He became an IAF ombudsman by default.

On other days, Lieutenant Colonel Pippert checked the upgrade assembly of UH-1H Iroquois (Huey) helicopters obtained through the U.S. Excess Defense Articles program. ARINC, an American aviation services company operating in Amman, rebuilt the Vietnam-vintage Hueys for use in the IAF. It also upgraded C-130 aircraft out at Mefraq Air Base. Radios, global positioning systems, and other components quickly became the priorities of the day for Lieutenant Colonel Pippert. He drafted Letters of Request to the State Department for Export Control Classification Numbers and to the U.S. Army Security Assistance Command for

Photo courtesy of Seabird Aviation Jordan

such essential helicopter upgrade components as infrared suppressors.

Of equal import to both Iraq and Jordan was the production of new aircraft. In existence for barely three years, Jordan Aerospace Industries (JAI) won the contract to set up manufacturing lines for the twin-seat surveillance aircraft, the Sama CH2000. Equipped with forward looking infrared equipment, this aircraft can fly missions both day and night. JAI now

Seeker aircraft.

MNSTC-I Air Cell.

builds these lightweight planes in its facility at the Queen Alia International Airport, just south of Amman. Valued at $5.8 million, this contract marked the first private venture in the Middle East for aircraft manufacture and maintenance. The 70th Squadron of the IAF began receiving initial deliveries of Sama CH2000s and readily put them into operation.

The Seeker is yet another surveillance aircraft now manufactured in Amman by Seabird Aviation Jordan, LLC. The Coalition Provisional Authority, the now-defunct transitional government in Iraq following the U.S.-led invasion, chose this aircraft for border patrol and security missions. With a helicopter-like cabin and wings behind the cockpit, the Seeker possesses excep-

tional surveillance capability. The Seeker also fit well within the Coalition's budget, with acquisition and operations costs equaling only one-third that of a similar twin-seat helicopter.

In June 2005, Lieutenant Colonel Pippert coordinated the funding of $210,000 and arranged the medical logistics training for the Iraqi Army at Marka Air Base. The Jordan Armed Forces fielded the medical logistics personnel and pharmacists to instruct and train during the fifteen-week program. Topics covered everything from warehouse selection criteria to blood storage and distribution. Two months later, ten Iraqi Army officers started the course.

By the time Lieutenant Colonel Pippert left Amman, Iraq now had the beginnings of an air force due to the largesse of Jordan and the United States. With his tour complete, Lieutenant Colonel Pippert would return home to Iowa just in time for the fall harvest.

Life on the

Home Front

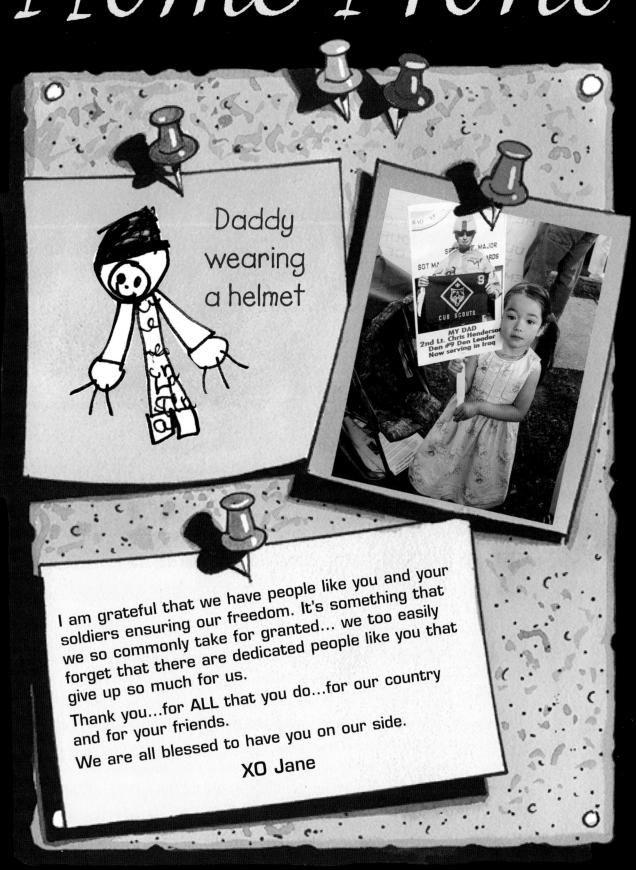

Daddy wearing a helmet

MY DAD
2nd Lt. Chris Henderson
Den #9 Den Leader
Now serving in Iraq

I am grateful that we have people like you and your soldiers ensuring our freedom. It's something that we so commonly take for granted... we too easily forget that there are dedicated people like you that give up so much for us.

Thank you...for ALL that you do...for our country and for your friends.

We are all blessed to have you on our side.

XO Jane

Family Readiness

Deployments and mobilizations are sources of great stress for both the soldiers involved and their families. Separation, role changes, and increases in responsibility, such as taking care of children, paying bills, and meeting other obligations that the deployed spouse or family member normally handled, can put a strain on the family and their relationships. Over the course of the 98th Division's deployment to Iraq, many Iroquois Division families faced challenges, and through their experiences were forever changed.

Some families faced trials they never imagined possible. Others were forced to become more than they may have thought they could be—more independent, more flexible, more resilient. This was hardly an effortless task, yet these families excelled. They were strong. They were supportive of their soldiers. They were faced with constant demands for their time and attention, yet they maintained a delicate balance so they could continue moving forward.

Other families refused to be brought down by seemingly overwhelming circumstances. For example, Yvonne King, wife of Sergeant First

Class Horace King, faced many battles while her husband was overseas, yet she never seemed to complain or let negativity overcome her. She was hopeful, supportive, and had such inspiring words. As the Family Readiness Group's coordinator, I called Yvonne and other spouses and family members to check on their well-being throughout the deployment. After speaking with Yvonne on the phone and listening to her positive attitude, I often felt as if she had done something for me—most likely without even knowing it.

Another incredible spouse, Helen Dawley, wife of Master Sergeant Jeff Dawley, had her own way of using her time during the deployment. She spent countless hours remodeling their house and attempting to perfect her gardens. Despite the hardship, she maintained a wonderful sense of humor, accomplished more than I ever thought possible, and welcomed me into her life in the physical absence of her best friend and husband, Jeff (although I get the feeling she would welcome anyone, anytime!)

Other spouses, such as Jodi Canty (wife of Staff Sergeant Doug Canty), Becca Wheeler (fiancée of Sergeant First Class Joe Butler), Kari Ward (wife of Major Scott Ward), and Nancy

"Women such as they are too often taken for granted for the work they do and the help they offer, but they are never forgotten."

by Jennifer Caffrey

Mobilization/Deployment Assistant • 98th Division Family Readiness Office

Jones (wife of Major Matt Jones), also left a permanent impression on me with their selflessness. All four of these women stepped up to help take care of other families who were in the same position as they were. They offered support, camaraderie, and an ear to listen. Was it simple for them to help others even though their soldiers were also overseas? They would probably say yes, and they made it look easy, too. Some of these women went even further; they physically helped those who needed it, took time out of their busy schedules to visit other Army Reserve family members, and penned and distributed newsletters to keep everyone informed. Women such as they are too often taken for granted for the work they do and the help they offer, but they are never forgotten.

One other interesting observation I have about 98th Division families during the deployment is that so many of them expressed concern for the well-being of others. I cannot tell you how many calls I made that started with the families asking "How is everyone else holding up?" and "Is there anything I can do to help someone else?" It quickly became clear to me that these families were truly concerned about one another, offering their assistance, patience, and experience to benefit people they may never even meet.

Over the course of the past year, our families accepted countless responsibilities without expectations of praise, reward, or compensation. They kept the home fires burning so their soldiers could protect our freedom. And they did so exceedingly well.

Town Hall Meetings

One word that stuck with me during the deployment of 98th Division soldiers is "expectations." Many of us who participated in the activities surrounding the deployment, whether overseas or back home, dealt with expectations on a daily basis. Prior to 9/11, who would have believed that soldiers from a training division would be mobilized and deployed to a war zone? In retrospect, did the families ever suspect that they would have to be self-sufficient during a deployment?

As Lieutenant General James R. Helmly, chief of the Army Reserve, stated recently, "The Global War on Terrorism (GWOT) has given us the opportunity to see how well-equipped we are to provide support and assistance to our Soldiers and Families." This support is vital because mission readiness depends not only on soldier readiness, but on family readiness as well. The Army Reserve community must be relevant and ready to provide

MG Robinson with CPT Joey Adam's parents.

responsive services to commanders in support of soldiers, civilian employees, and their families. By keeping families informed and supported during deployment, we empower and unify not only the community, but also the expeditionary force.

As the Army Reserve continues to support missions around the world, its family programs will evolve to meet families' needs, and the implementation of an accreditation program will standardize family program services across the board.

Recent changes to the program have included the addition of child and youth services positions and mobilization deployment assistants to support and assist families. In addition, an Army Reserve

MG Robinson speaking at a Town Hall meeting in West Hartford, CT.

by John Knope
Family Readiness Coordinator • 98th Division Family Readiness Office

Mr. John Knope.

Web site, www.MyArmyLifeToo.com, was developed to provide greater accessibility to family programs information online.

On the home front, the 98th Division Family Readiness Group's (FRG) goal was to establish a network that enabled family members to effectively gather information, resolve problems, and maintain mutual support, thereby reducing stress associated with military life. Each unit commander established an FRG that was tailored to the mission and focus of the unit. As the family program coordinator, I tried to act as a conduit for the FRGs by offering directions and assistance, but otherwise let the units carry through with whatever actions they deemed necessary to meet families' expectations.

In retrospect, what was accomplished in the family readiness arena was monumental. With the help of many volunteers, we conducted family readiness mobilization

CSM Grocott and SFC Travis May.

briefings, held conference calls with family members, organized fundraisers for the FRGs, held town hall meetings throughout the division, provided Family Readiness Academy and Deployment Cycle training, mailed care packages to deployed soldiers, received and distributed many donations for the families, produced a reunion DVD, and enlisted the services of 98th Division alumni to contact families. The success of the mission is centered on the commitment of our volunteers and on the families' resilience, and I personally want to thank everyone who participated during the deployment.

Theater Call from Paducah, Kentucky.

98th Division Families Donate Toys to Wounded Warriors at Walter Reed Army Medical Center

by SGM Dennis Martinson

Having experienced firsthand the financial and emotional burden endured by families of wounded soldiers recuperating at Walter Reed Army Medical Center (WRAMC), two 98th Division families from the Fort Dix NCO Academy (NCOA), New Jersey, spearheaded a campaign to help alleviate some of the burden. Sergeant First Class Christopher Peffley and his wife Laura and Sergeant Major Dennis Martinson and his wife Brenda delivered more than $1,800-worth of donated toys and health and comfort items to wounded soldiers and their families at the Mologne House, WRAMC, in December 2005.

"While Chris was at Mologne House, we got to know some of the brave soldiers and their families who are filled with hope and determination and are overcoming great odds. Most of the families arriving at Walter Reed bring very little in the way of food and clothing for an extended stay," said Laura Peffley. "By donating toys, clothes, and food, we are trying to ease some of that stress and are showing our support and gratitude to the sol-

diers and their families."

While serving at Kirkush Military Training Base, Iraq, Sergeant First Class Peffley sustained a severe nonbattle injury to his left arm that required medical evacuation to Landstuhl, Germany, and a transfer to Walter Reed.

Sergeant Major Martinson, who served with Peffley in Iraq, was also moved by what he saw at Walter Reed after visiting another member of his team who was recuperating there.

Most of the families arriving at Walter Reed bring very little in the way of food and clothing for an extended stay.

"I was both inspired and saddened by what I saw," Martinson said. "These soldiers, despite their physical injuries, still carry themselves as warriors and they are my heroes. When Peffley mentioned delivering toys to Walter Reed, I wanted in on it."

The donations were collected and provided by Sun National Bank of Browns Mills, New Jersey, and Colonel Nancy Prickett and the soldiers of the 4219th U.S. Army Hospital located at Picatinny Arsenal, New Jersey. Sun National Bank holds an annual holiday party for the children of deployed soldiers at its Browns Mills branch.

After the Sun National Bank holiday party in December 2004, there remained the question of distributing the leftover toys. Brenda and Laura, volunteers in the Family Readiness Group and founders of "Operation Soldier Success," a

SFC Christopher Peffley and SGM Dennis Martinson

nonprofit organization designed to provide support to the families of deployed soldiers, quickly came up with a solution. The two women went from barracks to barracks handing out the leftover toys to soldiers who were going on pass over the holidays before they deployed to Iraq.

With the memory of his stay at Walter Reed still fresh in his mind, Peffley suggested another way to share the extra toys from this past party. "All of us agreed to donate them to the Mologne House," Peffley explained. "We had made previous trips to Walter Reed with donations, but the holiday season is especially difficult for the wounded soldiers and their families staying at Walter Reed. We wanted to spread some holiday cheer."

Upon unloading the truck at Walter Reed, all the gifts and donations were gone within thirty minutes. One soldier explained that his wife and children were coming that evening. He had spent all his money on plane tickets and had no Christmas gifts for his children.

Another soldier stated that prior to his deployment to Iraq, he was at the Fort Dix Mobilization Station last Christmas and had received gifts from Sun National Bank's holiday party.

"I think it was wonderful that we could touch this soldier and his family both before and after his tour in Iraq," said Brenda Martinson.

"I can't remember a more fulfilling holiday season, being able to give a little holiday cheer to these soldiers who have given more than most. It made my whole Christmas," Sergeant Major Martinson echoed.

Adapted from an original story by SGM Dennis Martinson and published in *The Railsplitter*, Winter 2006.

National Military Family Association Announces Winners of the 2005 NMFA Family Award
Alexandria, VA, August 12, 2005

The NMFA Family Award is given to 15 families who exemplify the best of the military family lifestyle and demonstrate our theme of "Strong Family, Strong Force."

NMFA awarded $1,000 each to the families of SFC Christopher Peffley and SGM Dennis Martinson and made a donation of $500 in each family's name to the charity of their choice.

The Peffley Family: Christopher, Laura, Leland, Anastasia, Alexander, and Broderick.

The Martinson Family: Dennis, Brenda, Aaron, Jarod, Tonia, Christopher, and Jeremiah.

Good morning everyone,

As we were driving down to Walter Reed, I was thinking about all the soldiers there and I wrote down my thoughts. I hope you like this. I was touched by all the memories of the wounded soldiers I had the privilege to meet.

You will probably not see their names in the newspaper, or on a plaque on a building or monument, and yet they are just as much heroes as the soldiers who made the ultimate sacrifice for our country and our way of life. They are our wounded warriors. As a nation, I think we do a good job in honoring those that have paid for our freedom by giving their lives in the pursuit of liberty and justice, but I can't help ponder the question, do we do enough for those who were wounded in combat who will be fighting the battle for the rest of their lives? My wife and I have had the honor of speaking with some of the families and soldiers at Walter Reed who sacrificed more than just their time.

Her son's injuries were so bad that the doctors had to induce a coma for a month so they could amputate his arm and leg and treat the infection that was running rampant through his body.

One mother's story in particular touches our hearts. She traveled from her home in Alaska to be with her nineteen-year-old son who was severely wounded by an IED outside of Baghdad. Her son's injuries were so bad that the doctors had to induce a coma for a month so they could amputate his arm and leg and treat the infection that was running rampant through his body. We spoke with her every day, listened to her worries and concerns and tried to provide encouragement and solace for her the best we could.

When her son was awakened from his coma, I felt compelled to meet this warrior. In his presence, I felt unworthy and in awe of what he endured. I could see the fighting spirit in his eyes as he realized for the first time that his life was changed forever. He could not speak very well because his jaw was wired shut, but words were not needed. I sat next to his bed for a few minutes and I could tell he was in a lot of pain. I leaned over next to him and told him he was my hero. I couldn't think of anything else to say.

When I was discharged three months later, the soldier's mother had lost her job, her vehicle was repossessed and her home was on the verge of foreclosure.   As far as we know, she is still keeping her midnight vigil over her son in the intensive care unit. If any leader wants to see the fruits of their labor and the mentorship they impart to soldiers, visit Walter Reed and you will be greeted by soldiers who have sacrificed much and yet through all their pain, they will say "Good morning, Sergeant."

I have attached some pictures of Laura setting up the table at Walter Reed with the food donated by the NCO Academy. No sooner had we started placing the food out when soldiers and their families came to the table asking if they

*The families of the wounded warriors
endure a great emotional and financial burden
caring for and supporting their loved ones.*

could take some of the items. The pictures didn't turn out as well as I had hoped for but I was grateful to see the food donations being put to good use by the families and soldiers. Once again, the NCO Academy and Operation Soldier Success have joined forces to show their support and appreciation for the wounded soldiers returning from the war in the Middle East.

Operation Soldier Success was formed when some of the members of the NCO Academy's FRG volunteers decided that not only do the Academy's soldiers

deserve support, but all soldiers wearing the uniform fighting the war against terror also do. On October 20, 2005, the NCO Academy donated over $200.00-worth of food to the wounded soldiers and their families at Walter Reed Army Medical Center. Many of the soldiers are not able to leave the medical facility due to the severi-

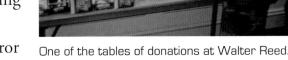

One of the tables of donations at Walter Reed.

ty of their injuries. The families of the wounded warriors endure a great emotional and financial burden caring for and supporting their loved ones. The donation of food from the NCO Academy is a small way of supporting and showing our gratitude to the soldiers fighting the good fight. For many of our wounded soldiers, their battle will never end.

Mrs. Laura Peffley

The NCO Academy and Operation Soldier Success embody the Warrior Ethos. They place the mission first, they never accept defeat, they never quit, and most importantly, they never leave, nor forget, a fallen comrade. This demonstration of kindness and support from volunteers across the country shows us in uniform that the Warrior Ethos equally applies to those not wearing the uniform. A special thanks goes out to the Fort Dix NCO Academy and FRG volunteers for their support.

Laura and I are planning another trip down to Walter Reed just before Christmas to bring donations of food and toys for the children.

Thank you.

Sergeant First Class Chris Peffley

The following was sent to LTC Timothy Hansen by Sue Morse, wife of 1SG Jeff Morse:

Sir,

Thought you might like to read something that my eleven-year-old daughter, Alyson wrote for school and was asked to read at our school's Memorial Day ceremony today. She read this in front of 1,000 students, 100+ staff and 3 TV stations! She was awesome and there weren't too many dry eyes among the adults.

A sidebar—we had three TV stations at school today observing because part of the ceremony was dedicated to three of our students—thirteen-year-old Justin, his eleven-year-old brother Josh, and their friend, eleven-year-old Allison -- who drowned in a river on Wednesday night.

I hope you enjoy Aly's writing piece.

Sue

MAJ Scott and Kari Ward and family.

What the Flag Means to Me

by Alyson Morse

What the flag means to me is freedom. It also means soldiers that are fighting for our country. All the colors of the flag mean something different to me. Red stands for all of the love the world has. The white of the stars are for my dad who is in Iraq fighting for our country. The blue, to me, is the blue sky. It looks so peaceful. The flag also means pride and sadness to me.

The flag stands for pride. The flag stands for pride because I am so proud of my dad who is in Iraq. My dad is in Iraq because he is training the Iraqi National Army. My dad is in the U.S. Army Reserve and is part of the 98th Division. I am proud of my dad because he got his Combat Infantry Badge and a Bronze Star when he was in Fallujah. He got another Bronze Star in April when his team was ambushed.

It is really sad having my dad gone. It is hard talking to him on the phone, but it is also nice to talk to him. His e-mails make me worried. Once we were able to see him on a web cam. It was really hard to say good-bye when we saw him on the web cam.

So, I think about so many things when I think about the flag.

A Busy Life, but Counting the Days

Every time the phone rings, every time there is a knock at the door, and every time there is a news alert for Iraq, my heart stops. I get a dizzy and sick feeling waiting to see who is on the other line, who is at the door, and what the news is in Iraq. That is how life is for me while my husband Sergeant First Class Dale P. Fair is in Iraq serving our country.

He left for Iraq only two short months after our wedding and only one week after our first son, Collin, was born. He is currently in Fallujah training the Iraqi troops for combat. Being a military wife has to be the hardest job I have ever had.

Lexi and Collin Fair.

I live in constant fear—will my husband come home? Will my two small children have a daddy? It's hard to stay positive when I receive that phone call from my husband at 2 am and can hear the strain in his voice after fighting for three hours straight, running in full gear in 107 degree weather with no time to stop and rest. I hear the bombs going off in the background as my husband needs to hear my voice desperately so he can make it through another night of fighting—not wanting to hang up when the calling card is about to run out, knowing I will lay in bed all night constantly wondering if he made it to his destination alive and well. This has been my life for the last ten months and we are not even sure how much longer we have to go at this time.

This is all new to me,

Dale as a very young soldier.

having my husband deployed, and believe me I have so much respect for all the other families that have to go through deployments! You don't realize the stress you are put through when a loved one is sent to war. No one could even begin to understand what you are going through unless they have lived through one. My days are a blur as I try to make it through each one knowing I am getting that much closer to my husband returning home. I am praying for the day all our soldiers will be home safe with their loved ones!

My husband is my heart and soul. I will always support him and am always thinking about him! I have sent either a care package or letter every week since he has left home and will continue to do so until he returns to the States! He is not only a great husband but also a great father to our small son and seven-year-old daughter, Lexi; a great son, brother, uncle and friend! He is adored by many and is a true hero to all of us!

God bless our troops! Let's bring them home!

Gina Fair,

Proud wife of
Sergeant First Class
Dale Fair

SFC Fair's promotion ceremony.

Rochester Red Wings
Opening Day

5732 Miles from Home

by Krista Diamond
Daughter of 1SG Bruce Diamond

It's a cold and sunny Saturday in March. Anyone outside would agree that it's one of the last winter weekends before spring, and the afternoon has never seemed so clear. But I'm not outside. Where I am is actually a room inside an army base in Manchester, New Hampshire. Where I'd rather be is, well, anywhere else.

In a few minutes, a meeting will start for families in Iraq. Around me is a large group of what appears to be mostly women with husbands, fathers, and sons overseas. No one looks happy. In fact, I can already feel the tension in the building. As a group of military men and women enter the room and begin speaking to us, I notice that there are three distinct groups of people present. There are the wives and mothers, who have stern faces and what I predict will be a lot of questions about the current situation in Iraq. Then there are the people in charge, dressed in standard camouflage, who have been in the war and are back to talk to us about it. Lastly, there's me. I feel very out of place because although my father is currently serving in Iraq, I don't know what to say about it, meanwhile everyone around me seems to have an answer for everything.

The war brings out strange things in people. I'm not talking about the soldiers and I'm not just talking about the enemy either. Mostly, I'm talking about the family. We hear a lot of information about how our troops will change while they're gone. Some sources even claim that they might not come back the same people. As my father put it in December 2004, the night before he left, "I just hope to come back alive." These kind of worries seem surreal to the average American family whose primary concerns have always been school, work, taxes, and holidays. But things change. For the father or husband in the family, being sent off to war is more than just a new job. It's also a new home, a new community, and basically, a new life. There are unbelievable risks, a bizarre culture, and for many, a homesickness which cannot be cured. But, there's also honor. There's a feeling of patriotism which most of us can only hope to admire. Serving overseas is, without a doubt, the most brave and noble act an American citizen can perform. Though there are hazards, frustrations and life-altering (if not life-threatening) situations every day, most people involved with the military will tell you that they are proud of their actions, and they are willing to accept the consequences.

We hear a lot of information about how our troops will change while they're gone.

But what about the rest of the family? At the meeting in Manchester, I start to realize why I feel so out of place. The room is filled up with mostly wives, and I can see in their faces the toll that the absence of their husbands has taken on them. It's the look I see on my mother's face every day. Single-handedly, these women are picking up extra hours at work, raising children, cooking, cleaning, and on top of that, trying to maintain contact with their husbands. They are all strong, whether by choice or by nature and they have all adapted to a huge change. But they're worried, and many are also angry. When the time comes during the meeting for questions, there is a brief moment of silence, broken by words, "I thought this was an army of one, but it's not like that at all." The woman who says this is speaking of the common fear that each soldier is not being treated like a person, but rather like a number. Other complaints include family support, the danger of war, and basically, the struggle of being thrust into the world of a single parent. Once one bold statement has been made, the others start coming in fast. Some people cry or use harsh words. Others, like me, don't say anything at all. There's a lot of emotion in the room, because the job of being a wife to a soldier in Iraq is probably the hardest one of all. Stephanie Mills, a chiropractor whose husband recently returned from southern Iraq knows about this struggle. "When he left, the first four to six weeks were the hardest," she says. "It was lonely and quiet." Despite the anxiety that many of these women feel, there isn't time to relax and adjust. There are kids depending on them to keep life as normal as possible. This is one of the many things that has caused so many wives at the family meeting to be upset. They are just plain exhausted.

Sitting there, I feel partially responsible for wearing them out, or at least for wearing my own mother out. The position of being a daughter or son with a missing father is a lot different than that of a mother, especially to a teenager. These are, after all, the most turbulent years of our lives.

1SG Bruce Diamond with wife, Kimberly and daughters Kelly and Krista.

Having a family member off fighting a war makes things much crazier. Steve McGrath, a junior at Bishop Brady, whose father returned from Kuwait this February, remembers the feeling. "There were a lot more responsibilities placed on me," he says, "And we'd just learned about soldiers' mental stress from summer reading, so I was worried." Most students, especially those at Brady, already deal with a demanding lifestyle. Every day we balance school, activities, friends, family, and of course, decisions about our futures. Any drastic change can throw this balance off, and having a father head off to Iraq certainly qualifies. It's been roughly five months since my own father left, and I'm still not adjusted. Despite what I tell people all the time, it really hasn't been easy.

The most noticeable change is how quiet things are at my house. With only one other person around, the place often feels huge. When my father calls, it sounds like he is in a different galaxy, rather than a different country. I still can't comprehend how far away he is, let alone the fact that he's part of a war. Having a father gone, just like having a husband gone, requires strength that

There's a lot of emotion in the room, because the job of being a wife to a soldier in Iraq is probably the hardest one of all.

most of us previously didn't know we had. Being seventeen years old, I want to be grown up, but most importantly, I want to be the same person I was before my father left. This is hard, because there's always something in the back of my mind, reminding me that things are different now, and even when my father returns to see me graduate from high school, things will still be different. Like I said before, the war does strange things to people. For me, it's created a sort of numbness, and it is the first time I've ever really spoken of it. Being part of a conflict that is so much bigger than the "he-said-she-said" dramas of the adolescent hallway, it's easy to feel isolated from the rest of society. At some point during the meeting, there is a much needed break, and I call my friends. What I thought would be comforting actually turns out to be very disorienting. I am surrounded by troubled faces, and the laughter on the other end of the line only serves to make me feel alone. And that's the hardest part of being the child in this situation. We don't have the huge responsibility that our mothers do, but sometimes, we still have to pretend that we're doing fine.

On that March afternoon, the officers talking to us say a lot about sacrifice. They say that we've

Unlike my father, I am not currently sleeping in the ruins of a soap factory. I am not eating breakfast in the company of rats.

made many. I say that the people who really deserve the credit are those who are actually overseas. There, in Iraq, is the real battle. Though it's hard at home, it's not a war. It's civilized. Unlike my father, I am not currently sleeping in the ruins of a soap factory. I am not eating breakfast in the company of rats. I am not conducting house-to-house searches in Fallujah, one of the most dangerous parts of Iraq. I am just here, at home, wondering why so many people believe that the war is a waste of time. Opinions like this are often influenced by the media's negative portrayal of the current situation. To those who believe that the American presence overseas is accomplishing nothing, I ask you to merely look at facts. Soldiers have been fighting in 118 countries for what was supposed to be four to six months (but has obviously lasted a lot longer) to earn Iraqi people their freedom. One of the most important freedoms is the right to vote, and with the recent election, that right was gained. As a result, Iraq is changing more and more every day. Since the elections, there has been a 30% decrease in attacks, plus more Iraqi informants for American troops. There has also been an increase in pride. Just two days after the elections, 10,000 people signed up to join the army of Iraq. This makes it a safer place, not just for our soldiers, but for the people who have been living there for their entire lives.

A lot of people may be hearing this information and thinking, "So what? Everyone over there still hates us." This is highly untrue. For a while, I believed that there could be no evidence to prove this claim wrong, especially since so many vehemently stand by it. Then, I received a package from my father in the mail. Enclosed was a letter sent to him from an Iraqi sergeant. Despite the fact that this particular Iraqi had two brothers executed by Saddam Hussein, his letter contained no bitter thoughts of his country's turmoil. Instead the feelings expressed were ones of gratitude toward America. "This is the day of working hard to build a new Iraq where our children can live with security," it reads. "Allah says in the Holy Koran: Work, Allah is going to see your work, prophet and believers as well."

If people who have experienced this level of tragedy can still talk about patriotism and believe in freedom, shouldn't we all be able to? Perhaps instead of protesting war, we should be getting informed about its benefits. Instead of just buying American flag bumper stickers, we should be learning things about what they really mean. And most importantly, instead of just missing our soldiers, we should be thankful that good people exist to fight for a cause that is going to change the world. If an Iraqi can lose a part of his family, and still smile about the goodwill of people, then so can I, and so can anyone. Instead of sulking in the back of a meeting, I should have been glad that I had the right to be there in the first place, because that's what freedom is. There is no reason why every living creature should not be entitled to such a thing.

It is a misconception to believe that our government is ripping loved ones away from us. These people are not being stolen. They have been given an opportunity to make a difference. Isn't that all anyone wants out of life? We discuss it during class and write essays about it at home, and now we have a living example of what it truly looks like. It's not just about pride, or courage. It's about someone like my dad being thousands of miles away, missing his family, missing his home, but still being able to say that he believes in America. For a long time I tried to seek out patriotism, catching glimpses of it in flags and anthems, but never really finding it at all. Now I know that it's my father, and thousands of other soldiers in Iraq. Now I know where I should have been looking all along.

Chaplain (COL) John Paul Womack.

Finding Comfort in Faith and Family

Hello! My name is Sherri. My husband, Staff Sergeant Bruce E. Boughton, is currently activated in Iraq. For those of you who have a loved one overseas, this will probably sound very familiar. Bruce and I have been married for seven wonderful years. We currently do not have any children. This had been the hardest time of our marriage. With Bruce half a world away, I have had to make all the major decisions without his input. We have always made every decision together from where we would go eat on a Friday night to which house to buy. Making some of these decisions myself has been very hard.

I know that my husband is doing something good by helping the Iraqi people. Every time he e-mails to let me know he's OK, he tells me how thankful the Iraqis he works with are. This does not make it easier to have my husband gone, but at least I know the work he is doing is appreciated.

SSG Boughton's godsons.

I have to say that this has been a very trying time for me—emotionally, spiritually, and financially. Every time the phone rings, someone knocks at the door, or I watch the news, I think, "OK, what happened? Is he OK?" The worry that comes along with your spouse being gone can be hard to handle. I'm very lucky to have my own and Bruce's parents close by. They are a great help.

Spiritually this is a real test of faith. I asked, "Why would God put me through this? What have we done to deserve this?"

After I got over the questions and the blame I started to understand that all I could do now was pray that Bruce and all the soldiers come home safely. My faith has become stronger and the church I have found has welcomed me with open arms. I am so thankful for my faith. I pray that someday every soldier will be safe and home with their families. Until then I pray that all the soldiers overseas and their families stay safe and can make it through this tough time.

Financially this has been very hard. I had to learn what bill gets paid today and what bill can wait until the next paycheck comes around. I learned to live on a lot less money coming in.

This has been a very hard year for me and all the spouses that sit at home and wonder if their loved one is OK. We look for e-mails to come, phones to ring, or letters to be delivered. Some of us are lucky. We hear from them two to three times a week. Some of us only hear from them once a month. Some of us don't hear from them at all.

Please remember your fellow soldiers when you are spending time with your loved ones. If you can, take time to call and see if there is anything you can do for a soldier's family. Let's pray that they all come home safely!

Sherri

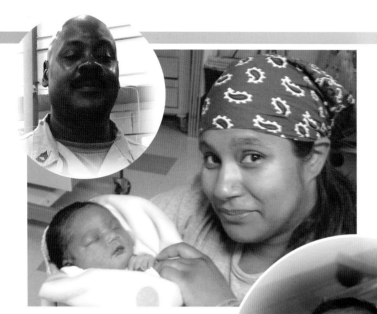

Maya Sophia
July 6, 2005 • 3:36 p.m.
8 lbs. 6 oz. • 21.5 in.
MSG Curtis and
Mrs. Adrian Yancey

RED CROSS COMES THROUGH!
Only 42 minutes after the TOC provided his location to the Red Cross, MSG Yancey e-mailed SGM Preston with the news!

McKenzie Joy
June 23, 2005 • 3:00 p.m.
6 lbs. 13 oz. • 20 in.
MAJ Kirk and Mrs. Kimberly Holmes
(and sister Kennady)

Born three hours after Dad stepped off the plane from Iraq for his two-week R&R. She was due July 1st and he was due to return on June 26th. Somehow it all worked out in just the nick of time.

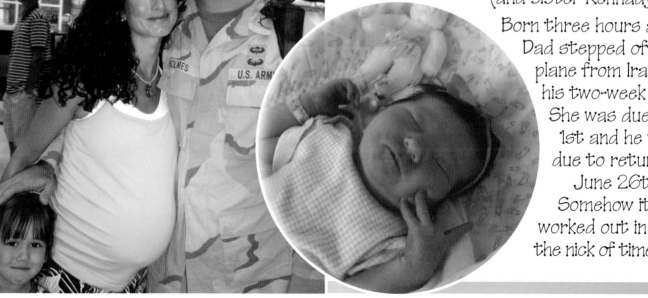

Alexis Catherine

October 26, 2004
(Just three weeks prior to Dad leaving for Iraq!)
LTC Joseph and
SFC Penelope Friedman

Camden

Born the morning SSG Kevin Baker left Camp Atterbury for Iraq. Members of the FAA printed a fax of baby's picture for Daddy to take on the plane.

The Paducah Dozen changed to the Baker's Dozen!

Babies • Babies • Babies

Baby Tennyson

My Brother Charles

I would like to start off by saying that this was my brother's second deployment since Desert Storm. It is very hard to explain what you are feeling. Until it happens to you, you will not fully understand. All I can do is tell you how it affected my family and me. The holidays were the worst. My mother cried. My dad was very quiet. I know what was going on in everyone's mind even though no one spoke about it. Is he safe, is he having a holiday, or being shot at?

What really saddens me is that I know somewhere out there sisters have lost their brothers. I really can never imagine not having Charles. Again, I can't even imagine what the families who have lost a loved one feel. You close your eyes at night saying a prayer that he and every soldier are safe. All you really can do is imagine what it is like there.

The worst is always on your mind especially when there is no contact, which, thank God, was not too bad this time because there is e-mail. We can only imagine how they lived for one year. This time it really took its toll on my parents. I tried to keep everything together while he was gone. I think I did a pretty good job of trying to keep my parents occupied. I really was okay at first when he e-mailed every day and I knew he was all right. In my mind as long as I heard from him every day, and I mean every day, I would reassure my parents and myself that he was fine. I'd say about six months in, when the moving around started, it got hard not knowing.

My brother and I are very close. Lately, even though he is home, I have started remembering things like they were yesterday. Like when he was born, I was nine years old and at my grandmother's. I wanted a sister so bad that when we got the call and found out it was a boy I remember crying and saying, " I am not going home I'm living here." Obviously, I did not understand why I couldn't have a sister. Then when I went home there was a beautiful baby boy. The minute I saw him I knew he would be my baby brother forever.

While he was growing up, the only person he wanted to know was his sister. It is too funny. Even today, we say the same things at the same time. At the dinner table, if I try to reach for something, he hands it to me knowing what I was reaching for without asking for it.

Charles returned home from Iraq on September 24, 2005, at 5:19 p.m. The plane was on time! A day and time I will never forget. When he came off the plane I just darted for him

by Debbie Marchione
Sister of SFC Charles Marchione

crying and really not believing he was finally here. He looked the same as when we said our good-byes. He did not change at all. As for what he experienced there I haven't asked as of yet. He is just so happy to be home with his daughter and family, there will be a time we will discuss that year of his life, but for now I just want him to be happy and adjust to being a civilian again.

I would also like to say that I don't think people fully understand what these soldiers are doing for us. On the day Chuck arrived, I ran to him, but

All in the family. Debbie with brother Charles.

noticed a lady also walking down the ramp from the plane and crying. My family asked her if she was all right. She just nodded and said sobbingly that her son was in the military. I knew what she was feeling because I feel the same every time I see a soldier.

When you hear that soldiers are killed or wounded it just really touches you even though your soldier is home. I feel for every family that has a soldier on active duty. I pray for their safe return. This really touched my heart when I read

in the *Post Standard* that Marine reservist Seanus Davey, 25, was killed in an explosion in Iraq. He was from Lowville, NY.

They flew Davey's body to Hancock Airport in Syracuse, New York. The part that touched my heart was that Sergeant Tom Connellan of the Syracuse Police Department sent sixteen police vehicles to escort Davey's remains with their lights flashing, driving slow on Interstate 81.

"We feel it's appropriate that we properly honor these soldiers that have given their lives for our country, rather than have them come back alone, with no fanfare," said Sergeant Connellan. "We want to show them the proper respect they deserve for their sacrifice." I commend Sgt. Connellan and wish that everyone would feel that way. God bless all our soldiers and their families!

98th Division Families

MSG John Demarco's son.

MSG Brian Kramer's daughter December 2004.

1LT Eric Booker and family.

LTC Douglas Henshaw and family.

1SG Nelson Soto's children and dog.

DAD

Daring man
Always working
Delivery of Love

ARMY

Active Duty
Rough rules
Military member
Yells commands

HOME

Heaven on Earth
Open arms
Memory place
Everlasting love

ALWAYS
AWAY

Across the world
Long from home
Ways away
Another year
Years away
Staying from home
Away forever
Will he come home?
A tear of sadness
Year of misery

Andrew Curwen, age 9,
March 2005.

MSG Steve Chriest and wife, Tina with children,
Jessica and Wyatt.

SFC Butler and
daughter, Gracie.

MAJ Shannon Clark's family.

Portrait by Christina Peterson, age 5, November 11, 2005.
Daughter of CPT Donald and Rose Marie Peterson.
(CPT Peterson is far right, wearing a helmet.)

SFC Doug Horan and children.

Dear Soldier,

I want to express my gratitude and thank you for all you have sacrificed being in harms way, and away from your families and loved ones, just to keep us safe here at home. I can only imagine what you have to deal with on a daily basis. Your strength and courage, just amaze me.

Please understand, that I among many, feel that you and your families are the true heroes of this Nation. You give so much, ask so little, and your spirit is so strong and enduring.

I have experienced the highs, the lows, the pain and the loneliness, you and your family have endured on a daily basis. I see this in my daughter's and grandson's eyes and faces, because my son-in-law is currently serving his country in Iraq.

Never will I forget the sad and tearful good byes at the airport, as my grandson's clung to their father. It was heart wrenching to say the least. But he knew he had a responsibility and a job to do, to keep us all safe. So off he went with a quivering chin, feeling nothing but gut wrenching pain in his heart and soul, as he looked back at his family. His courage left me weak with emotion.

As a young child, I experienced World War II, the soldiers saying good bye and the one's returning home. The rationing of meat, sugar, gas, etc. as well as the air raids. But at no time have I ever seen the Nation pull together in such a manner as they do now. Whether it is "support your troops banners" on the back of vehicles, or American Flags displayed everywhere.

When I see soldiers in their uniforms, sometimes I just want to salute them or hug them. The gratefulness runs just so high. A few weeks ago I went to the Post Office to mail out a package to my son-in-law and the Postal Clerk said to me, "please thank him for me". If I said it almost reduced me to tears, I would be telling you the truth. We are a grateful Nation.

Your strength and courage, in the face of danger and devastation is done with such love, compassion and dignity, I salute you. Please accept my humble and heart felt thank you, for all you do, for families every where. Somewhere, someplace, every moment of the day, someone is praying for your safe return.

Marcy Tiernay

SFC Leon Reed's son,
wearing the 98th DIV patch.

168

Welcome Home

Warriors

Welcome Home Warrior Ceremonies

One of the cornerstones of the American military has been the reservist or citizen soldier. For more than 230 years, the call to arms has been answered by private citizens willing to leave their civilian careers and families behind and risk their lives in defense of the nation. They have been doctors, lawyers, executives, teachers, fire fighters, police officers, clerks, writers, drivers, and more, all united in their patriotism and dual service to the nation.

Since the terrorist attacks on the World Trade Center and Pentagon in September 2001, America's reservists have been called upon increasingly to support their active-duty brothers and sisters, particularly for combat actions in Iraq and Afghanistan. The hardships endured by these citizen soldiers have been many. Some have lost their lives; others have suffered terrible wounds that have changed their lives forever; still others have experienced difficulties at home related to their service. All have sacrificed in one way or another.

The selfless sacrifices endured by reservists have not gone unnoticed or forgotten. In December 2004, the chief of the Army Reserve, Lieutenant General James R. Helmly, established the Welcome Home Warrior Citizen (WHWC)

award to honor citizen soldiers who served honorably in support of Operation Enduring Freedom and Operation Iraqi Freedom.

"This program honors in a small measure our soldiers who have willingly answered their nation's call to war," Helmly said. "It is a gesture of gratitude from a nation that wants to recognize them for their dedication, service, and sacrifice. The Welcome Home Warrior Citizen program provides an appropriate, timely, and enduring memento to soldiers and their families."

As the soldiers of the 98th Division returned home from service abroad, the division began instituting the WHWC program to publicly recognize their efforts. In ceremonies held across the country, soldiers were greeted with the inspirational sounds of the division band and heartfelt vocal performances. Senior leaders, including Major General Bruce Robinson and Command Sergeant Major William Grocott, honored the soldiers of the division, speaking of their accomplishments and sacrifices. Local and state representatives were also on hand to thank the citizen soldiers of the 98th on behalf of the community.

To serve as tangible recognition of their service, each soldier was presented with a personalized

> *"This program honors in a small measure our soldiers who have willingly answered their nation's call to war."*
>
> Lieutenant General James R. Helmly

encased American flag, a specially designed commemorative coin and certificate, a lapel pin set, and a Welcome Home Warrior Citizen flag. Families and civilian employers were also recognized with awards and profuse thanks, for their sacrifices were great as well.

Following are photographs taken at the 98th Division Welcome Home Warrior Citizen ceremonies held in late 2005. These images capture the joy, love, and gratitude felt by the soldiers, their friends and families, and members of the community.

2005 Welcome Home Warrior Ceremony Locations

August 31	Fort Bliss, TX
September 8 and 16	Fort Bliss, TX
September 16, 20, and 26	Camp Atterbury, IN
October 6	Lewiston, ME
October 7	Londonderry, NH
October 8	Devens, MA
October 8	Providence, RI
October 9	West Hartford, CT
October 9	Fort Dix, NJ
October 10	Fort Hamilton, NY
October 10	Schenectady, NY
October 11	Mattydale, NY
October 12	Rochester, NY
October 12	Amherst, NY
October 13	Atlanta, GA
October 14	Fort Knox, KY

"Warrior Citizen"

In appreciation for your faithful military service.

Your selfless sacrifice and excellent performance of duty is reflective of the Army's Warrior Ethos.

Your patriotic service as a true "Warrior Citizen" will never be forgotten.

173

HONOR ROLL OF VALOR

The photo galleys of this chapter are of the soldiers who served in support of the Foreign Army Training Assistance Command mission from June 2004 until March 2006.

The subsequent list contains the names of soldiers who served on active duty since September 11, 2001 for Operation Noble Eagle, Operation Enduring Freedom and Operation Iraqi Freedom.

SSG Kyle S. Abeline
Ovid, NY
98th Division (IT)
Fallujah, Iraq

CPT Joseph A. Adams Jr
Bardwell, KY
100th Division (IT)
An Numaniyah, Iraq

MSG Thomas L. Adkins Jr
Metropolis, IL
100th Division (IT)
Al Kasik, Iraq

SSG Diego A. Alvarez
North Providence, RI
98th Division (IT)
Mosul, Iraq

MSG Dennis G. Acevedo
Rincon, PR
108th Division (IT)
Tall Afar, Iraq

SSG Thomas B. Adams
Cary, NC
108th Division (IT)
Al Kasik, Iraq

MSG Armand L. Allen Jr
West Greenwich, RI
98th Division (IT)
Ar Rustamiyah, Iraq

1SG Clifford A. Alves Jr
Gloucester, MA
98th Division (IT)
Kirkush, Iraq

COL Cheryl Adams
Parlin, NJ
98th Division (IT)
Baghdad, Iraq

SFC Stephen F. Adelman
Middleboro, MA
98th Division (IT)
Tikrit, Iraq

COL Michele Altieri
Sackets Harbor, NY
98th Division (IT)
Baghdad, Iraq

CPT Kris B. Anderberg
London, OH
84th USARRTC
Baghdad, Iraq

MAJ George Adams
Franklin, IN
USAR IRR
Al Kut, Iraq

MAJ Brian M. Adelson
Gansevoort, NY
98th Division (IT)
Al Kasik, Iraq

LTC Hector F. Alvarado
Rochester, NY
98th Division (IT)
Baghdad, Iraq

SSG Richard Anderson Jr
Alma, AR
90th RRC
Al Kasik, Iraq

MSG Robert G. Anderson
Fort Huachuca, AZ
104th Division (IT)
Al Kasik, Iraq

MAJ Michael T. Ansay
Exeter, RI
98th Division (IT)
Al Kasik, Iraq

SGT Samuel E. Askins
Willis, TX
95th Division (IT)
Baghdad, Iraq

LTC Oscar J. Avery
Browns Mills, NJ
98th Division (IT)
Baghdad, Iraq

SSG Rodney S. Anderson
West Newbury, MA
98th Division (IT)
Al Kasik, Iraq

SFC Angel Aponte
Avenel, NJ
98th Division (IT)
Habbaniyah, Iraq

MAJ Paul Aufschlager
East Amherst, NY
98th Division (IT)
Baghdad, Iraq

SFC Ricky L. Avery
Rockford, IL
84th USARRTC
Al Kasik, Iraq

SSG Scotty R. Anderson
Berea, KY
100th Division (IT)
Baghdad, Iraq

SFC Alejandro J. Arroyo
Belleville, NJ
98th Division (IT)
Tall Afar, Iraq

SFC Andrew S. Austin
McKinney, TX
95th Division (IT)
Baghdad, Iraq

MSG Eugene A. Bacon
Bolton, CT
98th Division (IT)
Baghdad, Iraq

SSG Jose F. Andujar-Torres
Ponce, PR
108th Division (IT)
Kirkush, Iraq

SPC Jason M. Askew
Niantic, CT
98th Division (IT)
Baghdad, Iraq

SSG Deborah A. Austin
Rochester, NY
98th Division (IT)
Taji, Iraq

SFC Carlos A. Baez
Eastampton, NJ
98th Division (IT)
Habbaniyah, Iraq

LTC Theresa R. Baginski
Randolph, NY
98th Division (IT)
Taji, Iraq

SFC Christopher Balch
Waterloo, NY
98th Division (IT)
Fallujah, Iraq

MAJ Jamey J. Barcomb
Williamsville, NY
98th Division (IT)
Fallujah, Iraq

SFC Kevin C. Barry
Andover, NH
98th Division (IT)
Fallujah, Iraq

SFC Martin L. E. Bailey
Millerton, PA
98th Division (IT)
Tall Afar, Iraq

SFC Eric A. Ball
Sanford, ME
98th Division (IT)
Baghdad, Iraq

SSG Christopher M. Barnes
Fresno, CA
104th Division (IT)
Fallujah, Iraq

LTC Joseph A. Bartasius
Medford, NJ
98th Division (IT)
Fallujah, Iraq

LTC Robert W. Bailey
Dryden, NY
98th Division (IT)
Taji, Iraq

MSG Gino K. Banks
Philadelphia, PA
98th Division (IT)
Taji, Iraq

MSG Mark E. Barney
Jefferson, ME
98th Division (IT)
Mosul, Iraq

MAJ Robert W. Bartholomew
Somers, CT
98th Division (IT)
Baghdad, Iraq

SSG Kevin L. Baker
Boaz, KY
100th Division (IT)
Al Kasik, Iraq

SFC James M. Barber
Ithaca, NY
98th Division (IT)
Fallujah, Iraq

1LT Carlos Barragan
Saugus, CA
104th Division (IT)
Al Kasik, Iraq

1LT Byron Barton
Anderson, IN
98th Division (IT)
Tall Afar, Iraq

SSG Jonathan R. Bates
Grand Rapids, MI
88th RRC
Taji, Iraq

MAJ Jerome C. Bennett
Charleston, SC
108th Division (IT)
Tall Afar, Iraq

SSG John P. Blancart
Union City, NJ
98th Division (IT)
Al Kut, Iraq

MSG Kenneth J. Bolyard
Fort Smith, AR
95th Division (IT)
Ar Rustamiyah, Iraq

SSG James L. Bellamy
Fort Dix, NJ
98th Division (IT)
Taji, Iraq

SFC Kelly J. Bickford
Greenwood, ME
98th Division (IT)
Baghdad, Iraq

SFC Michael E. Blount
Danbury, CT
98th Division (IT)
Fallujah, Iraq

1LT Eric F. Booker
Henrietta, NY
98th Division (IT)
Taji, Iraq

SFC Michael D. Belton
Hamden, CT
98th Division (IT)
Al Kasik, Iraq

MSG Barton R. Bigsby
Alexander, NY
98th Division (IT)
Mosul, Iraq

SFC Matthew T. Boedeker
Murphysboro, IL
100th Division (IT)
An Numaniyah, Iraq

SGT Thomas J. Borders
Wartburg, TN
100th Division (IT)
Baghdad, Iraq

MAJ Curtis A. Bennett
Irmo, SC
81st RRC
Tall Afar, Iraq

MAJ John A. Bivona
Brooklyn, NY
98th Division (IT)
Fallujah, Iraq

CPT Paul Bollenbacher
Wyckoff, NJ
98th Division (IT)
An Numaniyah, Iraq

SSG Bruce E. Boughton
Horseheads, NY
98th Division (IT)
Al Kasik, Iraq

SFC Paul H. Bourque
Waterford, CT
98th Division (IT)
Fallujah, Iraq

SFC Paul E. Brady
Lake in the Hills, IL
100th Division (IT)
Iraq

1SG Michael P. Brodeur
Langdon, NH
98th Division (IT)
Ar Rustamiyah, Iraq

SFC Randol Brooks
Sachse, TX
USAR IRR
Ar Rustamiyah, Iraq

SFC William R. Bowie
Hopkinsville, KY
100th Division (IT)
An Numaniyah, Iraq

SFC Timothy R. Bragg
Sanford, ME
98th Division (IT)
Al Kut, Iraq

CPT Carl E. Bronson
Aloha, OR
104th Division (IT)
Al Kasik, Iraq

SFC Ronald L. Brooks
Waterboro, ME
98th Division (IT)
Tall Afar, Iraq

SSG Kenneth W. Bradley Jr
Castle Hayne, NC
108th Division (IT)
Mosul, Iraq

1SG Darrell K. Brantley
Murray, KY
100th Division (IT)
Al Kasik, Iraq

MSG Henry L. Brooks
Louisville, KY
100th Division (IT)
An Numaniyah, Iraq

SFC Andrew T. Brown
Dillsburg, PA
98th Division (IT)
Fallujah, Iraq

MAJ Lawrence Bradley
Williston Park, NY
USAR IRR
Samarra, Iraq

SFC Colin J. Briggs
Milwaukee, WI
84th USARRTC
Mosul, Iraq

MAJ Mark D. Brooks
Hartland, ME
98th Division (IT)
Taji, Iraq

MAJ Gregrick T. Brown
Hammond, IN
84th USARRTC
Baghdad, Iraq

SSG Kenneth Brown
Queensbury, NY
98th Division (IT)
Habbaniyah, Iraq

SSG Donald B. Bryan
Buchanan, VA
80th Division (IT)
An Numaniyah, Iraq

CPT Joseph D. Burkhart
Fairport, NY
98th Division (IT)
Baghdad, Iraq

SFC Michael A. Bushardt
Marcy, NY
98th Division (IT)
Kirkush, Iraq

SFC Lincoln S. Brown
North Brunswick, NJ
98th Division (IT)
Al Kasik, Iraq

MAJ Walter S. Bryant
Talbott, TN
100th Division (IT)
Basrah, Iraq

SFC Scott A. Burnside
Albion, NY
98th Division (IT)
Fallujah, Iraq

SFC Joseph S. Butler
Baldwinsville, NY
98th Division (IT)
Taji, Iraq

MSG Norman A. Brown
Jefferson, NH
98th Division (IT)
Taji, Iraq

SFC Dale Burgdoff
Mount Holly, NJ
98th Division (IT)
Taji, Iraq

LTC Malcolm S. Burr II
Georgetown, MA
98th Division (IT)
Taji, Iraq

SFC Miguel Caban-Villanueva
Manchester, CT
98th Division (IT)
Baghdad, Iraq

MAJ Scott P. Brownlee
Hooksett, NH
98th Division (IT)
Baghdad, Iraq

SSG James R. Burke
Peabody, MA
98th Division (IT)
Al Kasik, Iraq

SGT Nicholas S. Bush
Burnside, KY
100th Division (IT)
Taji, Iraq

CPT Gary A. Campbell
Barbourville, KY
100th Division (IT)
Baghdad, Iraq

SSG Steven N. Campbell
Brewer, ME
98th Division (IT)
Baghdad, Iraq

MSG Jeremiah F. Casey Jr
Buffalo, NY
98th Division (IT)
An Numaniyah, Iraq

SFC Michael J. Cawley
Seabrook, NH
98th Division (IT)
Fallujah, Iraq

SGT Gene F. Charboneau
Scotia, NY
98th Division (IT)
Baghdad, Iraq

SSG Sarah L. Carl
Spencerport, NY
98th Division (IT)
Rear Detachment

COL Edward P. Castle
Horseheads, NY
98th Division (IT)
Baghdad, Iraq

MAJ Jason L. Cawthorne
Alameda, CA
USAR IRR
Baghdad, Iraq

SSG Brian D. Charnock
Drexel Hill, PA
98th Division (IT)
Fallujah, Iraq

1SG Chris L. Carlisle
Mitchell, IN
84th USARRTC
Ar Rustamiyah, Iraq

SFC Christopher T. Catalano
Union, NJ
98th Division (IT)
Ar Rustamiyah, Iraq

SFC Berdj K. Cekic
Kendall Park, NJ
98th Division (IT)
Kirkush, Iraq

SSG Bradley P. Chase
Webster, NY
98th Division (IT)
Taji, Iraq

SFC John D. Carroll
Waterbury, CT
98th Division (IT)
Taji, Iraq

SFC David S. Catani
Troy, NH
98th Division (IT)
Taji, Iraq

SFC Matthew Centuori
Seymour, CT
98th Division (IT)
Ar Rustamiyah, Iraq

SSG David D. Chevalier
Williamsburg, MA
98th Division (IT)
Mosul, Iraq

SFC Dean A. Chilton
Schenectady, NY
98th Division (IT)
Taji, Iraq

SFC Kevin T. Clark
Barre, VT
98th Division (IT)
Kirkush, Iraq

COL William Clegg
East Greenwich, RI
98th Division (IT)
Baghdad, Iraq

LTC Edward C. Collazzo
Woonsocket, RI
98th Division (IT)
Basrah, Iraq

MSG Steven T. Chriest
Bemus Point, NY
98th Division (IT)
Fallujah, Iraq

SGT Michael L. Clark
Somerset, MA
98th Division (IT)
Baghdad, Iraq

1SG Troy A. Cline
Arundel, ME
98th Division (IT)
Kirkush, Iraq

SSG Derriel D. Collins
Meridian, MS
100th Division (IT)
Taji, Iraq

LTC Daniel J. Christian
Albany, NY
98th Division (IT)
An Numaniyah, Iraq

MAJ Shannon R. Clark
Painted Post, NY
98th Division (IT)
Kirkush, Iraq

SFC Peter M. Coffey
Plainfield, CT
98th Division (IT)
Kirkush, Iraq

MAJ Patricia A. Collins
Tonawanda, NY
98th Division (IT)
Baghdad, Iraq

MSG Robert F. Cicero
Yonkers, NY
98th Division (IT)
Rear Detachment

MAJ Calvin Clarke
Stafford, NY
USAR IRR
Baghdad, Iraq

SGT Christopher M. Coleman
Hamburg, NY
98th Division (IT)
Taji, Iraq

SSG Sean A. Collins
New Bedford, MA
98th Division (IT)
An Numaniyah, Iraq

CPT William Colon
Bayside, NY
98th Division (IT)
Baghdad, Iraq

MAJ David Conner
Allegany, NY
98th Division (IT)
Taji, Iraq

CPT Christopher Costello
Lansdale, PA
98th Division (IT)
Al Kasik, Iraq

SFC Eriberto Crespo
Perth Amboy, NJ
98th Division (IT)
Ar Rustamiyah, Iraq

MSG John F. Compitello
Rochester, NY
98th Division (IT)
Camp Arifjan, Kuwait

SSG Kenneth W. Cordaro
Palos Verdes Estates, CA
63rd RRC
Baghdad, Iraq

SSG Kevin J. Cowin
Springfield, MO
89th RRC
Al Kasik, Iraq

LTC Mark G. Crisci
Newberg, OR
104th Division (IT)
Baghdad, Iraq

LTC David J. Conboy
Grand Island, NY
98th Division (IT)
Baghdad, Iraq

SGT Julia T. Cordeiro
Attleboro, MA
98th Division (IT)
Taji, Iraq

MSG Robert E. Cradic
Crestwood, KY
100th Division (IT)
Al Kasik, Iraq

SFC Michael Crispens
Queensbury, NY
98th Division (IT)
Tall Afar, Iraq

SFC William J. Connell
Turnersville, NJ
98th Division (IT)
Dahuk, Iraq

LTC Michael R. Corriveault
Blackstone, MA
98th Division (IT)
Taji, Iraq

SSG John D. Crawford
Avon, IN
84th USARRTC
Baghdad, Iraq

SFC Ryan L. Crissy
Endicott, NY
98th Division (IT)
Baghdad, Iraq

LTC Terrence K. Crowe
Grand Island, NY
98th Division (IT)
Tall Afar, Iraq

SSG Charles P. Cutler
Rochester, NY
98th Division (IT)
Taji, Iraq

MAJ Lynn B. Daley
Rochester, NY
98th Division (IT)
Baghdad, Iraq

COL Jody J. Daniels
Cherry Hill, NJ
98th Division (IT)
Baghdad, Iraq

LTC George Crowell
Sayre, PA
98th Division (IT)
Baghdad, Iraq

SSG Tlaloc Cutroneo
Hyde Park, MA
98th Division (IT)
Baghdad, Iraq

SFC Dennis K. Daly
Queensbury, NY
98th Division (IT)
Taji, Iraq

MSG Wilbert D. Daniels
Brooklyn, NY
98th Division (IT)
Taji, Iraq

SFC Jeff N. Curd
Paducah, KY
100th Division (IT)
An Numaniyah, Iraq

SFC Daniel Cyr
Milford, CT
98th Division (IT)
Taji, Iraq

SSG Dannie R. Daniel
Rochester, NY
98th Division (IT)
Ar Rustamiyah, Iraq

MAJ Marc J. Dauria
Ramsey, NJ
98th Division (IT)
Baghdad, Iraq

MAJ John C. Curwen
Lowell, MA
98th Division (IT)
Kirkush, Iraq

SSG David K. Daily
Saco, ME
98th Division (IT)
Tall Afar, Iraq

MSG Frederick Daniels
Attica, NY
98th Division (IT)
Baghdad, Iraq

SFC Steven D. David
Rochester, NY
98th Division (IT)
Rear Detachment

CPT Adam G. Davidson
Rochester, NY
98th Division (IT)
Taji, Iraq

CPT Bryon L. Davis
New York, NY
98th Division (IT)
Fallujah, Iraq

CPT Jeffrey L. Davis
Albuquerque, NM
90th RRC
Al Kasik, Iraq

SSG Michael C. Dee
Palmer, MA
98th Division (IT)
Al Kindi, Iraq

SSG Clifford Davidson
San Antonio, TX
95th Division (IT)
Baghdad, Iraq

SSG Denise Davis
Bronx, NY
98th Division (IT)
Camp Buehring, Iraq

SFC Stephen C. Davis
Sullivan, IL
84th USARRTC
Ar Rustamiyah, Iraq

SFC Murray D. DeForce
Erie, PA
98th Division (IT)
An Numaniyah, Iraq

MAJ Karen P. Davies
Plattsburgh, NY
98th Division (IT)
Taji, Iraq

MAJ James C. Davis
Flandreau, SD
104th Division (IT)
An Numaniyah, Iraq

MSG Robert J. Dawley
Watertown, NY
98th Division (IT)
Kirkush, Iraq

SFC David A. De Jesus Jr
Bayside, NY
98th Division (IT)
Al Kasik, Iraq

SFC Anthony Davis
Philadelphia, PA
98th Division (IT)
An Numaniyah, Iraq

SFC James C. Davis
Ferriday, LA
95th Division (IT)
Kirkuk, Iraq

SFC Joseph P. Deady
Amesbury, MA
98th Division (IT)
Taji, Iraq

1SG Jimmy DeJesus
Roselle Park, NJ
98th Division (IT)
Camp Buehring, Kuwait

SGT Kevin A. Delahoy
Jamestown, NY
98th Division (IT)
Baghdad, Iraq

1SG Rocci R. DeRezza
Paducah, KY
100th Division (IT)
Al Kasik, Iraq

COL Joseph R. DeWitt
Hackettstown, NJ
77th RRC
Baghdad, Iraq

MAJ Roberto A. DiBacco
Rocky Hill, CT
98th Division (IT)
Baghdad, Iraq

MSG John DeMarco
Rochester, NY
98th Division (IT)
Al Kasik, Iraq

LTC Joseph M. Deserio
Staten Island, NY
98th Division (IT)
Taji, Iraq

MAJ Terry L. Dewitt
Arkadelphia, AR
95th Division (IT)
Al Kasik, Iraq

CPT Ramin Dilfanian
Englishtown, NJ
98th Division (IT)
Taji, Iraq

CPT Scott Demers
Rochester, NH
98th Division (IT)
Baghdad, Iraq

MSG Mark A. DeVaux
Haverville, MA
98th Division (IT)
Taji, Iraq

1SG Bruce T. Diamond
Pembroke, NH
98th Division (IT)
Fallujah, Iraq

CPT Kenneth H. Dilg
South Lyon, MI
84th USARRTC
Baghdad, Iraq

SFC Robert V. Derenda
Ledbetter, KY
100th Division (IT)
Al Kasik, Iraq

CPT Robert M. Devito
Windsor, CT
98th Division (IT)
Taji, Iraq

SSG Victor R. Diaz
Buffalo, NY
98th Division (IT)
Baghdad, Iraq

SSG Christopher Dill
Tonawanda, NY
98th Division (IT)
Kirkush, Iraq

MAJ James M. Dirisio
Olean, NY
98th Division (IT)
Baghdad, Iraq

COL Edward B. Downey
Guilderland, NY
98th Division (IT)
Baghdad, Iraq

SFC Michael D. Dustin
Mustang, OK
95th Division (IT)
Baghdad, Iraq

SSG Paul M. Eastman
Corinna, ME
98th Division (IT)
Baghdad, Iraq

SSG Yianiss N. Dolivramento
Providence, RI
98th Division (IT)
Kirkush, Iraq

MSG Robert F. Downing
Framingham, MA
98th Division (IT)
An Numaniyah, Iraq

MSG Daniel Dwyer
Mount Holly, NJ
98th Division (IT)
Kirkush, Iraq

SFC Keith B. Egan
Southington, CT
98th Division (IT)
Kirkush, Iraq

LTC Keith A. Donahoe
Bardstown, KY
100th Division (IT)
Al Kasik, Iraq

LTC Brian T. Duemling
Chatham, NJ
98th Division (IT)
Tikrit, Iraq

SSG Michael D. Dyer
Ellijay, GA
98th Division (IT)
Taji, Iraq

SFC Christopher Eliss
San Antonio, TX
95th Division (IT)
Iraq

MAJ Erin M. Dowd
West Hartford, CT
98th Division (IT)
Baqubah, Iraq

CPT Peter Dunleavy
Tulsa, OK
90th RRC
Baghdad, Iraq

SSG Arthur H. Eastman
Bradenton, FL
108th Division (IT)
Al Kasik, Iraq

MAJ Michael L. Eller
Coventry, CT
98th Division (IT)
An Numaniyah, Iraq

197

CW3 Mark Elsaesser
Amherst, NY
98th Division (IT)
Rear Detachment

LTC John J. Enright Jr
Tinton Falls, NJ
98th Division (IT)
Al Kasik, Iraq

SFC Dennis P. Ewing Jr
Celoron, NY
98th Division (IT)
An Numaniyah, Iraq

1LT Michael A. Fairbanks
Norman, OK
90th RRC
Baghdad, Iraq

CSM Kim F. Emerling
Salem, MA
98th Division (IT)
Fallujah, Iraq

CPT Joseph Erdek
Tulsa, OK
90th RRC
Baghdad, Iraq

SFC John A. Ezzo
Queensbury, NY
98th Division (IT)
Fallujah, Iraq

LTC Todd A. Falk
Wilton, NY
98th Division (IT)
Baghdad, Iraq

MSG Mark D. Emerson
Port Byron, NY
98th Division (IT)
Al Kasik, Iraq

LTC Thomas P. Evans
Columbus, NJ
98th Division (IT)
Taji, Iraq

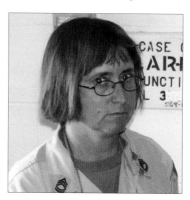
SFC Robin K. Fahey
Dracut, MA
98th Division (IT)
Baghdad, Iraq

SFC Thomas J. Falletta
New Egypt, NJ
98th Division (IT)
Kirkush, Iraq

SFC Corey W. Emmons
Gray, ME
98th Division (IT)
Tall Afar, Iraq

MSG Jack Evensizer
Dalton Gardens, ID
104th Division (IT)
Al Kasik, Iraq

SFC Dale P. Fair
Rochester, NY
98th Division (IT)
Fallujah, Iraq

SGT Mladenka Fangiullos
Liverpool, NY
98th Division (IT)
Baghdad, Iraq

SFC Mark A. Faulkner
Warsaw, NY
98th Division (IT)
Fallujah, Iraq

SSG Jaime T. Flores
San Antonio, TX
90th RRC
Baghdad, Iraq

SSG Michael A. Flynn
Lutz, FL
81st RRC
Fallujah, Iraq

SFC Andrew G. Forneris
Holbrook, NY
98th Division (IT)
Camp Arifjan, Kuwait

LTC William G. Fava
Batavia, NY
98th Division (IT)
Baghdad, Iraq

SGT Nicholas P. Flores
Fresno, CA
104th Division (IT)
Al Kasik, Iraq

MSG Kenneth A. Fogenay
Brooklyn, NY
98th Division (IT)
Kirkush, Iraq

LTC Louis A. Forrisi
Brooklyn, NY
98th Division (IT)
Taji, Iraq

SFC Zenen Figueroaquinones
Hartford, CT
98th Division (IT)
Baghdad, Iraq

MAJ Michael G. Floru
Riverside, CT
98th Division (IT)
Taji, Iraq

CPT Peter S. Fong
Castro Valley, CA
63rd RRC
Al Kasik, Iraq

SFC Bruce L. Forsyth
Pottstown, PA
98th Division (IT)
Ar Rustamiyah, Iraq

MAJ Dean A. Florence
Charlestown, NH
98th Division (IT)
Baghdad, Iraq

SFC Milton Flournoy
Chicago, IL
100th Division (IT)
Baghdad, Iraq

SFC Jason J. Ford
Brockton, MA
98th Division (IT)
Fallujah, Iraq

CPT David S. Fosdick
Hancock, NY
98th Division (IT)
Zakho, Iraq

SGT Randy J. Francis
East Greenwich, RI
98th Division (IT)
Baghdad, Iraq

SFC Diane C. Fredette
Farmingdale, ME
98th Division (IT)
Baghdad, Iraq

SGT Guadalupe Garcia
Rochester, NY
98th Division (IT)
Baghdad, Iraq

CW3 Mark Garvin
Mesa, AZ
USAR IRR
Baghdad, Iraq

SSG Gerardo J. Franco
Bayamon, PR
65th RRC
An Numaniyah, Iraq

SFC Thomas R. Freund
Lancaster, NY
98th Division (IT)
Al Kasik, Iraq

SFC Leonel Garcia
Natalia, TX
95th Division (IT)
Iraq

MSG Joey L. Gaskins Jr
Port Reading, NJ
98th Division (IT)
Kirkush, Iraq

SSG Robert G. Franklin
Converse, TX
95th Division (IT)
Habbaniyah, Iraq

LTC Joseph D. Friedman
Walworth, NY
98th Division (IT)
Taji, Iraq

SFC Bartholomew Garner
Newark, DE
98th Division (IT)
Kirkush, Iraq

MAJ Jerome A. Gaudino
Bath, NY
98th Division (IT)
Baghdad, Iraq

SFC Terry T. Frazier
Camden, AR
95th Division (IT)
Baghdad, Iraq

CPT Joseph Gagnon
Little Falls, NJ
98th Division (IT)
Fallujah, Iraq

1SG Roland B. Garrahan
Corning, NY
98th Division (IT)
Taji, Iraq

SFC Terry L. Gay Jr
Dahlgren, IL
100th Division (IT)
An Numaniyah, Iraq

SFC Bruce N. Genung
Hopatcong, NJ
98th Division (IT)
Camp Arifjan, Kuwait

CW2 Jeffry P. Gibbs
Kileen, TX
90th RRC
Baghdad, Iraq

SFC William K. Goguen
Winchendon, MA
98th Division (IT)
Taji, Iraq

SGT Joel V. Gomez
Leominster, MA
98th Division (IT)
An Numaniyah, Iraq

CPT Robert Gerstenzang
Jamestown, NY
98th Division (IT)
Fallujah, Iraq

1LT Michael F. Gillespie
Philadelphia, PA
98th Division (IT)
Baghdad, Iraq

CPT Brian Golas
West Kingston, RI
USAR IRR
Kabul, Afghanistan

CPT Johann Gomez
Rumford, RI
98th Division (IT)
Baqubah, Iraq

1LT James F. Gettens
Sterling, MA
98th Division (IT)
Baghdad, Iraq

CPT Thomas D. Gillis
Dover, NH
98th Division (IT)
Baghdad, Iraq

MSG Brett M. Goldstein
Newington, CT
98th Division (IT)
Kirkush, Iraq

MSG Howard J. Gooch
West Seneca, NY
98th Division (IT)
Baghdad, Iraq

MSG Frank M. Giannantonio
Hawthorne, NJ
98th Division (IT)
Kirkush, Iraq

LTC Martin Gilmore
Newark, NY
98th Division (IT)
Ar Rustamiyah, Iraq

MAJ Denise Golliday
Toledo, OH
98th Division (IT)
Camp Buehring, Kuwait

MAJ Andrew S. X. Gooden
Bloomfield, CT
98th Division (IT)
Tall Afar, Iraq

MSG Patricia A. Goodrich
Rome, NY
98th Division (IT)
Baghdad, Iraq

MAJ William J. Gordon
Chappaqua, NY
98th Division (IT)
Baqubah, Iraq

SGT Sherida T. Grant
Bridgeport, CT
98th Division (IT)
Baghdad, Iraq

LTC Edward M. Griffin Jr
Nashua, NH
98th Division (IT)
Basrah, Iraq

SSG Dennit W. Goodwin
Charlotte Hall, MD
98th Division (IT)
Baghdad, Iraq

CPT Aaron J. Gorges
Corning, NY
98th Division (IT)
Fallujah, Iraq

SSG Paulette Graves
Buffalo, NY
98th Division (IT)
Baghdad, Iraq

SSG Todd A. Griffin
Houston, TX
95th Division (IT)
Baghdad, Iraq

SGT Paul Goodwin
Piqua, OH
84th USARRTC
Taji, Iraq

SFC Scott F. Gould
North Smithfield, RI
88th RRC
Al Kasik, Iraq

MAJ Timothy M. Gray Sr
Dover, DE
98th Division (IT)
Kuwait

MAJ Rexall A. Griggs
St. George, UT
USAR IRR
Baghdad, Iraq

CPT Carlos E. Gorbea
Cambridge, MA
98th Division (IT)
Fallujah, Iraq

SGT David L. Graham
Lavaca, AR
90th RRC
Baghdad, Iraq

CSM Cedric D. Green
New York, NY
98th Division (IT)
Fallujah, Iraq

1LT William H. Gritsavage Jr
Lancaster, NY
98th Division (IT)
Baghdad, Iraq

1SG Gerard A. Guilbeault
Londonderry, NH
98th Division (IT)
Kirkush, Iraq

LTC James W. Hale
Marlborough, CT
98th Division (IT)
Baghdad, Iraq

SFC Victor D. Hamilton
Smithville, TN
100th Division (IT)
An Numaniyah, Iraq

SFC Timothy S. Harris
Horseheads, NY
98th Division (IT)
Fallujah, Iraq

SGT Ryan D. Haggerty
Amherst, NY
98th Division (IT)
Baghdad, Iraq

SSG Brandy Hall
San Antonio, TX
75th Division (TS)
Taji, Iraq

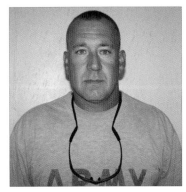

SSG William J. Hanifin
Fairport, NY
98th Division (IT)
Taji, Iraq

MSG Donna M. Harting
Niskayuna, NY
98th Division (IT)
Baghdad, Iraq

MAJ Luther Hahn
Colchester, CT
98th Division (IT)
Baghdad, Iraq

SGT Kenneth M. Hallstrom
Bethany, CT
98th Division (IT)
Baghdad, Iraq

LTC Timothy J. Hansen
Rochester, NY
98th Division (IT)
Rear Detachment

CPT Joseph P. Hartman
Greenville, SC
81st RRC
Kirkush, Iraq

SSG Clint T. Hale
Clarksville, TN
100th Division (IT)
Baghdad, Iraq

SSG Thomas H. Hamilton
Collingswood, NJ
98th Division (IT)
Tikrit, Iraq

MAJ Louis E. Harris
Waltham, MA
98th Division (IT)
Fallujah, Iraq

MSG Douglas C. Haskell
North Reading, MA
98th Division (IT)
Taji, Iraq

MAJ Shauna M. Hauser
North Hero, VT
98th Division (IT)
Baghdad, Iraq

MAJ Micah R. Hedrick
Mesa, AZ
USA PERSCOM
Baghdad, Iraq

SSG Robert F. Heintzelman
Ontario, NY
98th Division (IT)
Fallujah, Iraq

CPT Tommy E. Henry Jr
Alexandria, VA
80th Division (IT)
Mosul, Iraq

SFC Henry L. Hayes Jr
Pennsauken, NJ
98th Division (IT)
Baghdad, Iraq

MSG Gregg Hefner
Tigard, OR
104th Division (IT)
An Numaniyah, Iraq

1LT Christopher Henderson
Cranford, NJ
98th Division (IT)
Baghdad, Iraq

SFC Erik J. Herbert
Bronx, NY
98th Division (IT)
Baghdad, Iraq

LTC Keith N. Hayslett
Howell, NJ
98th Division (IT)
Baghdad, Iraq

MAJ Robert L. Hefner
Pewaukee, WI
100th Division (IT)
Camp Doha, Kuwait

SSG Ave M. Hendricks
Cheektowaga, NY
98th Division (IT)
An Numaniyah, Iraq

MAJ Steven R. Herold
Racine, WI
88th RRC
Baghdad, Iraq

SFC William J. Hazelton
Elmira, NY
98th Division (IT)
Kirkush, Iraq

LTC Christian J. Heidorf
Gansevoort, NY
98th Division (IT)
Baghdad, Iraq

SSG Michael J. Hendriks
Glenwood Landing, NY
USAR IRR
Fallujah, Iraq

MSG Neil T. Hertzler
LeRoy, NY
98th Division (IT)
Taji, Iraq

MAJ John I. Hetherington
Manchester, CT
98th Division (IT)
Ar Rustamiyah, Iraq

MSG Peter T. Hoffman
Framingham, MA
98th Division (IT)
Tall Afar, Iraq

SFC James C. Holoman
Arcadia, LA
95th Division (IT)
Tall Afar, Iraq

SGT Donald D. Hull II
Somerset, KY
100th Division (IT)
Al Kasik, Iraq

SGT Kendra M. Hinson
Jamestown, NY
98th Division (IT)
Baghdad, Iraq

MAJ Ronald P. Holden
Channahon, IL
85th Division (TS)
Fallujah, Iraq

SFC Edward L. Hotin
Leominster, MA
98th Division (IT)
Kirkush, Iraq

SFC Lavere L. Hunter
Horseheads, NY
98th Division (IT)
Ar Rustamiyah, Iraq

LTC George S. Hluck
Painted Post, NY
98th Division (IT)
Baghdad, Iraq

1SG John C. Hollenbeck
Bayville, NY
98th Division (IT)
Al Kasik, Iraq

CH (COL) Gary W. Howard
Johnstown, NY
98th Division (IT)
Kirkush, Iraq

CPT Victor Ingram
Las Vegas, NV
USAR IRR
Baghdad, Iraq

MSG Thomas W. Hoefs
Fonda, NY
98th Division (IT)
Kirkush, Iraq

MAJ Kirk H. Holmes
Troy, NY
98th Division (IT)
Tall Afar, Iraq

MAJ Juan Howie
Willimantic, CT
98th Division (IT)
Baghdad, Iraq

SSG Christopher E. Jackson
San Antonio, TX
95th Division (IT)
Habbaniyah, Iraq

MSG Rogelio A. James Jr
Rosedale, NY
98th Division (IT)
Kirkush, Iraq

CPT Timothy Jeffers
Indianapolis, IN
USAR IRR
Baghdad, Iraq

1SG Robert M. Johnson
Sylvan Beach, NY
98th Division (IT)
An Numaniyah, Iraq

1SG Christopher A. Jones
Middletown, NY
98th Division (IT)
Al Kasik, Iraq

MSG Scott R. James
Andover, MA
78th Division (TS)
Iraq

LTC David J. Johns
Salem, NH
98th Division (IT)
Baghdad, Iraq

LTC Stephen C. Johnson
Northborough, MA
98th Division (IT)
Camp Arifjan, Kuwait

SSG Jerry E. Jones Jr
Albany, KY
100th Division (IT)
An Numaniyah, Iraq

MSG Jason C. Jaskula
Niagara Falls, NY
98th Division (IT)
Fallujah, Iraq

1SG Kenneth L. Johnson
Burlington, NJ
98th Division (IT)
Ar Rustamiyah, Iraq

1SG Joseph B. Joie
Denison, TX
95th Division (IT)
An Numaniyah, Iraq

MAJ Matthew T. Jones
Eden, NY
98th Division (IT)
Fallujah, Iraq

SFC Richard G. Jean
Nashua, NH
98th Division (IT)
Fallujah, Iraq

MAJ Paul A. Johnson
Glastonbury, CT
98th Division (IT)
Baghdad, Iraq

SGT Aundre R. Jones
Brooklyn, NY
98th Division (IT)
An Numaniyah, Iraq

LTC Stephen B. Jones
Douglassville, PA
98th Division (IT)
Baghdad, Iraq

CPT Charles Jordan
Paducah, KY
100th Division (IT)
Al Kasik, Iraq

MAJ Joann Kartes
Fairfax, VA
USAR IRR
Baghdad, Iraq

MSG Martha B. KellyChalas
Wollaston, MA
98th Division (IT)
Baghdad, Iraq

SSG Jeffery M. Kilmer
Owego, NY
98th Division (IT)
Ar Rustamiyah, Iraq

CPT Susan M. Kane
West Roxbury, MA
94th RRC
Baghdad, Iraq

SFC Joseph R. Kaufman
New Bedford, MA
98th Division (IT)
Tikrit, Iraq

MSG Levi N. Kenner
Colorado Springs, CO
USAR IRR
Baghdad, Iraq

CPT Brian L. Kilpatrick
Edmond, OK
95th Division (IT)
Al Kasik, Iraq

LTC Glenn P. Kapiloff
Farmington, ME
98th Division (IT)
Baghdad, Iraq

MAJ Brian P. Keith
Easley, SC
108th Division (IT)
Baghdad, Iraq

CW4 Albion Kenney
South Thomaston, ME
98th Division (IT)
Baghdad, Iraq

SFC Michael I. Y. Kim
Lumberton, NJ
98th Division (IT)
Fallujah, Iraq

MSG Paul D. Karpowich
Bridgeport, PA
98th Division (IT)
Mosul, Iraq

COL Lawrence J. Kelly
Pittsford, NY
98th Division (IT)
Baghdad, Iraq

CSM Ronald P. Kilby
Dennysville, ME
98th Division (IT)
Kirkush, Iraq

SFC Horace L. King
Prattsburgh, NY
98th Division (IT)
Taji, Iraq

SGT Morris A. Klock
Geneva, NY
98th Division (IT)
Kirkush, Iraq

MSG Andrew C. Krom
Tillson, NY
98th Division (IT)
Al Kut, Iraq

SGT Almitra A. Lambert
New York, NY
98th Division (IT)
Baghdad, Iraq

SSG Phillip G. Langley
Mount Pleasant, MI
84th USARRTC
Baghdad, Iraq

SFC Robert G. Kluzinski
Middletown, CT
98th Division (IT)
Mosul, Iraq

SSG Anthony J. Kuhn
Buffalo, NY
98th Division (IT)
Kirkush, Iraq

SGT Paul A. Lamora Jr
Webster, NY
98th Division (IT)
Baghdad, Iraq

MSG John V. Langton
Wakefield, MA
98th Division (IT)
Al Kut, Iraq

SGT Sean M. Knox
Ludlow, MA
98th Division (IT)
Baghdad, Iraq

SSG Roger E. Labrie
Manchester, NH
98th Division (IT)
An Numaniyah, Iraq

MSG Ramiro Landeros
Rumford, RI
98th Division (IT)
Al Kasik, Iraq

SFC James F. Lantvet
Cooperstown, NY
98th Division (IT)
Fallujah, Iraq

MSG Brian R. Kramer
Blasdell, NY
98th Division (IT)
Taji, Iraq

MAJ Benny Lamanna
North Massapequa, NY
98th Division (IT)
Baghdad, Iraq

LTC Alan M. Lane
Dixmont, ME
98th Division (IT)
Ad Diwaniyah, Iraq

CPT Ronald A. Lanzo
Bridgeport, CT
98th Division (IT)
Baghdad, Iraq

SSG William G. LaRock
Plattsburgh, NY
98th Division (IT)
Taji, Iraq

COL Robert J. Lawless Jr
Lake Mary, FL
98th Division (IT)
Taji, Iraq

SFC Jeffrey N. Leach
Winterport, ME
98th Division (IT)
Kirkush, Iraq

SSG Trevor D. LeFever
Unadilla, NY
98th Division (IT)
Fallujah, Iraq

MAJ Matthew R. Larson
Omaha, NE
84th USARRTC
Taji, Iraq

SSG Isaiah J. Lawrence
Westport, MA
98th Division (IT)
Taji, Iraq

MAJ James R. Leady
Danville, KY
100th Division (IT)
Baghdad, Iraq

SGT Marilyn M. LeMay
Scarborough, ME
98th Division (IT)
Taji, Iraq

CPT Krzysztof Laski
Boston, MA
98th Division (IT)
Tall Afar, Iraq

SFC Robert J. Lawrence
Peru, NY
98th Division (IT)
Baghdad, Iraq

SFC Lisa Lee
Plattsburgh, NY
98th Division (IT)
Baghdad, Iraq

MAJ Michael D. Lemieux
Pittsford, NY
98th Division (IT)
Baghdad, Iraq

SFC Bruce G. Laude
Seneca Falls, NY
98th Division (IT)
Kirkush, Iraq

MAJ Harry M. Lawson
Hudson, NH
98th Division (IT)
Baghdad, Iraq

SFC Timothy P. Lee
Elmira, NY
98th Division (IT)
Mosul, Iraq

SSG Dennis W. Lenz
Clifton Park, NY
98th Division (IT)
Baghdad, Iraq

SFC Gary R. Lessard
North Chelmsford, MA
98th Division (IT)
An Numaniyah, Iraq

SFC Marvin Lewis
Irmo, SC
108th Division (IT)
Baghdad, Iraq

CPT Alex E. Limkin
Albuquerque, NM
90th RRC
Baghdad, Iraq

LTC Robert J. Logan
Voorheesville, NY
98th Division (IT)
Taji, Iraq

MSG Emil Leum
Florence, SC
98th Division (IT)
Taji, Iraq

SFC Freddy Leyton
Piscataway, NJ
98th Division (IT)
Tall Afar, Iraq

1LT Jennifer E. Linnemeyer
San Antonio, TX
90th RRC
Baghdad, Iraq

MAJ Paul A. Loncle
Rochester, NY
98th Division (IT)
Kirkush, Iraq

SFC Paul M. Levesque
Nashua, NH
98th Division (IT)
Fallujah, Iraq

CSM Randall A. Liberty
Benton, ME
98th Division (IT)
Fallujah, Iraq

SFC Richard T. Llewellyn
Ballston Spa, NY
98th Division (IT)
Tall Afar, Iraq

SGT Carmen D. Lord
Cherry Hill, NJ
98th Division (IT)
Taji, Iraq

SGT Jason Lewis
Ft. Gordon, GA
95th Division (IT)
Habbaniyah, Iraq

MAJ Jeffrey A. Liebentritt
Canandaigua, NY
98th Division (IT)
Rear Detachment

SSG Brian S. Locatelli
Altamont, NY
98th Division (IT)
Fallujah, Iraq

SGT Natesha G. Lovell
Albany, NY
98th Division (IT)
Umm Qasr, Iraq

CPL Terrance M. Low
Scituate, NY
98th Division (IT)
Kirkush, Iraq

SFC Armando L. Lugo
Louisville, KY
100th Division (IT)
Baghdad, Iraq

LTC Andrew A. Lyons Jr
Floral Park, NY
98th Division (IT)
Taji, Iraq

SFC David K. MacMullen
Groveland, MA
98th Division (IT)
Al Kut, Iraq

SFC Benjamin C. Lowery III
West Branch, MI
84th USARRTC
Taji, Iraq

SPC William Lugo
Walden, NY
98th Division (IT)
Baghdad, Iraq

SFC Francisco Maciel
Dumont, NJ
98th Division (IT)
Habbaniyah, Iraq

SSG Daniel D. Maher
Woodside, NY
98th Division (IT)
Samarra, Iraq

SFC Richard W. Luck Jr
Voorheesville, NY
98th Division (IT)
Baghdad, Iraq

MAJ Gregory L. Lusardi
Hackettstown, NJ
98th Division (IT)
Kirkush, Iraq

MAJ Karen M. Mack
East Haven, CT
98th Division (IT)
Baghdad, Iraq

SFC Gerald F. Mahoney Jr
Norton, MA
98th Division (IT)
Samarra, Iraq

COL Jeffrey H. Lueck
Winona, MN
84th USARRTC
Al Kasik, Iraq

SFC Bradley B. Lutz
Madisonville, KY
100th Division (IT)
An Numaniyah, Iraq

SGT Jessica E. MacMullan
Bridgton, ME
98th Division (IT)
Baghdad, Iraq

SSG David W. Maiden
North Branford, CT
98th Division (IT)
Taji, Iraq

1SG Martin E. Maloney
Painted Post, NY
98th Division (IT)
Baghdad, Iraq

SFC Charles S. Marchione Jr
Syracuse, NY
98th Division (IT)
Al Kasik, Iraq

CPT Larry E. Martin
Milledgeville, GA
87th Division (TS)
Taji, Iraq

SSG Patricia Matt
St. Ignatius, MT
USAR IRR
Baghdad, Iraq

MAJ Peter H. Mangerian
Fairport, NY
98th Division (IT)
Baghdad, Iraq

CPT Jonathan W. Mark
Wauwatosa, WI
84th USARRTC

SSG Steven L. Martin
Grand Gorge, NY
98th Division (IT)
An Numaniyah, Iraq

SFC Robert Matthews Jr
Rochester, NY
98th Division (IT)
Rear Detachment

CPT Thomas Manion
St. Bonaventure, NY
98th Division (IT)
Fallujah, Iraq

SFC Robert J. Marshall Jr
Plymouth, MA
98th Division (IT)
Mosul, Iraq

SGT Jose A. Martinez Jr
Albany, NY
98th Division (IT)
Al Kasik, Iraq

SSG Travis J. May
Metropolis, IL
100th Division (IT)
An Numaniyah, Iraq

MAJ Michael F. Manni
Cranston, RI
98th Division (IT)
Mosul, Iraq

SPC Sylvester C. Marshall
Lakewood, NJ
98th Division (IT)
Taji, Iraq

SGM Dennis Martinson
Fort Dix, NJ
98th Division (IT)
Kirkush, Iraq

MAJ Martin A. Mayerchak
Otsego, MN
USARRTC-SWIOC
Ar Rustamiyah, Iraq

CPT Keith L. McBride
Katy, TX
75th Division (TS)
An Numaniyah, Iraq

SSG Glen R. McGee II
Quincy, IL
84th USARRTC
Baghdad, Iraq

SFC Ronald H. McNary
Friendswood, TX
95th Division (IT)
Al Kasik, Iraq

SSG Antone R. Mello
Marion, MA
98th Division (IT)
Baghdad, Iraq

LTC Kenneth A. McClellan
Middletown, CT
98th Division (IT)
Kirkush, Iraq

LTC Philip S. McGrath
North Kingstown, RI
98th Division (IT)
Taji, Iraq

SGT Juan Medina Jr.
Brooklyn, NY
98th Division (IT)
Al Kasik, Iraq

SFC Kathleen S. Menard
Hardwick, VT
98th Division (IT)
Taji, Iraq

MAJ Scott P. McConnell
Rochester, NY
98th Division (IT)
Kirkush, Iraq

MSG Robert E. McGuire
Piscataway, NJ
98th Division (IT)
Kirkush, Iraq

SFC Juan A. Medrano
Houston, TX
75th Division (TS)
Baghdad, Iraq

SSG Dennis P. Mendes
Rumford, RI
98th Division (IT)
Tall Afar, Iraq

SFC Patty McFarland
San Antonio, TX
95th Division (IT)
Taji, Iraq

MSG Dale L. McMahon
Plattsburgh, NY
98th Division (IT)
Kirkush, Iraq

SGT Roberto E. Melecio
Rochester, NY
98th Division (IT)
Baghdad, Iraq

SPC Keith H. Mendiola
Springfield, OR
104th Division (IT)
Baghdad, Iraq

SPC Jose L. Mendozaduran
Phoenix, AZ
63rd RRC
Baghdad, Iraq

MAJ William G. Mergner
Walled Lake, MI
84th USARRTC
Al Kasik, Iraq

SFC Charles E. Miller Jr
Staten Island, NY
98th Division (IT)
Ar Rustamiyah, Iraq

CPT Calvin E. Miner
Concord, CA
104th Division (IT)
Baghdad, Iraq

MAJ Carmen R. Mercer
Cinnaminson, NJ
98th Division (IT)
Baghdad, Iraq

SGM Christopher Miele
Westfield, NJ
98th Division (IT)
An Numaniyah, Iraq

SSG Michael S. Miller Jr
Albany, NY
98th Division (IT)
Kabul, Afghanistan

LTC Robert Minkewicz
Lavallette, NJ
98th Division (IT)
Fort A.P. Hill, VA

SSG Ronald W. Mercier II
Gilmanton, NH
98th Division (IT)
Taji, Iraq

MAJ Michael S. Mikulski
Southampton, NJ
98th Division (IT)
Fallujah, Iraq

LTC Richard G. Miller
Carthage, NY
98th Division (IT)
Baghdad, Iraq

LTC Richard F. Monczynski
Rochester, NY
98th Division (IT)
Rear Detachment

LTC Kevin B. Meredith
Louisville, KY
81st RRC
Baghdad, Iraq

MAJ Brian E. Miller
Red Bank, NJ
98th Division (IT)
Taji, Iraq

MSG Michael E. Mills
Willits, CA
104th Division (IT)
Al Kasik, Iraq

LTC Lisa G. Montoya
El Paso, TX
USAR IRR
Baghdad, Iraq

SGT Amanda L. Moody
Keene, NH
98th Division (IT)
Baghdad, Iraq

1SG Shawn R. Morgan
Poestenkill, NY
98th Division (IT)
Baqubah, Iraq

CPT Ari A. Moskowitz
Middletown, NY
98th Division (IT)
Taji, Iraq

SSG Richard E. Mustone
Saratoga Springs, NY
98th Division (IT)
Fallujah, Iraq

MAJ Thomas W. Moody
Clarksville, TN
100th Division (IT)
Al Kasik, Iraq

MAJ George Morrison
Colorado Springs, CO
USAR IRR
Baghdad, Iraq

SFC Roy J. Moweary
Greensburg, PA
98th Division (IT)
Baghdad, Iraq

MAJ Kevin F. Myers
Syracuse, NY
98th Division (IT)
Ad Diwaniyah, Iraq

SSG John L. Moore
Framingham, MA
98th Division (IT)
Fallujah, Iraq

1SG Jeffrey K. Morse
Barre, VT
98th Division (IT)
Kirkush, Iraq

MAJ Peter R. Mucciarone
Margate City, NJ
98th Division (IT)
Samarra, Iraq

LTC Randall W. Myers
Fulton, NY
98th Division (IT)
Baghdad, Iraq

LTC Antonio Morales
Spencerport, NY
98th Division (IT)
Camp Arifjan, Kuwait

SSG Gary J. Mosier
Lake View, NY
98th Division (IT)
Baghdad, Iraq

SSG Brian P. Murphy
Mahomet, IL
84th USARRTC
Baghdad, Iraq

MAJ Catherine A. Nadal
Yonkers, NY
98th Division (IT)
Baghdad, Iraq

SSG Edmond F. Nadeau
Hiram, ME
98th Division (IT)
Baghdad, Iraq

SGT Quan D. Nguyen
Worchester, MA
98th Division (IT)
Al Kasik, Iraq

MAJ Reginald Norwood
Willingboro, NJ
78th Division (TS)
Al Kasik, Iraq

SFC Cesar A. Ochaita
Plymouth, MA
98th Division (IT)
Baghdad, Iraq

LTC Alan B. Neidermeyer
Howell, NJ
98th Division (IT)
Baghdad, Iraq

LTC Steven R. Niblett
Budd Lake, NJ
98th Division (IT)
Baghdad, Iraq

SFC Bennie B. Nunnally
Rochester, NY
98th Division (IT)
Fallujah, Iraq

MAJ William J. O'Donnell
Warwick, RI
98th Division (IT)
Rear Detachment

CSM Milton Newsome
Rochester, NY
98th Division (IT)
Taji, Iraq

MAJ Bradley C. Nindl
Rutland, MA
98th Division (IT)
Mosul, Iraq

MAJ Martin J. O'Brien
Troy, NY
98th Division (IT)
Fallujah, Iraq

CPT Stacey E. O'Keefe
Chelmsford, MA
98th Division (IT)
Taji, Iraq

SSG Saleem Newsome
Middletown, NY
98th Division (IT)
Taji, Iraq

SGT Kenneth L. Northrop
Thomaston, ME
98th Division (IT)
Baghdad, Iraq

SFC Michael S. O'Bryan
Plattsmouth, NE
95th Division (IT)
Al Kasik, Iraq

SGT Jason D. Oliver
Ballston Lake, NY
98th Division (IT)
Taji, Iraq

MAJ Godfrey E. Onye
Providence, RI
98th Division (IT)
Taji, Iraq

SFC Monty E. Otwell
Wesley, AR
95th Division (IT)
Al Kasik, Iraq

SSG Everton G. Palmer
West Hartford, CT
98th Division (IT)
Kirkush, Iraq

MAJ Russell W. Partridge
Honeoye Falls, NY
98th Division (IT)
Baghdad, Iraq

MAJ Richard Orsino
Webster, NY
98th Division (IT)
Rear Detachment

SSG Raymond J. Padilla
Kent City, MI
88th RRC
An Numaniyah, Iraq

MAJ Frank A. Palombaro
West Seneca, NY
98th Division (IT)
Basrah, Iraq

SFC Chad V. Pastrick
Beaver Dams, NY
98th Division (IT)
Abu Ghurayb, Iraq

SFC Angel Ortolaza
Hartford, CT
98th Division (IT)
Taji, Iraq

MAJ Fedencia E. Pagaduan
Princeton, MA
98th Division (IT)
Baghdad, Iraq

SFC Carl L. Paris III
Hempstead, NY
98th Division (IT)
Baghdad, Iraq

SSG Claude E. Patrick
Swanzey, NH
98th Division (IT)
Baghdad, Iraq

SGT Juan Osorio
St. Louis, MO
84th USARRTC
Baghdad, Iraq

CPT Christian M. Pajak
Glassboro, NJ
98th Division (IT)
Taji, Iraq

SSG Cedric J. Parks
McDonough, GA
81st RRC
Al Kasik, Iraq

SSG Craig E. Patrick
Rock Island, IL
84th USARRTC
Taji, Iraq

MAJ Brian L. Patterson
Louisville, KY
100th Division (IT)
Al Kasik, Iraq

SSG Jose F. Pedroza Jr
Norwalk, CA
63rd RRC

SFC Randall G. Pendleton
Isleboro, ME
98th Division (IT)
Kirkush, Iraq

SFC Jeremy T. Peterson
Elmira Heights, NY
98th Division (IT)
Baghdad, Iraq

SFC James W. Patterson II
Stockton, CA
98th Division (IT)
Baghdad, Iraq

SFC Christopher L. Peffley
Fort Dix, NJ
98th Division (IT)
Kirkush, Iraq

MSG Douglas R. Pepin
Oakdale, CT
98th Division (IT)
Kirkush, Iraq

CPT Jeffrey M. Pfeiffer
Draper, UT
96th RRC
Al Kasik, Iraq

CPT Julius N. Pearl
Warrenton, VA
80th Division (IT)
An Numaniyah, Iraq

MAJ John N. Pekol
Robbinsville, NJ
98th Division (IT)
Baghdad, Iraq

CPT David A. Peterson
Hollywood, FL
84th USARRTC
Baghdad, Iraq

MSG James E. Philips
Niagara Falls, NY
98th Division (IT)
Baghdad, Iraq

MAJ Randy G. Pedretti
Algonquin, IL
USAR IRR
Baghdad, Iraq

MAJ Ann M. Pellien
Lackawanna, NY
98th Division (IT)
Baghdad, Iraq

CPT Donald W. Peterson
Williamsville, NY
98th Division (IT)
Tall Afar, Iraq

SGT Elgin C. Physic
Lewiston, ME
98th Division (IT)
Taji, Iraq

MAJ Robert J. Piccirillo
Schenectady, NY
98th Division (IT)
Baghdad, Iraq

SFC John J. Poirier
Cushing, ME
98th Division (IT)
Kirkush, Iraq

MAJ Christopher T. Powers
Cumberland, ME
98th Division (IT)
Fallujah, Iraq

MAJ Ralph S. Pruitt
El Centro, CA
91st Division (TS)
Fallujah, Iraq

SFC Neil J. Pierce
Paducah, KY
100th Division (IT)
An Numaniyah, Iraq

SFC Todd E. Pomelow
Fairfield, ME
98th Division (IT)
Al Kut, Iraq

SSG Mario Pratcher
Memphis, TN
95th Division (IT)
Baghdad, Iraq

SSG George R. Puente Jr
Clarksville, TN
81st RRC
Fallujah, Iraq

CH (LTC) David A. Pillsbury
Durham, ME
98th Division (IT)
Taji, Iraq

MAJ Andrew J. Pottle
Perry, ME
98th Division (IT)
Baghdad, Iraq

SGM Jocene D. Preston
Penfield, NY
98th Division (IT)
Rear Detachment

MAJ Timothy G. Pulley
Bloomfield, MO
84th USARRTC
Baghdad, Iraq

LTC James R. Pippert
Dysart, IA
USAR IRR
Baghdad, Iraq

MAJ Donald C. Powell Jr
Rochester, NY
98th Division (IT)
Baghdad, Iraq

LTC Roland W. Prilliman
Central Valley, NY
98th Division (IT)
Kirkuk, Iraq

MAJ Alex E. Punsalan
Niantic, CT
98th Division (IT)
Baghdad, Iraq

SFC Wilmer M. Quarles
Naugatuck, CT
98th Division (IT)
Baghdad, Iraq

SGT Juan Quinones
Holyoke, MA
98th Division (IT)
Balad, Iraq

SFC Arturo Ramirez
San Antonio, TX
95th Division (IT)
Baghdad, Iraq

SSG Thomas A. Ray
Austin, TX
95th Division (IT)
Baghdad, Iraq

SSG Jennifer L. Quayle
North Chili, NY
98th Division (IT)
Taji, Iraq

1LT Andrew Radano
Rochester, NY
98th Division (IT)
Baghdad, Iraq

MAJ Robert F. Ramirez
Albany, NY
98th Division (IT)
Kirkush, Iraq

MSG Dylan E. Raymond
Brooklyn, NY
98th Division (IT)
Kirkush, Iraq

CPT Kevin Quinlan
Taunton, MA
98th Division (IT)
Baghdad, Iraq

SFC Todd M. Raley
Doylestown, WI
84th USARRTC
Abu Ghurayb, Iraq

SFC Eric C. Ransom
Nutley, NJ
98th Division (IT)
Al Kasik, Iraq

SFC Leon D. Reed
Painted Post, NY
98th Division (IT)
Al Kasik, Iraq

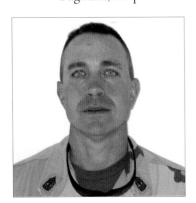

1SG John Quinn
Holbrook, NY
98th Division (IT)
Kirkush, Iraq

SFC Floyd P. Ralph Jr
Duluth, MN
84th USARRTC
Fallujah, Iraq

MSG Joseph C. Ray
Orchard Park, NY
98th Division (IT)
Samarra, Iraq

MAJ James Reese
Rochester, NY
98th Division (IT)
Baghdad, Iraq

SFC Randy Relyea
Berne, NY
98th Division (IT)
Tall Afar, Iraq

CPT Peter C. Richard
Wesley Chapel, FL
98th Division (IT)
Fallujah, Iraq

SFC Mark A. Ridgeway
Gorham, ME
98th Division (IT)
Habbaniyah, Iraq

1SG Andrew M. Rippel
Chatham, NY
98th Division (IT)
Tall Afar, Iraq

SSG Julio Reyes
Chicago, IL
84th USARRTC
Baghdad, Iraq

SSG Michael A. Richards
Spencerport, NY
98th Division (IT)
Taji, Iraq

SFC Darryl Riley
Brooklyn, NY
98th Division (IT)
Al Kasik, Iraq

CSM Robert J. Riti
Cortlandt Manor, NY
98th Division (IT)
Al Kasik, Iraq

SSG Mark C. Rhodes
Rochester, NY
98th Division (IT)
An Numaniyah, Iraq

SGT Jarred Rickey
Cranston, RI
98th Division (IT)
Taji, Iraq

SSG Steven J. Rinaldi
Hawthorne, NJ
98th Division (IT)
Taji, Iraq

MSG Monique Ritz
Edmond, OK
95th Division (IT)
Taji, Iraq

MAJ Mark J. Ricchiazzi
North Tonawanda, NY
98th Division (IT)
Rear Detachment

SFC Angie R. Rideout
Portland, ME
98th Division (IT)
Baghdad, Iraq

CPT David I. Rios
Paterson, NJ
98th Division (IT)
Baghdad, Iraq

LTC Eugene F. Rivera
Rochester, NY
98th Division (IT)
Baghdad, Iraq

SSG Fabian Rivera
Macedon, NY
98th Division (IT)
Baghdad, Iraq

SSG Jose Rodriguezsoba
Adjuntas, PR
65th RRC
An Numaniyah, Iraq

MAJ Keith A. Root
Enfield, CT
98th Division (IT)
Baghdad, Iraq

SSG Christina M. Rowe
Laconia, NH
98th Division (IT)
Taji, Iraq

SPC Gregory A. Roark
Malvern, AR
95th Division (IT)
Baghdad, Iraq

MSG Kenneth V. Roederer Jr
Louisville, KY
100th Division (IT)
Baghdad, Iraq

CPT Christopher B. Rose
Laurel, NY
98th Division (IT)
Al Kasik, Iraq

SSG Ronald J. Russell Jr
Lambertville, NJ
98th Division (IT)
Baghdad, Iraq

CPT Jorge L. Rodriguez
Hartford, CT
98th Division (IT)
Al Kasik, Iraq

SSG Patrick Romero
North Haven, CT
98th Division (IT)
Baghdad, Iraq

SSG Michael Rouse
Murrieta, CA
USAR IRR
Taji, Iraq

SFC Thomas J. Rutherford
Conesus, NY
98th Division (IT)
Rear Detachment

SFC Jorge L. Rodriguez Jr
Lowell, MA
98th Division (IT)
Baghdad, Iraq

LTC Daniel Rook
Pittsford, NY
98th Division (IT)
Rear Detachment

1LT Matthew D. Rousseau
Manchester, NH
98th Division (IT)
Al Kasik, Iraq

CPT Joseph W. Ryser
Mason, OH
84th USARRTC
An Numaniyah, Iraq

MAJ Gregario V. M. Sablan Jr
Saipan, MP
9th RRC
Al Kasik, Iraq

SFC Dale A. Sanderlin
Sicklerville, NJ
98th Division (IT)
Al Kasik, Iraq

MSG Thomas E. Santmyer
Syracuse, NY
98th Division (IT)
Kirkush, Iraq

SFC Michael Scannell
Eden, WI
84th USARRTC
Taji, Iraq

MSG Everett H. Samms
South Plainfield, NJ
98th Division (IT)
Kirkush, Iraq

SGT David T. Santana
Buffalo, NY
98th Division (IT)
Taji, Iraq

SSG Raymond Saucier
Sanford, ME
98th Division (IT)
Camp Arifjan, Kuwait

SFC Anthony C. Scaringi
Walden, NY
98th Division (IT)
An Numaniyah, Iraq

SSG Felix Sanchez
Browns Mills, NJ
98th Division (IT)
Al Kasik, Iraq

MSG Raul C. Santiago
Dorado, PR
108th Division (IT)
Al Kasik, Iraq

SFC Juan J. Saul
Los Angeles, CA
104th Division (IT)
Baghdad, Iraq

SSG Donald K. Scee
Alamogordo, NM
USAR IMA
Al Kasik, Iraq

SSG Jose Sanchez Jr
Chicago, IL
84th USARRTC
Fallujah, Iraq

CPT Victor Santiago
Walworth, NY
98th Division (IT)
Baghdad, Iraq

SFC Shawn M. Saville
Hudson Falls, NY
98th Division (IT)
Taji, Iraq

LTC Thomas Schalk
Massapequa, NY
98th Division (IT)
Zakho, Iraq

MAJ Richard Schau
Edison, NJ
98th Division (IT)
Baghdad, Iraq

MAJ James Scott
Prince George, VA
USAR IRR
Taji, Iraq

SFC Walter N. Serra
New York, NY
98th Division (IT)
Fallujah, Iraq

MAJ Edward D. Shelton
Oklahoma City, OK
95th Division (IT)
Al Kasik, Iraq

SGT Troy A. Schneider
Tonawanda, NY
98th Division (IT)
Baghdad, Iraq

LTC Richard W. Sellner
Hooksett, NH
98th Division (IT)
Baghdad, Iraq

SFC Susan D. Sevigny
Berlin, NH
98th Division (IT)
Taji, Iraq

COL Douglas R. Shipman
South Glastonbury, CT
98th Division (IT)
Al Kasik, Iraq

SFC Michael I. Schreiber Jr
Elmira, NY
98th Division (IT)
Samarra, Iraq

LTC Christopher Semler
Fairport, NY
98th Division (IT)
Baghdad, Iraq

MSG Alfred J. Seydler III
Amsterdam, NY
98th Division (IT)
Tall Afar, Iraq

SFC William J. Shortino
Omaha, NE
95th Division (IT)
Al Kasik, Iraq

SSG Ethan E. Schweitzer
Middletown, CT
98th Division (IT)
Habbaniyah, Iraq

SFC Richard C. Semo
Rochester, NH
98th Division (IT)
Baghdad, Iraq

MSG Christopher D. Sharpe
Jackson, NJ
98th Division (IT)
Tikrit, Iraq

MSG Robert T. Shown
Owensboro, KY
100th Division (IT)
Baghdad, Iraq

MAJ Robert F. Sile
Rochester, NY
98th Division (IT)
Baghdad, Iraq

SGT Destry Singh
Ozone Park, NY
98th Division (IT)
Baghdad, Iraq

MAJ Michael K. Slowinski
North Tonawanda, NY
98th Division (IT)
Baghdad, Iraq

SFC Matthew T. Smith
Webster, NY
98th Division (IT)
Kirkush, Iraq

MSG Jose M. Silva
Jersey City, NJ
98th Division (IT)
Kirkush, Iraq

SFC Billy Rae Singpracha
Cranston, RI
98th Division (IT)
Al Kut, Iraq

MAJ Mark Small
Gallatin, TN
USAR IRR
Al Kasik, Iraq

SFC Michael A. Smith
Columbus, WI
84th USARRTC
Baghdad, Iraq

MSG Jeffery M. Sims
Ladson, SC
81st RRC
Baghdad, Iraq

SFC Everett K. Sloan
Egg Harbor Township, NJ
98th Division (IT)
Kirkuk, Iraq

MAJ James M. Smith
Williamsburg, KY
100th Division (IT)
Kirkush, Iraq

LTC Stanley B. Smith
Easton, PA
98th Division (IT)
Baghdad, Iraq

SFC Kenneth W. Sinclair
Nashua, NH
98th Division (IT)
Kirkush, Iraq

LTC Mark S. Slowik
Horseheads, NY
98th Division (IT)
Baghdad, Iraq

MAJ John Smith
Fuquay-Varina, NC
USAR IRR
Al Kasik, Iraq

MAJ Evelyn G. Smith-Florence
Fort Washington, MD
99th RRC
Baghdad, Iraq

MSG Harry L. Snellings
Jamestown, NY
98th Division (IT)
Kirkush, Iraq

1SG Nelson V. Soto
Rochester, NY
98th Division (IT)
Baghdad, Iraq

MAJ Elmer J. St. Vil
Brooklyn, NY
98th Division (IT)
Ad Diwaniyah, Iraq

SFC Jeffrey L. Stout
Willow Grove, PA
98th Division (IT)
An Numaniyah, Iraq

SPC Tia Snyder
Norton, MA
98th Division (IT)
Baghdad, Iraq

SFC Clayburn C. Sowell
Inverness, FL
81st RRC
Fallujah, Iraq

SFC Edward J. Stefik
North Tonawanda, NY
98th Division (IT)
Baghdad, Iraq

1SG Anthony W. Straus
Saratoga Springs, NY
98th Division (IT)
Kabul, Afghanistan

CPT Terrence Sommers
Augusta, GA
108th Division (IT)
Baghdad, Iraq

SFC Martin P. Spears
Katy, TX
95th Division (IT)
Al Kasik, Iraq

MAJ Stephen L. Steiner
Little Falls, NY
98th Division (IT)
Baghdad, Iraq

SGM James Strickland
Four Oaks, NC
81st RRC
Baghdad, Iraq

CPT David R. Sonnek
Hickory, NC
108th Division (IT)
Sinjar, Iraq

CPT Traci A. St. Denis
Cohoes, NY
98th Division (IT)
Baghdad, Iraq

1SG Robert Stochel
Mount Laurel, NJ
98th Division (IT)
Mosul, Iraq

SSG James W. Strother Jr
Lexington, SC
81st RRC
Mosul, Iraq

1SG Gilbert Suarez Jr
Merrick, NY
98th Division (IT)
Al Kasik, Iraq

MSG Carol Y. Swan
Rochester, NY
98th Division (IT)
Rear Detachment

CPT Michael A. Szalma
Orlando, FL
98th Division (IT)
Al Kasik, Iraq

SSG Andres Talavera Jr
Bridgeport, CT
98th Division (IT)
Baghdad, Iraq

LTC Sean P. Sullivan
Northville, NY
98th Division (IT)
Baghdad, Iraq

MAJ Dean F. Swartwood
Cortland, NY
98th Division (IT)
Kirkush, Iraq

SSG Marcy J. Szebenyi
Old Bridge, NJ
98th Division (IT)
Taji, Iraq

SSG Douglas Taylor
Tuppers Plains, OH
88th RRC
Al Kasik, Iraq

LTC Chester W. Sutphen
Warwick, RI
98th Division (IT)
Fallujah, Iraq

MAJ Roger B. Swartwood
Burdett, NY
98th Division (IT)
Fallujah, Iraq

1SG Charles D. Szostecki
Chapmansboro, TN
100th Division (IT)
Fallujah, Iraq

CPT Gordon S. Taylor
Ponca City, OK
95th Division (IT)
Baghdad, Iraq

SFC Larry D. Sutton
Rochester, NY
98th Division (IT)
Taji, Iraq

MSG Martin A. Swiss III
Franklin, NJ
98th Division (IT)
Baghdad, Iraq

MAJ Peter J. Taft
Bradley, ME
98th Division (IT)
Basrah, Iraq

SGT Jackie Taylor
Ocean View, NJ
98th Division (IT)
Baghdad, Iraq

SFC James F. Taylor
Concord, NC
108th Division (IT)
Tall Afar, Iraq

LTC Edward J. Tennent
Red Oak, TX
95th Division (IT)
Baghdad, Iraq

SFC Allen R. Thomas
Gurley, AL
108th Division (IT)
Baghdad, Iraq

MAJ James A. Timmerman
Randolph, NJ
USAR IRR
Baghdad, Iraq

SFC Joseph B. Taylor
New Hartford, NY
98th Division (IT)
Taji, Iraq

CPT Jeffery E. Tennyson
Batavia, NY
98th Division (IT)
Tall Afar, Iraq

SGT Michael L. Thomas
Houston, MN
84th USARRTC
An Numaniyah, Iraq

MAJ Juan A. Torres
Waterbury, CT
98th Division (IT)
An Numaniyah, Iraq

SFC Marlene A. Taylor
Waterloo, NY
98th Division (IT)
Baghdad, Iraq

SSG Christopher J. Thallemer
Bloomingdale, IL
84th USARRTC
An Numaniyah, Iraq

MSG Kenneth S. Thompson
Lincoln, NE
95th Division (IT)
An Numaniyah, Iraq

CSM Brendan R. Toth
Pawcatuck, CT
98th Division (IT)
Kirkush, Iraq

CPT Phillip A. Taylor
Norman, OK
95th Division (IT)
Tall Afar, Iraq

SFC Patrick E. Thiel
Tonawanda, NY
98th Division (IT)
Baghdad, Iraq

CPT Michael K. Threlfall
Goshen, NH
98th Division (IT)
Fallujah, Iraq

SGT Harold E. Towlson
Buffalo, NY
98th Division (IT)
Baghdad, Iraq

SFC Ricky N. Treece
Holden, MO
95th Division (IT)
Fallujah, Iraq

SGT Nick A. Trumble
Friendship, NY
98th Division (IT)
Baghdad, Iraq

LTC Stephen Udovich
Newark, DE
99th RRC
Al Kasik, Iraq

SFC Ricardo Valenzuela
Elmhurst, NY
98th Division (IT)
Baghdad, Iraq

SSG Ralph J. Trenchard
Owego, NY
98th Division (IT)
Baghdad, Iraq

MSG Alfred J. Tugaoen
Rochester, NY
98th Division (IT)
Baghdad, Iraq

SGT Tariq Umaru
Glenolden, PA
98th Division (IT)
Baghdad, Iraq

SGT Joseph G. Van Dyck
Statesville, NC
108th Division (IT)
Taji, Iraq

MAJ Paul R. Trometer
Gasport, NY
98th Division (IT)
Fallujah, Iraq

MSG Bobby Turner
Rochester, NY
98th Division (IT)
Rear Detachment

SFC Patricia Uyechi
Webster, NY
98th Division (IT)
Camp Buehring, Kuwait

SFC Stephen N. Van Son
Webster, NY
98th Division (IT)
Al Kasik, Iraq

LTC Stephen M. Truhan
Brattleboro, VT
98th Division (IT)
Baqubah, Iraq

MAJ James Tyrrell
Gainsville, VA
USAR IRR
Ad Diwaniyah, Iraq

SFC Stephen M. Vail
Portland, ME
98th Division (IT)
Fallujah, Iraq

MAJ Douglas VanValkenburg
Farmington, CT
98th Division (IT)
Baghdad, Iraq

MAJ Norma J. Vargus
Middletown, NY
98th Division (IT)
Baghdad, Iraq

MSG Ernest J. Vigil
Lakewood, CO
104th Division (IT)
Mosul, Iraq

CW2 Michael Wade
El Paso, TX
90th RRC
Baghdad, Iraq

MAJ John J. Waldron Jr
Fishers, IN
100th Division (IT)
Baghdad, Iraq

MAJ Jose Vazquez
Melbourne, FL
87th Division (TS)
Baghdad, Iraq

CPT Stephen D. Vile Jr
Marlton, NJ
98th Division (IT)
Samarra, Iraq

CPT Doyle L. Wadhams
Albion, NY
98th Division (IT)
Fallujah, Iraq

SFC Keith W. Walker
Erie, PA
98th Division (IT)
Taji, Iraq

1SG Jon M. Venturin
Killbuck, NY
98th Division (IT)
Fallujah, Iraq

LTC Peter C. Vogel
Howell, NJ
98th Division (IT)
Baghdad, Iraq

LTC David P. Wait
Graniteville, VT
98th Division (IT)
An Numaniyah, Iraq

SFC Scott W. Wallace
South Newbury, NH
98th Division (IT)
Tall Afar, Iraq

SFC James B. Vible
Peacedale, RI
98th Division (IT)
Mosul, Iraq

1SG Robert Voll
Southbury, CT
98th Division (IT)
An Numaniyah, Iraq

SFC Jerry L. Walden
Keota, OK
95th Division (IT)
Al Kasik, Iraq

SFC Albert C. Ward
Hannibal, NY
98th Division (IT)
Tall Afar, Iraq

CSM Randal T. Ward
Lockport, NY
98th Division (IT)
Rear Detachment

SFC Herman B. Welch
Saco, ME
98th Division (IT)
Samarra, Iraq

SSG Eric M. West
Ogdensburg, NY
98th Division (IT)
Kirkush, Iraq

SFC Dyana R. White
Corinna, ME
98th Division (IT)
Baghdad, Iraq

MAJ Scott M. Ward
Bath, NY
98th Division (IT)
Fallujah, Iraq

MAJ Scott T. Wels
Waterford, ME
98th Division (IT)
Ad Diwaniyah, Iraq

SSG Joseph West
Fayetteville, NC
USAR IRR
An Numaniyah, Iraq

SFC Nelson E. White
Akron, NY
98th Division (IT)
Kirkush, Iraq

SGT Raj Watkins
Vineland, NJ
98th Division (IT)
Rear Detachment

SFC Randolph L. Weltch
North Bergen, NJ
98th Division (IT)
Taji, Iraq

MSG Trevor C. Weston
Nashwauk, MN
84th USARRTC
Al Kasik, Iraq

SFC Richard W. White
Manchester, NH
98th Division (IT)
Baghdad, Iraq

MAJ Henry L. Weber
Rochester, NY
98th Division (IT)
Baghdad, Iraq

MSG Darren West
Maplewood, NJ
98th Division (IT)
Taji, Iraq

CPT Darren K. Whiddon
Perry, FL
108th Division (IT)
Al Kasik, Iraq

SFC Roger G. White Jr
Oceanport, NJ
98th Division (IT)
Baghdad, Iraq

SSG Terrance White
Sicklerville, NJ
98th Division (IT)
Tall Afar, Iraq

MAJ Albert F. Williams
Radcliff, KY
100th Division (IT)
Kirkush, Iraq

MAJ Michael Williams
Columbia, SC
USAR IRR
Tall Afar, Iraq

SSG Ronald Wilson
Rochester, NY
98th Division (IT)
Rear Detachment

SGT Sonya Whorley
Killeen, TX
USAR IRR
Baghdad, Iraq

CPT Christiane L. Williams
Springfield, OR
104th Division (IT)
Baghdad, Iraq

MSG Samuel H. Williams
Vinton, VA
98th Division (IT)
Baghdad, Iraq

SFC Eric D. Winfield
La Place, LA
95th Division (IT)
Baghdad, Iraq

1SG Matthew W. Widner
Knoxville, TN
81st RRC
Kirkush, Iraq

SFC Efrem V. Williams
Orange, NJ
98th Division (IT)
Camp Doha, Kuwait

SFC Torrance A. Williams
Franklin, LA
95th Division (IT)
Taji, Iraq

SGT Julian F. With
Schenectady, NY
98th Division (IT)
Kirkush, Iraq

MSG Paul S. Wilcock
Andover, NJ
98th Division (IT)
Fallujah, Iraq

MSG Jeffrey M. Williams
Waterford, CT
98th Division (IT)
Kirkush, Iraq

MSG John D. Wilson
Woonsocket, RI
98th Division (IT)
Camp Buehring, Kuwait

MSG Paul D. Witten
Auburn, ME
98th Division (IT)
An Numaniyah, Iraq

1SG Robert Wolff
Galloway Township, NJ
98th Division (IT)
An Numaniyah, Iraq

MAJ Angela D. Woods
Yonkers, NY
98th Division (IT)
Taji, Iraq

SGT Antonio R. Xavier
Milford, CT
98th Division (IT)
Baghdad, Iraq

1SG Edward Yurek
Bath, ME
98th Division (IT)
Fallujah, Iraq

LTC Tezeon Y. Wong
Newbury, OH
84th USARRTC
Taji, Iraq

MAJ Ashley Worboys
Broken Arrow, OK
90th RRC
Mosul, Iraq

MSG Curtis S. Yancey
Detroit, MI
88th RRC
Al Kasik, Iraq

SSG Bradley H. Ziverk
Springfield, MO
95th Division (IT)
Baghdad, Iraq

SFC Sherman J. Wood
Omaha, NE
95th Division (IT)
Kirkush, Iraq

MSG Joel E. Wright
North Tonawanda, NY
98th Division (IT)
Baghdad, Iraq

MAJ David A. Yasenchok
Rochester, NH
98th Division (IT)
Ar Rustamiyah, Iraq

MAJ Cecil Woode
Decatur, TX
75th Division (TS)
Baghdad, Iraq

SSG Filip Wyszynski
Williamstown, NJ
98th Division (IT)
Samarra, Iraq

LTC David A. Youngberg Jr
New York, NY
98th Division (IT)
Baghdad, Iraq

SPC Joshua K. Abbott	Auburn, ME	7 BDE 3/304 (USMA)
SFC Ralph Adjaye	Bronx, NY	4 BDE 7/98 (OD)
1LT Joseph D. Affinito	Oradell, NJ	1 BDE 1/385 (BCT)
SFC Michael P. Agate	Glendale, NY	3 BDE 6/98 (MI)
SGT Syed S. Ahmad	Syracuse, NY	2 BDE 2/389 DET 1 CO B&C
1LT Seth T. Aitken	Swansea, MA	1 BDE 2/385 (BCT) (-)
1LT Tariq S. Alam	Media, PA	1 BDE 3/385 (BCT) (-)
MAJ Ortiz R. Alicea	Liverpool, NY	HQ 6TH BDE (PD SCH)
SPC Brantley M. Allen	Fairport, NY	7 BDE 1/391 DET 3 CO C
SFC Christopher F. Allen	Tobyhanna, PA	4 BDE 8/98 (PS)
MSG Mark A. Alston Sr.	South Ozone Park, NY	3 BDE 3/98 (SC)
SSG Priscila P. Alvarez	Passaic Park, NJ	3 BDE 2/98 (MP)
SFC Chibuzo C. Amadi	S. Richmond Heights, NY	7 BDE 2/391 (REC) (-)
MSG Jesse B. Amado	Hope, RI	3 BDE 3/98 (SC)
SSG John W. Ammermann	Utica, NY	3 BDE 5/98 (CA/PO)
SSG Alma M. Andersen	Lunenburg, MA	3 BDE 6/98 (MI)
CW3 Eric G. Andersen	Putnam, CT	3 BDE 6/98 (MI)
SSG Rodney S. Anderson	West Newbury, MA	1 BDE 1/304 DET 2 CO D&E
SFC Demetry A. Anemojanis	Flushing, NY	1 BDE 3/385 DET 1 CO D&E
CPT Darren P. Annis	Newport , VT	7 BDE 1/391 DET CO B
SPC Andrea T. Antonelli	Newburgh, NY	3 BDE 1/98 (EN) (-)
SGT David Arias	Brooklyn, NY	HQ 98TH DIVISION (IT)
MSG Velda S. Armstrong	Valley Stream, NY	4 BDE 9/98 (-)
SSG Patrick A. Arrigoni	Coventry, CT	HQ 8TH BDE (SROTC)
SSG Nelson E. Arroyo Jr.	Woodside, NY	5 BDE 11/98 DET 4
SGT Christopher C. Arsenault	Springfield, MA	1 BDE 2/417 (BCT) (-)
SSG David L. Asay	Dixon, MO	2 BDE 1/390 (EN OSUT) (-)
SGT Andrea Y. Ashterman	New Rochelle, NY	3 BDE 2/98 (MP)
SPC Mark A. Austin	Rockway, NY	1 BDE 1/304 (BCT) (-)
SFC Michael T. Avery	Spencer, NY	2 BDE 2/390 DET 2
SGT Domingo Ayala II	Bronx, NY	5 BDE 11/98 (HS) (-)
SSG Jeanine M. Babic	Port Chester, NY	4 BDE 9/98 (-)
SFC Nicholas D. Baboolal	Hartford, CT	3 BDE 2/98 (MP)
SFC James A. Bach	Manchester, CT	HQ 4 BDE (CSS SCH)
SPC Michael W. Bailey	Albion, IL	1 BDE 1/304 (BCT) (-)
LTC Mark S. Bajko	Newburyport, MA	6 BDE 12/98 (C&GS)
SFC Christopher M. Bak	Bronx, NY	3 BDE 2/98 (MP)
SSG John E. Bakowski	Elma, NY	2 BDE 2/390 DET 2
SFC Janet E. Baldridge	Bel Air, MD	6 BDE T DET DSS
SSG Anthony A. Balestrieri	Midland Park, NJ	7 BDE 2/391 (REC) (-)
SGT Mark J. Baptiste II	Taunton, MA	1 BDE 2/417 DET 1 CO B&C
SGT Penni L. Barbeau	Bangor, ME	7 BDE 1/391 DET 1 CO A
SGT Daniel C. Barber	Salamanca, NY	7 BDE 1/391 DET 3 CO C
SSG Richard Barber	Windsor, CT	3 BDE 6/98 (MI)
SSG Jeremy J. Barcomb	Keene, NH	1 BDE 1/304 DET 2 CO D&E
CPT Lee Baroldy	Orchard Park, NY	2 BDE 1/390 (BCT) (-)
SGT Elaine Barreto	Brooklyn, NY	5 BDE 11/98 DET 4
SSG Robert L. Battle	Teaneck, NJ	4 BDE 10/98 (QM)

SSG Christopher S. Bean	Wayne, PA	1 BDE 1/417 (BCT)
SSG Omayra Bedward	Pleasant Valley, NY	4 BDE 9/98 (-)
SGT Joshua D. Beers	Flushing, NY	3 BDE 5/98 (CA/PO)
SGT Eric S. Bellas	Westwood, NJ	1 BDE 3/385 DET 1 CO D&E
SFC Michael D. Belton	Hamden, CT	1 BDE 2/417 DET 2 CO D&E
SGT Leonora J. Benn	Hamburg, NY	4 BDE 9/98 DET 1
SSG Lisa L. Benson	Clarksville, TN	4 BDE 9/98 DET 1
SPC Shirley A. Benton	Fort Hood, TX	7 BDE 2/391 (REC) (-)
SGT Matthew S. Bernard	Milford, NH	1 BDE 1/304 (BCT) (-)
SSG Rafael A. Berrios	New Windsor, NY	3 BDE 2/98 (MP)
SGT Manisha T. Bhatt	Cherry Hill, NJ	7 BDE 2/391 (REC) (-)
SGT Luciano Biancaniello	Derry, NH	1 BDE 1/304 (BCT) (-)
SSG John M. Bieber	Trumansburg, NY	5 BDE 11/98 (HS) (-)
SSG John W. Biehn III	Meriden, CT	3 BDE 2/98 (MP)
CPT David J. Biggins	Falls Church, VA	3 BDE 6/98 (MI)
1LT Travis J. Birkholz	Warrensburg, NY	6 BDE 12/98
SSG Ernest E. Bishop	Arlington, TX	1 BDE 2/417 DET 2 CO D&E
SPC Kelli A. Blanco	New York, NY	1 BDE 2/304 DET 1 CO A&D
SFC Daniel P. Blodgett	Hilton, NY	4 BDE 7/98 (OD)
SSG Sarah L. Blood	Oxford, NY	2 BDE 2/390 DET 2
SPC Eric J. Boisse	Saco, ME	1 BDE 2/304 (BCT) (-)
SFC Franklin L. Booker Jr.	Central Islip, NY	4 BDE 10/98 DET 1
SGT Michael J. Boone	Long Branch, NJ	1 BDE 3/385 (BCT) (-)
SSG Harold P. Borden III	Johnstown, NY	4 BDE 7/98 (OD)
SFC Andre L. Bostic	Brooklyn, NY	1 BDE 1/385 (BCT)
MSG Michael D. Boucher	Enfield, CT	4 BDE 9/98 (-)
SPC Anthony W. Bouley Jr.	Schenectady, NY	7 BDE 1/391 DET 1 CO A
SSG Dale A. Bourque	Waterboro, ME	5 BDE 11/98 DET 4
2LT Bryce N. Bouton	Biddeford, ME	1 BDE 2/304 (BCT) (-)
SSG Michael D. Boyce	Falmouth, ME	1 BDE 1/304 DET 1 CO B&C
SGT Erzcel J. Boyd	Piscataway, NJ	7 BDE 2/391 (REC) (-)
MAJ Ross M. Boyer	Freeville, NY	HQ 8TH BDE (SROTC)
CPT Scott D. Boyington	Randolph, ME	1 BDE 2/304 (BCT) (-)
SFC Joseph R. Bradbury	Windsor, ME	7 BDE 3/304 DET 6
1SG Peter G. Brade	Batavia, NY	HQ 2D BDE(EN OSUT)
SFC William T. Brightman	Newark, NY	7 BDE 3/391 LS DET 1 TM 1
SPC Jinger A. Brinkley	Royal Oak, MI	7 BDE 3/304 (USMA)
LTC Mark Brittain	Rochester, NY	HQ 98TH DIVISION (IT)
SFC Lisa A. Brooks	Long Island City, NY	4 BDE 10/98 DET 1
SFC Carl L. Brown	Islip, NY	5BDE 11/98 DET4
CPT James L. Brown Jr.	East Haven, CT	1 BDE 2/417 DET 1 CO B&C
SFC Philip E. Brown	Gillett, PA	3 BDE 1/98 (EN) DET 1
SFC Phyllis M. Brown	Orange, NJ	1 BDE 3/385 (BCT) (-)
CSM Shawn P. Browne	Lancaster, NY	6 BDE 9801 DET (DSS) (-)
SSG Michael S. Bruno	Horsham, PA	7 BDE 2/391 (REC) (-)
SPC Robert I. Bruttomesso	Middletown Springs, VT	7 BDE 1/391 DET 2 CO B
SGT David R. Bryant	Winthrop, ME	7 BDE 3/304 (USMA)
SSG Marcus E. Buckley	Gouldsboro, ME	7 BDE 1/391 DET 1 CO A

SSG Bethannie J. Bugbee	Scarborough, ME	1 BDE 2/304 (BCT) (-)
SFC Raymond G. Bullock Jr.	Springfield, VT	4 BDE 9/98 (-)
SFC Charmetri A. Bulluck	New Britain, CT	7 BDE 3/391 DET 6
SGT Justin T. Burke	Niagara Falls, NY	4 BDE 9/98 DET 1
SSG Elizabeth N. Burnham	Weymouth, MA	3 BDE 5/98 (CA/PO)
SGT Jared M. Bush	North Tonawanda, NY	2 BDE 1/390 (BCT)
SGT Kelly E. Butler	Adelphi, MD	3 BDE 6/98 (MI)
SPC Sean T . Butler	Newington, CT	1 BDE 2/417 (BCT) (-)
CPL William F. Butler	Wakefield, ME	3 BDE 6/98 (MI)
CPT Justen G. Byrne	Asbury Park, NJ	1 BDE 3/385 (BCT) (-)
SSG Ronald A. Cabell	Centerville, MA	5 BDE 11/98 DET 4
SSG Robert A. Cain	Holland, NY	2 BDE 1/390 (BCT) (-)
MAJ Michael M. Calamito	Maywood, NJ	4 BDE 10/98 (QM)
MSG Agustin Calderon	Gainesville, VA	3 BDE 6/98 (MI)
SPC Shawn M. Caldwell	Bowie, MD	3 BDE 6/98 (MI)
MSG Harold R. Call	Cazenovia, NY	HQ 8TH BDE (SROTC)
SSG Matthew D. Callahan	Ayer, MA	3 BDE 2/98 (MP)
SPC Gomez M. Camacho	Fort Kent, ME	7 BDE 1/391 DET 1 CO A
SPC Adam T . Cambridge	Bangor, ME	3 BDE 6/98 (MI)
MSG Abby A. Campbell	Bronx, NY	3 BDE 5/98 (CA/PO)
SGM Karen A. Campbell	Chicopee, MA	HQ 4TH BDE(CSS SCH)
SSG Vinson Campos	Bronx, NY	3 BDE 2/98 (MP)
SFC Douglas E. Canty	Camillus, NY	2 BDE 2/389 DET 1 CO B&C
LTC Randall W. Carlson	Milford, PA	3 BDE 1/98 (EN) (-)
SFC David P. Carney	Eastbrook, ME	7BDE 1/391 DET 7
COL Brian M. Carpenter	Bangor, ME	HQ 1ST BDE (BCT)
MSG Johnny L. Carpenter	Etna, ME	7 BDE 1/391 DET 1 CO A
SGT David B. Carr	Rochester, NY	4 BDE 9/98 DET 1
SSG Tommy K. Carr	Mattydale, NY	6 BDE 9801 DET (DSS) (-)
SFC Richard G. Carrion	Milton, FL	3 BDE 5/98 (CA/PO)
SFC Andrew L. Carter	Boston, MA	3 BDE 6/98 (MI)
MAJ John Carvajal	East Northport, NY	3 BDE 2/98 (MP)
LTC Paul E. Casazza	Rockville Center, NY	4 BDE 9/98 (-)
SFC James A. Castello	Elmira, NY	3 BDE 1/98 (EN) DET 1
SGT Michael E. Catellier Jr.	Troy, NY	3 BDE 1/98 (EN) (-)
SGT William Celestino	Yonkers, NY	3 BDE 2/98 (MP)
LTC Robert D. Cendrowski	Mount Holly, NJ	6 BDE 13/98 (CAS3)
MAJ Mark J. Cepiel	Mechanicville, NY	HQ 8 BDE (SROTC)
SSG Wing W. Chan	Brooklyn, NY	1 BDE 3/385 (BCT) (-)
CPT David L. Chandler	Springville, NY	HQ 2D BDE (EN OSUT)
SSG Warren Chen	Linden, NJ	1 BDE 3/385 (BCT) (-)
SGT Chann E. Chhim	Philadelphia, PA	1 BDE 1/417 (BCT)
SSG Kevin R. Chiasson	Arlington, VA	3 BDE 6/98 (MI)
LTC George Chin	Staten Island, NY	6 BDE 13/98 (CAS3)
SSG Mark L. Christian	Salisbury Mills, NY	3 BDE 2/98 (MP)
LTC Paul J. Ciesinski	East Hampton, CT	4 BDE (CSS SCH)
SSG Stacey Claiborne	Cambria Heights, NY	1 BDE 3/385 DET 1 CO D&E
SFC Charles Clark Jr.	Riverton, WY	1 BDE 2/385

MSG David K. Clark	Buffalo, NY	7 BDE 1/391 DET 3 CO C
SSG Mario H. Clarke	Bloomfield, NJ	1 BDE 3/385 DET 1 CO D&E
CW3 Mario J. Claussell	Port Jefferson, NY	3 BDE 6/98 DET 9
SFC Philip D. Clohecy	Barrington, NH	7 BDE 3/304 (USMA)
SFC Russell D. Coffill	Chester, NH	3 BDE 6/98 (MI)
SFC Phyllis M. Collier	Edison, NJ	1 BDE 3/385 (BCT) (-)
SFC Patrick A. Collins	Buffalo, NY	7 BDE 1/391 DET 3 CO C
MSG Gladys I. Colon	Marlton, NJ	HQ 3 BDE (CS SCH)
MAJ Benedict J. Conboy	Delmar, NY	HQ 8TH BDE (SROTC) DIV IT
MSG Joseph Conicelli	Topsham, ME	7 BDE 3/304 DET 6
MSG Gregory O. Cook	Agawam, MA	4 BDE 9/98 (-)
1LT Joseph M. Corso Jr.	Hampton, CT	1 BDE 2/417 DET 1 CO B&C
CPT Mark D. Cossar	Tonawanda, NY	7 BDE (TS)
SFC Edward R. Cote	Childwold, NY	3 BDE 1/98 (EN) (-)
MSG Edward B. Cotton	Jamaica, NY	7 BDE 2/391 (REC) (-)
MAJ George C. Cressman Jr.	North Wales, PA	1 BDE 1/417 (BCT)
SFC Jeffery E. Crippen	Rome, NY	3 BDE 3/98 (SC)
SSG Howard A. Crosby Jr.	Marion, NY	HQ 7TH BDE (TS)
CPT John D. Crow	Depew, NY	2 BDE 1/390 (BCT) (-)
CPT Charles E. Crusha Jr.	Corning, NY	HQ 8TH BDE (SROTC)
SFC Anthony Cruz	Maspeth, NY	1 BDE 3/385 DET 1 CO D&E
SSG Geoffrey M. Cummings	East Granby, CT	7 BDE 3/304 (USMA)
SFC Billy J. Cummins	Winthrop, ME	7 BDE 3/304 (USMA)
SPC James C. Cunha	Weymouth, MA	1 BDE 2/385 (BCT)
SFC John B. Cunningham	Westfield, NY	3 BDE 1/98 (EN) DET 1
SFC Lawrence Cupidore	Brooklyn, NY	4 BDE 9/98 (-)
SSG George A. Dadson Jr.	Rochester, NY	HQ 7TH BDE (TS)
MSG Audra Y. Damondawson	Brooklyn, NY	HQ 3 BDE (CS SCH)
MSG Frederick R. Dana	East Meadow, NY	4 BDE 9/98 DET 2
MAJ Christopher P. Daniels	Rochester, NY	HQ 98TH DIVISION (IT)
SFC Stanley Dash	Bronx, NY	5 BDE 11/98 DET 4
SGT Charles A. Davenport	Little Compton, RI	3 BDE 6/98 (MI)
SSG Charles Davis Jr.	East Elmhurst, NY	4 BDE 10/98 DET 1
SFC David J. Davis	West Valley, NY	2 BDE 1/390 DET 1 CO D&E
MSG Gary W. Davis	Tewksbury, MA	3 BDE 4/98 (CM)
1SG Gerald R. Davis	Saunderstown, RI	3 BDE 5/98 (CA/PO)
SSG Rosemary A. Davis	New Rochelle, NY	3 BDE 2/98 (MP)
SGT Terrance M. Davison	Trenton, NJ	7 BDE 2/391 (REC) (-)
MSG Phillip M. Deangelo	Binghamton, NY	HQ 8TH BDE (SROTC)
SFC Reed F. Degolier	Mayville, NY	3 BDE 1/98 (EN) DET 1
MSG Jesus Dejesus	Mount Holly, NJ	4 BDE 8/98 (PS)
MSG Rafael Delvalle Jr.	Bristol, CT	4 BDE 9/98 (TC) DET 1
SFC Thomas Demarco	Rochester, NY	7 BDE 1/391 DET 3 CO C
COL Raymond Denisewich	Providence, RI	HQ 1ST BDE (BCT)
LTC Eric H. Deravin III	Bronx, NY	HQ 8TH BDE (SROTC) DIV IT
SFC Michael W. Desens	Williamson, NY	2 BDE 2/389 DET 2 CO D&E
SSG Gregg M. Desiato	Granville, NY	4 BDE 7/98 (OD)
MSG Charles A. Destival II	Danbury, CT	4 BDE 10/98 (QM)

PFC John C. Deveau Jr.	Caribou, ME	1 BDE 2/304 DET 1
SGT Sean R. Dever	Waterbury, CT	1 BDE 2/417 DET 2 CO D&E
CPT Joseph R. Devine	Orland, ME	1 BDE 1/304 DET 1 CO B&C
SGT Anthony Diangelo	Plymouth, MA	3 BDE 6/98 (MI)
MSG Lugo E. Diaz	West Haverstraw, NY	4 BDE 9/98 (TC)
CW2 Joan Dickerson	Tampa, FL	HQ 98TH DIV (IT)
SSG Bridget A. Dickson	Bronx, NY	3 BDE 6/98 (MI)
PFC Michael D. Digregorio	Fall River, MA	3 BDE 3/98 (SC)
PFC John N. Dimillo	Portland, ME	1 BDE 2/304 (BCT) (-)
SSG Michael J. Dipetta	Erin, NY	3 BDE 1/98 (EN) DET 1
SFC David G. Dispenza	Buffalo, NY	2 BDE 1/389 (EN OSUT) (-)
SFC Christopher M. Ditizio	Swedesboro, NJ	3 BDE 5/98 (CA/PO)
MAJ Brian T. Dixon	Blossvale, NY	HQ 6TH BDE (PD SCH)
SFC Nathan A. Dolson Jr.	Niagara Falls, NY	2 BDE 1/390 (BCT) (-)
SPC April Dorch	Plainfield, NJ	4 BDE 8/98 (PS)
SGT Jacqueline Dorval	Ashland, MA	3 BDE 6/98 (MI)
SFC Michael E. Doughty	Limerick, ME	7 BDE 3/304 DET 6
1LT Thomas J. Doyle	Germantown, MD	3 BDE 6/98 (MI)
SSG Todd Doyle	Yarmouth, ME	7 BDE 3/304 DET 6
SFC Celene M. Doyley	Bronx, NY	HQ 3 BDE (CS SCH)
SGT Travis A. Drew	Guilford, ME	7 BDE 3/304 (USMA)
SFC Todd M. Drickel	Webster, NY	2 BDE 2/389 DET 2 CO D&E
SSG Ioan Dubovici	New York, NY	3 BDE 6/98 (MI)
SSG Christina A. Duggan	Webster, MA	5 BDE 11/98 DET 4
MAJ Zolten L. Dukes	Rochester, NY	7 BDE 1/391 DET 3 CO C
SSG Jefferson J. Duncan II	Jersey City, NJ	3 BDE 5/98 (CA/PO)
SPC Alexander R. Dunn	Lackawanna, NY	2 BDE 1/390 (BCT) (-)
SGT Andrea L. Dunn	Germantown, NY	5 BDE 11/98 DET 4
SFC Herron R. Dunston	South Orange, NJ	1 BDE 3/385 DET 1 CO D&E
SFC Nancy Durieux	Highland Park, NJ	1 BDE 3/385 (BCT) (-)
SGT Angela L. Ebert	Unity, ME	3 BDE 1/98 (EN) DET 1
1LT Adrian A. Edwards	Somerset, MA	3 BDE 6/98 (MI)
SPC David C. Edwards	Columbia, MS	1 BDE 2/417 (BCT)
LTC Jesse C. Edwards Jr.	Fairport, NY	HQ 98TH DIVISION (IT)
SPC Nathaniel N. Edwards	Piscataway, NJ	7 BDE 3/391 (LOG SPT) (-)
MSG Paul A. Edwards	South Burlington, VT	HQ 8TH BDE (SROTC)
SPC Eric Egan	Hillsboro, OR	3 BDE 3/98 (SC)
SPC Ralph W. Egbert	Manheim, PA	7 BDE 2/391 (REC) (-)
SFC James E. Eggleston IV	Rochester, NY	7 BDE 2/391 DET 1 CO B
SFC Tyler L. Ekwell	Rochester, NY	3 BDE 5/98 (CA/PO)
MSG Monique M. Eldridge	Kennebunk, ME	5 BDE 11/98 (HS) (-)
COL James A. Elliott Jr.	Bangor, ME	HQ 98TH DIVISION (IT)
SSG Charles E. Emerson	Penn Yan, NY	2 BDE 2/389 DET 2 CO D&E
SGT Christopher J. English	West Seneca, NY	2 BDE 1/390 (BCT) (-)
SGT Bradley R. Erdmann	Downingtown, PA	1 BDE 1/417 (BCT)
SFC Craig E. Ernst Jr.	Marlboro, NY	3 BDE 1/98 (EN) (-)
MAJ Jose L. Escobar	Clifton, NJ	7 BDE 2/391 (REC) (-)
SPC Diana R. Espinosa	Rutherford, NJ	1 BDE 3/385 DET 1 CO D&E

SFC Michael J. Esposito	Ft Huachuca, AZ	3 BDE 6/98 (MI)
SSG Corey S. Estes	Madison, ME	1 BDE 1/304 DET 1 CO B&C
SSG Robert N. Estrada	Perth Amboy, NJ	1 BDE 3/385 (BCT)
SSG Carita V. Fant	Brooklyn, NY	5BDE 11/98 DET4
MAJ Kathleen C. Farrell	Cumberland, RI	3 BDE 6/98 (MI)
SFC Robert K. Farrow	New York, NY	4 BDE 9/98 (-)
SSG Dennis Febles	Billerica, MA	3 BDE 6/98 (MI)
SGT Carmen I. Feliz	Freeport, NY	HQ 98TH DIV (IT) DET 20
SFC Gregory R. Ferguson	Farmington, NY	2 BDE 2/389 DET 2 CO D&E
SGT Meghan K. Ferguson	Farmington, NY	2 BDE 2/389 DET 2 CO D&E
SSG Lorraine C. Fernandes	Brooklyn, NY	6 BDE 14/98 (NCOES) DET 2
MSG Vernon C. Ficcaglia	Geneva, NY	2 BDE 2/389 (EN OSUT) (-)
SFC Gary D. Field	Malone, NY	3 BDE 1/98 (EN) DET 1
SSG Edualdo Figueroa	Clifton, NJ	1 BDE 3/385 DET 1 CO D&E
SSG Christine A. Fillgrove	Chili, NY	7 BDE 3/391 LS DET 1 TM 1
MAJ Thomas D. Fillgrove	Chili, NY	HQ 98TH DIVISION (IT)
SGT Kelly M. Finn	St. Catharines, Ontario,	2 BDE HQ (EN OSUT)
SGT Tiffany Finn	Arverne, NY	HQ 5TH BDE (HS SCH)
MAJ Erin J. Fish	Round Lake, NY	HQ 8TH BDE (SROTC)
MAJ Richard S. Flacinski	Hopewell Junction, NY	3 BDE 2/98 (MP)
SSG Kevin M. Fleming	South Portland, ME	7 BDE 3/304 (USMA)
SSG Kevin R. Flinn	Brandon, VT	7 BDE 1/391 DET 2 CO B
SFC Martin M. Flores A	Flanders, NJ	6 BDE 9801 T DET DSS TM 3
SSG Joy M. Flynn	New Haven, CT	4 BDE 9/98 DET 4
SSG Rafael Fonseco Jr.	Bridgeport, CT	1 BDE 2/417 (BCT) (-)
MAJ Sandra L. Forrest	Dunellen, NJ	3 BDE 5/98 DET 1
MAJ Kenneth R. Foulks Jr.	Belford, NJ	4 BDE 8/98 (PS)
SFC John J. Fountain	Laconia, NH	HQ 98TH DIV (IT) DET 1
CPT Jahn K. Foy	Brooklyn, NY	1 BDE 1/385 (BCT) (-)
SPC Robert J. Fragale	Buffalo, NY	2 BDE 1/390 (BCT) (-)
MSG Michelle L. Frankson	East Elmhurst, NY	HQ 8TH BDE (SROTC)
SFC Patricia A. Fraser	Piffard, NY	HQ 98TH DIVISION (IT)
SFC Gary J. Fraske	Saugerties, NY	3 BDE 6/98 (MI)
SSG David J. Fredricksen	West Milford, NJ	3 BDE 1/98 (EN) (-)
1LT Alice C. French	Minot, ME	7 BDE 3/304 (USMA)
SSG Peter P. Fusco	New Bedford, MA	3 BDE 3/98 (SC)
SSG Steven E. Gajan	Newark, NY	HQ 98TH DIVISION (IT)
SFC Efrain Garcia	Brooklyn, NY	5 BDE 11/98 DET 4
SSG Maritza Garcia	Astoria, NY	5 BDE 11/98 DET 4
SGT Peter M. Garian	Medway, MA	3 BDE 6/98 (MI)
SFC Clifford R. Garrettson Jr.	Freeport, NY	3 BDE 1/98 (EN) (-)
SFC Gregory A. Gauthier	Buffalo, NY	2 BDE 2/390 DET 2
PFC Matthew J. Geboskie Jr.	Indian Orchard, MA	1 BDE 1/304 (BCT) (-)
SSG Christopher A. Gentiluomo	Ballston Spa, NY	4 BDE 7/98 (OD)
SPC Frank Genua	Cliffside Park, NJ	1 BDE 3/385 (BCT) (-)
SSG Elizabeth G. Germano	Middletown, CT	3 BDE 6/98 (MI)
SGT Fred J. Ghanim	Ringoes, NJ	3 BDE 5/98 (CA/PO)
SFC Anthony M. Giancola	Buffalo, NY	HQ 8TH BDE (SROTC)

SFC Joseph A. Giardina	Denville, NJ	3 BDE 2/98 (MP)
CPT James G. Gill Jr.	Millville, NJ	7 BDE 3/391 (LGSPT) (-)
SSG William E. Gillespie	Oneonta, NY	2 BDE 2/390 DET 2
SFC Hayward K. Gillies	Concord, NH	3 BDE 6/98 (MI)
CPT Joseph H. Gingold	Rochester, NY	2 BDE 2/390 (BCT) (-)
MAJ Gregory D. Ginnetti	Cromwell, CT	3 BDE 6/98 DET 12
SGT Nicholas R. Goff	Cheektowaga, NY	2 BDE 1/390 (BCT) (-)
SGT Maria Y. Gomez	Roselle, NJ	3 BDE 5/98 DET 1
MAJ Joseph B. Gonsalves	Greenville, RI	3 BDE 3/98 (SC)
MAJ Lester Gonzalez	Cicero, NY	HQ 98TH DIVISION (IT)
LTC Darryl H. Goodman	Johns Island, SC	108 7 BDE HQ
SFC Kevin M. Gosler	Auburn, MA	1 BDE 2/417 DET 2 CO D&E
CPT Benjamin K. Grabski	Rochester, NY	2 BDE 2/390 DET 2
SFC Heather Gray	Hernando, FL	3 BDE 6/98 (MI)
SGT Reid F. Gray	Framingham, MA	3 BDE 6/98 (MI)
SFC Sheldon Gray	Elkins Park, PA	1 BDE 1/417 (BCT)
SPC David W. Greenawalt Jr.	Blasdell, NY	4 BDE 9/98 DET 1
SFC Trevor C. Greene	Brooklyn, NY	5 BDE 11/98 DET 4
COL Donald H. Greenwood	Quincy, MA	HQ 8TH BDE (SROTC)
SGT Samuel Gregory Jr.	Henrietta, NY	7 BDE 1/391 DET 4 CO D
SFC Darrell C. Grover	St. Petersburg, FL	7 BDE 2/391 (REC) (-)
SFC Walter L. Guertin	Attleboro, MA	3 BDE 6/98 (MI)
SGT Jeffrey A. Gurnsey	Nedrow, NY	2 BDE 2/389 DET 1 CO B&C
1LT Bryan J. Haas	Watertown, CT	1 BDE 2/417 (BCT) (-)
MAJ Adam W. Hackel	Doylestown, PA	HQ 98TH DIVISION (IT)
SPC Stacey L. Hackmack	Waretown, NJ	1 BDE 3/385 (BCT) (-)
SSG Dawn J. Hage	Castleton, NY	2 BDE 2/390 DET 2
SGT Kim E. Hall	Philadelphia, PA	4 BDE 8/98 (PS)
SSG Reinaldo F. Hall	Brooklyn, NY	4 BDE 9/98 (TC)
SSG James D. Hamilton	Philadelphia, PA	1 BDE 1/417 (BCT)
SFC Karl A. Hanson	Manchester, NH	1 BDE 1/304 (BCT) (-)
SFC Michael J. Harper	Lumberton, NJ	3 BDE 5/98 (CA/PO)
SSG Patrick J. Harrington	Alexandria, VA	3 BDE 6/98 (MI)
SGT Tom N. Harrington	Dumont, NJ	1 BDE 1/385 (BCT)
SSG Richard T. Harris	Rochester, NY	HQ 98TH DIVISION (IT)
SFC Rhys Harrison	Phippsburg, ME	7 BDE 3/304 (USMA)
MAJ Scott K. Harrison	Milford, CT	HQ 8TH BDE (SROTC)
SPC Augustine C. Hartman	Scarborough, ME	1 BDE 1/304 DET 1 CO B&C
SFC Francis S. Haste	Fulton, NY	3 BDE 1/98 (EN) (-)
CW3 Terri L. Hathaway	Rochester, NY	HQ 98TH DIV (IT) DET 5
MSG Patricia Hawkins	Danbury, CT	HQ 4TH BDE(CSS SCH)
MAJ Robert P. Hedden Jr.	Rochester, NY	6 BDE 12/98 (C&GS)
SFC Matthew Heinbockel	Denville, NJ	1 BDE 3/385 DET 1 CO D&E
LTC Derek Henshaw	West Seneca, NY	6 BDE 13/98 (CAS3)
MAJ Derek Henshaw	West Seneca, NY	6 BDE 13/98 (CAS3)
SSG Ernesto A. Hernandez	Hackensack, NJ	1 BDE 3/385 DET 1 CO D&E
MAJ Kimberly G. Hicks	Theresa, NY	6 BDE 12/98 (C&GS)
SFC Marion C. Hill	Brooklyn, NY	3 BDE 4/98 (CM)

Name	Hometown	Unit
SFC Michael J. Hill	Philadelphia, PA	1 BDE 1/417 (BCT)
LTC Thomas C. Hillman	Gardiner, ME	6 BDE 12/98 (C&GS)
MAJ Christopher J. Hilton	Annapolis, MD	5 BDE 11/98 (HS)
MSG Cheryl Hiltonvadner	Rushville, NY	HQ 98TH DIVISION (IT)
CPT Gregory T. Hinton II	Little Rock, AR	HQ 98TH DIVISION (IT)
MAJ John D. Hitchcock	Ballston Spa, NY	7 BDE 1/391 (CMTE) (-)
SPC Stacy L. Hogg	Schenectady, NY	7 BDE 1/391 DET 3 CO C
CPT Andrew K. Holland	Hamburg, NY	2 BDE 1/390 (BCT) (-)
CPT Peter J. Holley	Liverpool, NY	HQ 6TH BDE (PD SCH)
SSG Christina M. Holst	Clifton Park, NY	7 BDE 1/391 (CMTE) (-)
SFC Douglas F. Horan	Hemlock, NY	2 BDE 2/390 DET 2
LTC James A. Horton Jr.	Somerville, NJ	7 BDE 2/391 (REC) (-)
SGM William D. Hotham	Mechanicsburg, PA	3 BDE 5/98 (CA/PO)
PFC Bradford A. Howard	Kennebunk, ME	1 BDE 2/304 (BCT) (-)
SSG Mark J. Howe	Ithaca, NY	2 BDE 2/389 (EN OSUT) (-)
SPC Maurice Howie	Providence, RI	1 BDE 2/385 (BCT)
SFC Paul W. Hrynio	Canastota, NY	2 BDE 2/389 DET 1 CO B&C
SSG Sheldon L. Hunt	New York, NY	4 BDE 10/98 (QM)
SSG Alexander M. Hunter	Rochester, NY	7 BDE 1/391 DET 3 CO C
SFC Donald J. Hunter II	Attica, NY	2 BDE 2/390 DET 1 CO D&E
MSG Richard H. Hussey	Lewiston, ME	7 BDE 3/304 DET 6
SFC Willie D. Hutchinson	Norwalk, CT	4 BDE 9/98 DET 4
SFC David J. Incorvaia Sr.	St. Robert, MO	2 BDE 1/390 (EN OSUT) (-)
1SG James F. Ingerick	Henrietta, NY	2 BDE 2/389 DET 2 CO D&E
SPC Jeffrey T. Irons	Pawtucket, RI	1 BDE 2/385 (BCT) (-)
SFC David W. Irwin	Piffard, NY	2 BDE 1/390 (BCT) (-)
SGT Cynthia Jacinthe	Brooklyn, NY	5BDE 11/98 DET4
SFC Ralph K. Jackson	Wilton, ME	7 BDE 1/391 DET 1 CO A
SSG Ansilla V. James	Stratford, CT	4 BDE 9/98 (-)
MSG Dennis James	Neversink, NY	HQ 98TH DIVISION (IT)
CSM Donna M. James	Cumberland, RI	4 BDE 9/98 (-)
SGT Jennifer R. James	Brunswick , ME	7 BDE 3/304 (USMA)
SFC Scott E. Janaski	West Falls, NY	2 BDE 1/390 (EN OSUT) (-)
MSG Craig S. Jandreau	LeRoy, NY	2 BDE 2/389 (EN OSUT) (-)
SSG David J. Jindra	Buffalo, NY	4 BDE 9/98 DET 1
SGT Carl O. Johnson Jr.	Troy, NY	4 BDE 7/98 (OD)
MSG Denise J. Johnson	Willingboro, NJ	4 BDE 10/98 DET 1
SGT Jamelah Johnson	Philadelphia, PA	7 BDE 2/391 (REC) (-)
SFC Jay M. Johnson	Voorhees, NJ	1 BDE 1/417 (BCT)
CSM Michael E. Johnson	Irvington, NJ	1 BDE 1/417 (BCT)
SSG Thomas W. Johnson Jr.	Buffalo, NY	7 BDE 2/391 DET 1 CO B
SGT Wayne P. Johnson	Marshfield, ME	7 BDE 1/391 DET 1 CO A
SGT Jada L. Jones	Rochester, NY	3 BDE 5/98 DET 1
SSG Mark R. Jones	Olean, NY	2 BDE 1/390 DET 7
SFC Melissa N. Jones	Brooklyn, NY	5 BDE 11/98 DET 4
SFC Timothy Jones	Bristol, ME	7 BDE 3/304 (USMA)
SPC Derik R. Jordan	Elizabeth, NJ	7 BDE 2/391 (REC) (-)
1SG Joseph J. Joyce	East Pembroke, NY	2 BDE 1/390 (BCT) (-)

SGT Derrick G. Justice	Rochester, NY	7 BDE 3/391 LS DET 1 TM 1
SGT Michael C. Kaifas	Niagara Falls, NY	7 BDE 1/391 DET 3 CO C
SSG Daniel J. Kalagian	Bridgeport, CT	3 BDE 2/98 (MP)
LTC Christopher J. Kamide	Deferiet, NY	6 BDE 12/98 (C&GS)
SGT Alison R. Kastner	Rochester, NY	HQ 98TH DIVISION (IT)
SGT Scott A. Kauker	Brunswick, OH	1 BDE 1/385 (BCT)
SPC Avery D. Kearse	Somerset, NJ	7 BDE 2/391 (REC) (-)
MSG Freddie P. Keating	Severn, MD	3 BDE 6/98 (MI)
SFC Christopher Keeling	Naugatuck, CT	1 BDE 2/417 (BCT) (-)
SFC Alvin A. Kellman	Brooklyn, NY	5 BDE 11/98 (HS) (-)
CPT Sharon K. Kelsey	Maynard, MA	3 BDE 6/98 (MI)
MSG Eithnea M. Kenny	North Quincy, MA	4 BDE 10/98 (QM)
SGT Komsai Keo	Brockport, NY	7 BDE 1/391 DET 3 CO C
LTC Alberto Kercado	Amsterdam, NY	HQ 8TH BDE (SROTC)
SSG Abdul K. Khan	York, ME	1 BDE 2/304 (BCT) (-)
SGT Martin R. Kidder	Springfield, VT	7 BDE 1/391 DET 2 CO B
SSG Laura J. Kilgour	Ipswich, MA	3 BDE 6/98 (MI)
SSG Joseph N. Kilmer	Towanda, PA	3 BDE 5/98 (CA/PO)
SGT David M. Kingsland	Schenectady, NY	7 BDE 1/391 (CMTE) (-)
SSG Shane G. Kinney	Natural Bridge, NY	4 BDE 7/98 (OD)
SSG Robert A. Kitchen	Bainbridge, NY	2 BDE 1/389 (EN OSUT) (-)
SFC Scott D. Kleinhenz	Cherry Hill, NJ	3 BDE 1/98 (EN) (-)
SSG Lee A. Kliss	Nashua, NH	1 BDE 1/304 (BCT) (-)
SSG John A. Knappe	Brewer, ME	1 BDE 2/304 DET 1 CO A&D
SFC James M. Knoeller	Arlington, VA	3 BDE 6/98 (MI)
SGT Korwyn Y. Kolewe	Binghamton, NY	3 BDE 1/98 (EN) DET 1
SFC Clarence R. Kratzer	Cookstown, NJ	3 BDE 1/98 (EN) (-)
SSG Robert A. Kraus	Nashua, NH	4 BDE 10/98 DET 1
SFC John A. Krautwurst Jr.	Rochester, NY	2 BDE 2/389 DET 2 CO D&E
SFC Frank P. Kren	Orchard Park, NY	7 BDE 2/391 DET 1 CO B
SFC James W. Krueger Jr.	Cortland, NY	2 BDE 2/389 (EN OSUT) (-)
SGT Marina A. Kulesz	Cheektowaga, NY	4 BDE 9/98 DET 1
CPT Edward P. Kuppinger	Rochester, NY	7 BDE 1/391 DET 3 CO C
CW2 Tracy L. Labrie	Accokeek, MD	3 BDE 6/98 DET 11
SSG Jennifer R. Labuda	Tonawanda, NY	4 BDE 9/98 DET 1
SGM Larry Laduca	Alden, NY	HQ 7TH BDE (TS)
LTC Paul P. Lally Jr.	Northford, CT	7 BDE 3/304 DET 6
SFC Patrick J. Laporte	Mohawk, NY	3 BDE 5/98 (CA/PO)
MSG Lynn A. Laracuente	Utica, NY	3 BDE 5/98 (CA/PO)
SGT Kendrick N. Lau	Newton, MA	3 BDE 5/98 (CA/PO)
SGT Travis W. Lawrence	Rochester, NY	2 BDE 2/389 DET 2 CO D&E
MSG Linda M. Leader	Niverville, NY	5 BDE 11/98 DET 4
SSG Rafael Lebron	Patterson, NY	1 BDE 2/417 (BCT) (-)
SGT Eun S. Lee	Bear, DE	3 BDE 5/98 (CA/PO)
LTC Linda D. Leibhart	Bath, NY	HQ 2D BDE(EN OSUT)
SSG Rom L. Lemay	Niagara Falls, NY	4 BDE 9/98 DET 1
CPT Christopher W. Lemmer	Burlington, NJ	1 BDE 1/417 (BCT)
SFC George E. Leonard	Camillus, NY	HQ 6TH BDE (PD SCH)

LTC Daniel M. Lepage	East Hampton, CT	6 BDE 12/98 (C&GS)
SGT Joseph J. Lepinskie	Buffalo, NY	2 BDE 1/390 (BCT) (-)
SGT Brian D. Lewis	Maynard, MA	5 BDE 11/98 (HS) (-)
SGT Gregory J. Lewis	Rochester, NY	2 BDE 2/389 DET 2 CO D&E
LTC Stuart K. Lhommedieu	Oxford, NY	7 BDE 1/391 (CMTE) (-)
SFC James J. Liberatore	Depew, NY	4 BDE 9/98 DET 1
SGT Erik Livingston	Philadelphia, PA	1 BDE 3/385 DET CO D&E
SGT Samie J. Lizzio	Johnstown, NY	7 BDE 1/391 DET 2 CO B
SGT Jennifer C. Loayza	Newton Highlands, MA	1 BDE 1/304 (BCT) (-)
SGT John A. Look	South Portland, ME	7 BDE 3/304 (USMA)
SFC Steven C. Loos	Killeen, TX	7 BDE 1/391 DET 1 CO A
SFC Carlos M. Lopez	Bronx, NY	4 BDE 9/98 (-)
SSG Fernando Lopez	South Ozone Park, NY	1 BDE 3/385 (BCT) (-)
SGT Israel Lopez	Bronx, NY	3 BDE 4/98 (CM)
SGT Jeremy N. Lounder	Worcester, MA	3 BDE 6/98 (MI)
SFC Marshall M. Lowery	Watertown, NY	2 BDE 2/389 DET 1 CO B&C
SFC James A. Luckenbach	Dansville, NY	2 BDE 2/390 (BCT) (-)
MAJ Edmund L. Luzine Jr.	Rensselaer, NY	HQ 98TH DIVISION (IT)
SGM Jon S. Lycett	Hamburg, NY	HQ 2D BDE(EN OSUT)
SFC Jack C. Lyon Jr.	Brasher Falls, NY	3 BDE 1/98 (EN) DET 1
MAJ William F. Lyons Jr.	Hudson, MA	3 BDE 6/98 (MI)
MAJ Kevin J. Macfarlane	Glastonbury, CT	HQ 8TH BDE (SROTC)
MSG Bernard A. Mack	Mount Vernon, NY	5 BDE 11/98 DET 4
SFC Lee M. Mackay	Depauville, NY	3 BDE 1/98 (EN) (-)
SFC Jason R. Maddocks	Readfield, ME	7 BDE 3/304 (USMA)
1LT Emanuel Mahand	Swedesboro, NJ	1 BDE 3/385 (BCT) (-)
MSG Samuel Maldonado	Hicksville, NY	4 BDE 9/98 DET 2
SSG William D. Maldonado	Lowell, MA	1 BDE 1/304 DET 2 CO D&E
MAJ William S. Mandrick	Rochester, NY	HQ 98TH DIVISION (IT)
SFC Lansford G. Manley	Brooklyn, NY	3 BDE 3/98 (SC)
SGT Israul Marrero	Dorchester, MA	3 BDE 6/98 (MI)
SGT Albert L. Marshall	Lumberton, NJ	1 BDE 1/417 (BCT)
SFC Dwight O. Martin	Bronx, NY	4 BDE 10/98 (QM)
SFC Herbert L. Martin Jr.	Avon, NY	7 BDE 1/391 DET 4 CO D
SFC Jason G. Martin	East Taunton, MA	5 BDE 11/98 (HS) (-)
SFC Neil C. Martin	Gasport, NY	2 BDE 2/390 DET 1 CO D&E
SFC Robert J. Martinchek Jr.	Newington, CT	4 BDE 9/98 (-)
SFC Maria D. Martinez	Paterson, NJ	1 BDE 3/385 DET 1 CO D&E
MSG Raul Martinez	Montgomery, NY	5 BDE 11/98 DET 4
SSG Wilson A. Martinez Jr.	Bronx, NY	HQ 3 BDE (CS SCH)
SSG Janet A. Mason	Bridgeport, CT	4 BDE 9/98 (TC)
SGT Richard L. Mathews Jr.	Elmira, NY	3 BDE 1/98 (EN) DET 1
SSG Douglas L. Mauran	Moriah, NY	7 BDE 1/391 DET 2 CO B
MSG George A. Maxsimic I	Holden, ME	1 BDE 2/304 (BCT) (-)
MSG Jacqueline M. Mays	Templeton, MA	HQ 8TH BDE (SROTC)
SFC David S. McCargo	Pike, NY	4 BDE 7/98 (OD)
SSG Michelle L. McCarthy	Brick, NJ	3 BDE 5/98 (CA/PO)
SGM Sharon L. McCarthy	Etna, ME	HQ 4TH BDE(CSS SCH)

SPC Antoine J. McCloud	Rochester, NY	7 BDE 3/391 LS DET 1 TM 1
MSG William J. McDonald Sr.	Middletown, CT	4 BDE 9/98 DET 2
SFC Anthony M. McDowell	Pennsauken, NJ	1 BDE 1/417 (BCT)
SFC Albert A. McDuffie	Bronx, NY	4 BDE 9/98 (TC) DET 1
SSG John B. McGowan	Long Beach, NY	5 BDE 11/98 DET 4
SSG James F. McGrath	Toronto, Canada	2 BDE 1/390 (EN OSUT) (-)
SSG Keith L. McGrath	Hudson, FL	7 BDE 1/391 DET 2 CO B
MAJ Terence G. McGuire	Williamsville, NY	HQ 8TH BDE (SROTC)
SPC Andrew D. McKenna	Farmington, NY	HQ 98TH DIVISION (IT)
1SG Sean P. McMullan	Topsham, ME	7 BDE 3/304 DET 6
SSG Sean H. McNeal	East Haven, CT	1 BDE 2/417 (BCT) (-)
SFC Cecil J. McNear III	Montgomery, AL	4 BDE 10/98 DET 1
SFC Gregg A. Medley	Great Neck, NY	7 BDE 3/391 DET 6
CPT Craig A. Meling	Quincy, MA	1 BDE 2/417 DET 1 CO B&C
SGT David T. Menzies	North Andover, MA	3 BDE 3/98 (SC)
LTC Dana M. Merrill	Burlington, NJ	1 BDE 1/417 (BCT)
MSG Steven B. Messinger	Hanson, MA	3 BDE 6/98 (MI)
MAJ Charles M. Meyer	Bloomfield, NY	HQ 8TH BDE (SROTC)
SSG Colby S. Miller	Edgewater, NJ	3 BDE 6/98 (MI)
SGT David S. Miller	Rockland, ME	1 BDE 1/304 DET 1 CO B&C
SPC James C. Miller	Cortland, NY	2 BDE 2/389 DET 1 CO B&C
SGT John R. Miller	Langhorne, PA	7 BDE 2/391 (REC) (-)
SPC Scott A. Miller Jr.	Chesterton, IN	1 BDE 2/304 DET 1 CO A&D
SSG Thomas E. Miller	Copenhagen, NY	2 BDE 2/389 DET 1 CO B&C
SSG Tamecole T. Millington	Bridgeport, CT	3 BDE 4/98 (CM)
CSM Augusto A. Minardi	Sewell, NJ	7 BDE 2/391 (REC) (-)
SSG Jason J. Minorczyk	West Seneca, NY	2 BDE 1/390 (BCT) (-)
SSG Ramon J. Miranda	Perth Amboy, NJ	7 BDE 2/391 (REC) (-)
SSG Carl A. Mitchell Jr.	Jamaica East, NY	5 BDE 11/98 DET 4
SSG Luis D. Molina	Rochester, NY	HQ 98TH DIVISION (IT)
SSG Evel A. Morales Jr.	Bellerose, NY	3 BDE 2/98 (MP)
SFC Peter J. Moran	Hudson, NY	6 BDE 9801 DET (DSS) (-)
MSG Charles C. Morgan	Maple Shade, NJ	HQ 8TH BDE (SROTC) DIV IT
SSG David N. Morin	Hermon, ME	7 BDE 1/391 DET 1 CO A
SFC Timothy P. Morrell	Chester, PA	HQ 98TH DIVISION (IT)
SSG Fred R. Morrill	Milton Mills, NH	1 BDE 2/304 (BCT) (-)
SGT Fana S. Moseley	Brooklyn, NY	5 BDE 11/98 DET 4
SGT Kelvin L. Mote	Ellsworth, ME	4 BDE 9/98 DET 5
MAJ Richard B. Motsinger	Pittsford, NY	HQ 98TH DIVISION (IT)
LTC James J. Mountain	Hope, RI	3 BDE 3/98 (SC)
MAJ Joseph K. Mubaraz	Dearborn, MI	7 BDE 2/391 (REC) (-)
SPC Lewis H. Mumford Jr.	Kansas City, KS	7 BDE 3/391 (LOG SPT) (-)
SFC James F. Murphy	Utica, NY	3 BDE 1/98 (EN) (-)
SFC Thomas P. Muscolino	Newark, NY	2 BDE 2/390 DET 2
SSG Titus A. Myers	Warwick, RI	3 BDE 6/98 (MI)
SFC Peter Naboka	Centereach, NY	7 BDE 3/391 DET 6
SSG Simone M. Nairne	Bronx, NY	3 BDE 2/98 (MP)
SGT Samantha M. Nanni	Worcester, MA	3 BDE 6/98 (MI)

SFC Mona E. Narcisse	Baldwin, NY	5 BDE 11/98 DET 4
MSG Vincent M. Natali	Liverpool, NY	3 BDE 5/98 (CA/PO)
SGT Michael P. Naughton Jr.	Cheektowaga, NY	2 BDE 1/390 (BCT) (-)
1SG Joel C. Neal Jr.	Rockland, ME	7 BDE 3/304 (USMA)
SSG Manuel F. Negron	Passaic, NJ	7 BDE 2/391 (REC) (-)
SSG Lester E. Newsom	Eddington, ME	7 BDE 1/391 DET 1 CO A
SSG Suphora T. Newsome	Middletown, NY	7 BDE 2/391 (REC) (-)
SFC Lawrence J. Nialetz	Westwood, MA	1 BDE 1/304 DET 2 CO D&E
SSG Kevin J. Nolan	Philadelphia, PA	1 BDE 1/417 (BCT)
MSG Greg R. Notholt	Bradley Beach, NJ	4 BDE 9/98 (-)
SFC Julissa J. Novillo	Roselle, NJ	7 BDE 2/391 (REC) (-)
1SG Miguel A. Nunez	Howell, NJ	1 BDE 1/417 (BCT)
SSG Elizabeth M. Nurse	Saint Albans, NY	5 BDE 11/98 DET 4
SGT Margaret M. O' Connor	Merrill, NY	7 BDE 1/391 (CMTE) (-)
MAJ Joseph G. O' Donnell	Mullica Hill, NJ	7 BDE 3/391 (LOG SPT) (-)
SPC Bryan J. O' Donovan	Rochester, NY	7 BDE 3/391 DET 2
SGT Daniel M. Oler	Erie, PA	2 BDE 1/390 DET 1 CO D&E
SFC Janice Oliver	Brooklyn, NY	1 BDE 3/385 DET 1 CO D&E
SSG Samantha S. Oliver	Watkins Glen, NY	2 BDE 2/389 (EN OSUT) (-)
SFC Luis F. Ontaneda	Ridgewood, NY	5 BDE 11/98 DET 4
1SG James M. Opperman	Lockport, NY	2 BDE 1/390 (BCT) (-)
SSG Michael S. Orourke	Bloomfield, NJ	1 BDE 3/385 DET 1 CO D&E
SFC Donna Ortiz	Warwick, RI	3 BDE 6/98 (MI)
SGT Edwin Ortiz	Bronx, NY	7 BDE 3/391 (LOG SPT) (-)
SFC Gin Ortiz	Yonkers, NY	3 BDE 2/98 (MP)
SFC James P. Ortiz	Bayonne, NJ	3 BDE 2/98 (MP)
SFC Kristen E. Ortiz	Rahway, NJ	3 BDE 5/98 (CA/PO)
SSG Omar Ortiz	Jersey City, NJ	3 BDE 2/98 (MP)
SGT Kennedy O. Osara	Claymont, DE	1 BDE 1/417 (BCT) (-)
MSG Matthew G. Osman	E. Rochester, NY	3 BDE 5/98 DET 1
MSG Doris Otero	Corona, NY	1 BDE 3/385 DET 1 CO D&E
LTC James O. Otwell	Buffalo, NY	HQ 98TH DIVISION (IT)
SFC Pasongsouk Oudom	Poughkeepsie, NY	3 BDE 1/98 (EN) (-)
SPC Robert R. Ouellette	Lowell, MA	7 BDE 3/391 (LGSPT) DET 1
SSG Mark R. Pabis	Fort Johnson, NY	4 BDE 7/98 (OD)
SGT Kelly L. Pai	Cortland, NY	2 BDE 2/389 (EN OSUT) (-)
LTC Douglas J. Paley	Somers, CT	HQ 4TH BDE (CSS SCH)
SGT Yetzabel Palma	Lawrenceville, NJ	7 BDE 2/391 (REC) (-)
SFC Andrew H. Panton	Rochester, NY	HQ 6TH BDE (PD SCH)
SGT Scott A. Paradis	West Gardiner, ME	7 BDE 3/304 (USMA)
MAJ Richard A. Parsons Jr.	Churchville, NY	HQ 98TH DIVISION (IT)
SFC Marvin Patterson Jr.	Webster, NY	3 BDE 5/98 (CA/PO)
LTC Gary J. Pawlak	Rochester, NY	HQ 98TH DIVISION (IT)
SFC Burton A. Pearman Jr.	Buffalo, NY	4 BDE 10/98 DET 1
SSG Albert G. Peckham Jr.	North Attleboro, MA	4 BDE 7/98 (OD)
SFC Debra C. Pedraza	Rochester, NY	6 BDE 14/98 (PD)
MSG Connie J. Penner	Mansfield, PA	3 BDE 1/98 (EN) DET 1
1SG Thomas D. Pennington	Newburgh, NY	1 BDE 2/417 DET 2 CO D&E

SFC Juan E. Perez	Freeport, NY	7 BDE 2/391 (REC) (-)
SPC Carla A. Perieradebrito	Stafford, VA	1 BDE 2/385 (BCT)
SSG Edward J. Perrin	Old Town, ME	HQ 98TH DIV (IT) DET 1
MSG David R. Peters	Framingham, MA	HQ 8TH BDE (SROTC)
MAJ Scott R. Peters	Rochester, NY	2 BDE 2/390 (BCT) (-)
MSG James W. Peterson II	E. Rochester, NY	3 BDE 5/98 DET 1
SGT Latonya D. Peterson	Trenton, NJ	7 BDE 2/391 (REC) (-)
SSG Sherry L. Petronsky	Cheektowaga, NY	2 BDE 1/390 (BCT) (-)
SSG Raffaele Petti	Bronx, NY	3 BDE 6/98 (MI)
COL Philip G. Piccini	Lake Orion, MI	HQ 98TH DIV (IT)
SPC Katherine A. Pickowicz	Gilmanton, NH	1 BDE 1/304 (BCT) (-)
SSG Richard D. Pierce Jr.	North Waterboro, ME	7 BDE 3/304 (USMA)
SGT Shawn M. Pierce	Leominster, MA	7 BDE 3/391 (LGSPT) DET 1
SFC Marie D. Pierre	Brentwood, NY	HQ 3 BDE (CS SCH)
SSG Rosie N. Pinkerton	Elizabeth, NJ	3 BDE 5/98 DET 1
SFC David P. Pittari	Southbury, CT	3 BDE 5/98 DET 1
SGT Sean R. Poage	South Portland, ME	7 BDE 3/304 (USMA)
MAJ William Ponce Jr.	Smithtown, NY	3 BDE 6/98 (MI)
MAJ Melovee D. Porter	Ballston Lake, NY	HQ 8TH BDE (SROTC)
MSG Gerald Posner	Lindenhurst, NY	3 BDE 4/98 (CM)
SFC Thomas J. Potter	Milton, VT	4 BDE 7/98 (OD)
SSG Robert L. Powers II	Merrimack, NH	3 BDE 6/98 (MI)
SGT Meredith N. Poyner	Devens, MA	3 BDE 6/98 (MI)
SSG Steven M. Press	Cheektowaga, NY	7 BDE 1/391 DET 3 CO C
SSG Duenean N. Pressley	Philadelphia, PA	1 BDE 1/417 (BCT)
SSG Henry A. Printup Jr.	Buffalo, NY	4 BDE 9/98 DET 1
SGT Brian E. Puff	Newark, NY	2 BDE 1/390 (BCT) (-)
SGT James D. Purcell	Cumberland, RI	7 BDE 3/391 (LGSPT) DET 1
SSG Herbert R. Quarterman	Hainesport, NJ	3 BDE 1/98 (EN) (-)
SFC Patricia Quigley	Spencerport, NY	7 BDE 3/391 LS DET 1 TM 1
SFC Queen S. Ragland	Kissimmee, FL	4 BDE 10/98 (QM)
SPC Troy L. Ragsdale	Philadelphia, PA	1 BDE 1/417 (BCT)
PFC Francisco Ramirez	Hackensack, NJ	1 BDE 1/385 (BCT)
LTC Michael J. Reed	Syracuse, NY	HQ 8TH BDE (SROTC)
SGT Robert T. Regan	Vienna, VA	3 BDE 6/98 (MI)
SSG James C. Reichert	Hamlin, NY	3 BDE 1/98 (EN) (-)
MAJ Stephen V . Reinis	Cherry Hill, NJ	1 BDE 1/417
MAJ William Renaldo	Buffalo, NY	HQ 2D BDE(EN OSUT)
SGT Raymond Reyes	Staten Island, NY	3 BDE 4/98 (CM)
SSG Jonathan J. Rhoads	Franklin, NH	6 BDE 14/98 (NH) DET 6
SSG Carl G. Rice	Syracuse, NY	3 BDE 1/98 (EN) DET 1
SSG Todd M. Rice	Irving, NY	2 BDE 1/390 (BCT) (-)
SSG Clifford R. Rich	Cave Creek, AZ	3 BDE 6/98 (MI)
SFC Willie Richbourgh	Fort Lee, VA	4 BDE 10/98 DET 1
SSG Eric F. Rivera	Islip Terrace, NY	1 BDE 1/385 (BCT)
SFC Victor P. Rivera Jr.	North Hampton, NH	HQ 98TH DIV (IT) DET 1
SGT Richard E. Robida Sr.	Nashua, NH	1 BDE 1/304 (BCT) (-)
SFC Hill R. Robinson	McDonough, GA	4 BDE 9/98 (-)

SFC Hector L. Robles	Union City, NJ	3 BDE 5/98 (CA/PO)
SSG Nicholas J. Rock	Norwich, CT	1 BDE 2/417 DET 1 CO B&C
SGT Charles A. Rodgers	Franklinville, NY	2 BDE 1/390 DET 1 CO D&E
SPC Douglas J. Rodoski	Polk City, FL	1 BDE 2/304 (BCT) (-)
SFC Dagoberto Rodriguez	West Point, NY	3 BDE 1/98 (EN) (-)
PFC Josue F. Rodriguez	Pemberton, NJ	7 BDE 3/391 (LOG SPT) (-)
SGT Luis A. Rodriguez	Framingham, MA	1 BDE 1/304 (BCT)
SPC Nicholas E. Rodweller	Bordentown, NJ	1 BDE 3/385 (BCT) DET 1
CW4 William H. Rogers	Braintree, MA	3 BDE 6/98 (MI)
SSG Darcy F. Rohloff	Clifton Park, NY	6 BDE 9801 DET (DSS) (-)
SGT Jason M. Roman	Cheektowaga, NY	2 BDE 1/390 (EN OSUT) (-)
SGT Josephine A. Roman	New York, NY	4 BDE 9/98 (TC)
SFC Ricardo Romero Jr.	Bethpage, NY	1 BDE 2/417 (BCT) (-)
CW2 Clifford M. Rose	Wrentham, MA	HQ 1ST BDE (BCT)
SPC Brandy A. Ross	Fairfield, ME	7 BDE 1/391 DET 1 CO A
SFC Scott Ross	Clifton Park, NY	6 BDE 12/98 (C&GS)
SPC Theodore W. Rothfuss	Williamson, NY	7 BDE 1/391 DET 4 CO D
SGT Lawrence A. Roukey	Westbrook, ME	7 BDE 3/304 (USMA)
SFC Lee T. Rowland	Orchard Park, NY	2 BDE 2/389 (EN OSUT) (-)
SFC Andre M. Roy	West Hartland, CT	4 BDE 9/98 (-)
CSM Suzanne D. Rubenstein	Commack, NY	4 BDE 10/98 (QM)
SFC Anthony W. Ruff	Wheatley Heights, NY	4 BDE 9/98 (-)
SGM Joseph T. Ruggiero	Marcy, NY	3 BDE 1/98 (EN) DET 1
SPC Robert H. Sabins	Bangor, ME	7 BDE 1/391 DET 1 CO A
SGT Robert N. Salgado	Haverstraw, NY	1 BDE 3/385 DET 1 CO D&E
SFC Elijah C. Salters	Rochester, NY	3 BDE 3/98 (SC)
CPT Rene O. Samayoa	Belleville, NJ	HQ 98TH DIV (IT) DET 19
MSG Alethea L. Samuels	Brooklyn, NY	5 BDE 11/98 DET 4
SPC Steven J. Sanborn	Buxton, ME	1 BDE 2/304 (BCT) (-)
SPC Emilio Sanchez Jr.	Browns Mills, NJ	7 BDE 3/391 (LOG SPT) (-)
SSG Priscilla Sanchez	West Paterson, NJ	3 BDE 2/98 (MP)
SFC Dale A. Sanford	Whitney Point, NY	2 BDE 2/390 DET 2
LTC Richard B. Sanford	Chepachet, RI	6 BDE 12/98 (C&GS)
SFC Blanca R. Santiago	Avenel, NJ	5 BDE 11/98 DET 4
SPC Juan P. Santiago	Brooklyn, NY	7 BDE 3/391 DET 2 TM 1
SFC Providencia Santiago	Hampton, VA	4 BDE 10/98 DET 1
SPC Robert L. Santiago	Tonawanda, NY	4 BDE 9/98 DET 1
MSG Louis M. Santos	Fall River, MA	3 BDE 3/98 (SC)
SFC Robert M. Sapiro	Shelton, CT	3 BDE 2/98 (MP)
LTC Douglas R. Satterfield	Shuykill Haven, PA	5 BDE HHC
SFC Charles F. Savage	Champlain, NY	4 BDE 7/98 (OD)
SSG Sean M. Scanlon	Montour Falls, NY	2 BDE 2/389 (EN OSUT) (-)
SGT Lara Scarpato	Fayetteville, NC	3 BDE 6/98 (MI)
LTC Miyako N. Schanely	Black River, NY	HQ 6TH BDE (PD SCH)
SSG David K. Schlicher	Centuria, WI	2 BDE 2/389 (EN OSUT) (-)
SGM Joann M. Schneider	Hamburg, NY	HQ 98TH DIV (IT) DET 15
CW4 Kent P. Schneider	Palmyra, NY	HQ 98TH DIV (IT)
MSG Timothy E. Schreiber	Middletown, DE	4 BDE 9/98 (-)

SSG Murray Schroeder	Palmyra, NY	7 BDE 1/391 DET 3 CO C
SFC Paul L. Schuler Jr.	Attica, NY	4 BDE 9/98 DET 1
SGT Claudius R. Scott	Rochester, NY	HQ 98TH DIVISION (IT)
SFC William R. Scritchfield	Buffalo, NY	4 BDE 10/98 (QM)
MAJ Robert F. Searle	Wolcott, NY	HQ 7TH BDE (TS)
SSG Danilda M. Serrette	Fishkill, NY	3 BDE 1/98 (EN) (-)
SGT Kevin A. Sexworth	Philadelphia, PA	7 BDE 2/391 (REC) (-)
SFC Douglas R. Shalley	Pengilly, MN	3 BDE 6/98 DET 10
SFC Albert R. Shanklin	Bangor, ME	1 BDE 1/304 DET 1 CO B&C
SGT Lorraine Sharkey	Willow Grove, PA	7 BDE 2/391 (REC) (-)
SFC Carson K. Shaw	Bridgeport, CT	1 BDE 2/417 (BCT) (-)
SSG David L. Shaw	Hazlet, NJ	1 BDE 3/385 (BCT) (-)
MAJ Ronald W. Shaw	Amherst, NY	HQ 8TH BDE (SROTC)
SGT Jonathan P. Shealy	Dunellen, NJ	1 BDE 3/385 (BCT)
CPT Nicholas J. Sheldon	Guilderland, NY	2 BDE 1/389 DET 1 CO D&E
SFC Lawrence Shen	Wethersfield, CT	3 BDE 3/98 (SC)
SFC Norma J. Shetron	Albany, NY	7 BDE 1/391 (CMTE) (-)
CPT Billie J. Shingledecker	Alden, NY	2 BDE 1/390 (BCT) (-)
SFC William L. Shirden	Jersey City, NJ	3 BDE 3/98 (SC)
LTC David J. Showerman	Scottsdale, AZ	HQ 1ST BDE (BCT)
SFC Steven M. Sick	Cohocton, NY	3 BDE 1/98 (EN) DET 1
SPC Laura J. Siedschlag	Pattersonville, NY	2 BDE 1/389 (EN OSUT) (-)
SGT Kathryn A. Sikorski	Liverpool, NY	6 BDE (PD)
CPT William J. Simpson	Milford, CT	3 BDE 2/98 (MP)
MSG Shawn Singleton	Syracuse, NY	HQ 8TH BDE (SROTC)
SGT Sherly I. Skeete	Bronx, NY	3 BDE 2/98 (MP)
SFC Jeffrey B. Slauenwhite	Somerville, ME	7 BDE 3/304 (USMA)
SGT Michael D. Slauenwhite	Somerville, ME	7 BDE 1/391 DET 1 CO A
SGT Keith Smalls	New York, NY	3 BDE 2/98 (MP)
CPT David L. Smith	Kennebunkport, ME	1 BDE 2/304 (BCT) (-)
MAJ Herbert N. Smith	Franklin Park, NJ	7 BDE 2/391 (REC)
SPC Jeremiah D. Smith	Buffalo, NY	2 BDE 1/390 DET 7
SSG Thomas J. Snieg	Greenfield, WI	3 BDE 6/98 (MI)
MSG Jose B. Soler	Jamaica, NY	3 BDE 2/98 (MP)
SPC Erick E. Soto	Rochester, NY	7 BDE 2/391 (REC) DET 2
SGT David Z. Sotolopez	Wappingers Falls, NY	3 BDE 1/98 (EN) (-)
SSG Michael A. Soule	Branchville, NJ	1 BDE 3/385 DET 1 CO D&E
SSG Nelson M. Sousa	Fall River, MA	HQ 1ST BDE (BCT)
1SG Karen L. Speckman	Gardner, MA	1 BDE 1/304 (BCT) (-)
SPC Kristin A. Spence	Watertown, NY	3 BDE 6/98 (MI)
SGT Jeffery L. Spino	Rochester, NY	HQ 98TH DIVISION (IT)
LTC Gregg A. Sponburgh	Mohawk, NY	HQ 8TH BDE (SROTC)
SFC Patricia I. Springer	Brooklyn, NY	4 BDE 10/98 DET 1
MSG Peter M. Stabile	Highland Mills, NY	3 BDE 1/98 (EN) (-)
SGT Ronald L. Steen	Bordentown, NJ	4 BDE 7/98 (OD)
MAJ Walter Steenson	Hilton, NY	HQ 2D BDE(EN OSUT)
SFC Lisa K. Steiner	Hamburg, NY	2 BDE 2/390 DET 2
LTC Douglas J. Stelmach	Boston, NY	HQ 2D BDE(EN OSUT)

SFC Leonard D. Stephens	Syracuse, NY	6 BDE 9801 DET (DSS) (-)
SFC Sharon L. Stevens	Saratoga Springs, NY	3 BDE 1/98 (EN) (-)
SGT Brendan J. Stewart	Nanuet, NY	4 BDE 10/98 (QM)
SPC Nilda Stewart	Mount Holly, NJ	7 BDE 3/391 (LOG SPT) (-)
SGT Brian M. Sticht	Gasport, NY	2 BDE 1/389 (EN OSUT) (-)
1SG Mark J. Stovall	Cresskill, NJ	1 BDE 3/385 DET 1 CO D&E
1SG Jason C. Stowe	Sicklerville, NJ	1 BDE 1/417 (BCT)
SPC James W. Strange Jr.	Las Vegas, NV	1 BDE 2/417 (BCT) (-)
SPC Trineisha S. Stutheit	New London, CT	2 BDE 1/389 (EN OSUT) (-)
MAJ Elmer J. Stvil	Brooklyn, NY	1 BDE 3/385 (BCT) (-)
SSG Joseph A. Styslinger	Worcester, NY	4 BDE 7/98 (OD)
CSM Annie L. Suggs	Brooklyn, NY	7 BDE 3/391 (LOG SPT) (-)
SGT John J. Sullivan	Woodbridge, CT	1 BDE 2/417 (BCT) (-)
MSG Steven Swindell	Warwick, NY	3 BDE 4/98 (CM)
SSG Jason M. Szostak	Webster, NY	7 BDE 1/391 DET 3 CO C
SGT Stanley J. Tarquinio Jr.	Woodbridge, NJ	3 BDE 5/98 (CA/PO)
SPC Kristen M. Tharpe	Riverton, NJ	7 BDE 2/391 (REC) (-)
SFC Curtis R. Thomas	South Plainfield, NJ	4 BDE 10/98 DET 1
1LT Nicholas A. Thomas	Tonawanda, NY	2 BDE 2/390 DET 2
SFC Andre M. Thompson	Rochester, NY	2 BDE 2/389 DET 2 CO D&E
SFC Corey A. Thompson	Rochester, NY	2 BDE 2/389 DET 2 CO D&E
SSG Gerald D. Thompson	St. Robert, MO	2 BDE 1/390 (EN OSUT) (-)
SFC Anthony D. Timmons	Middletown, NY	4 BDE 9/98 DET 5
MSG Samuel Tlumac	Manchester, ME	4 BDE 9/98 (-)
SPC Mark A. Toderico	Gray, ME	1 BDE 2/304 (BCT) (-)
MSG Tyrenna D. Tolbert	White Plains, MD	4 BDE 8/98 (PS)
SSG Anthony J. Toleman	Waterford, NY	2 BDE 1/389 (EN OSUT) (-)
MSG Chad M. Tooke	Whitesboro, NY	2 BDE 1/389 DET 1 CO D&E
SFC Abimael Torres	Cambria Heights, NY	1 BDE 3/385 DET 1 CO D&E
MSG Daniel S. Torres	Hamburg, NY	3 BDE 1/98 (EN) (-)
SPC George R. Torrise	Browns Mills, NJ	3 BDE 5/98 (CA/PO)
SPC Sean J. Toubman	Schenectady, NY	2 BDE 1/389 (EN OSUT) (-)
LTC David W. Towle	Black River, NY	HQ 98TH DIVISION (IT)
SSG Wayne Townsend	Bronx, NY	3 BDE 6/98 DET 8
SGT Ovidio N. Traverso Jr.	Mechanicsburg, PA	1 BDE 3/385 DET 1 CO D&E
MSG Fleurette R. Tredway	Briarwood, NY	4 BDE 10/98 (QM)
MAJ Gabriel Troiano	Leesburg, VA	3 BDE 6/98 (MI)
SGT John Tsohandaridis	Framingham, MA	5 BDE 11/98 DET 4
SGT Christopher W. Tucker	Frankport, NY	7 BDE 1/391 DET 2 CO B
SGM Jennifer L. Turner	Norwich, NY	HQ 98TH DIVISION (IT)
SSG Lyndon S. Tuttle	Lowville, NY	4 BDE 7/98 (OD)
SFC James J. Udis	Clifton, NJ	4 BDE 9/98 (TC)
SFC Todd M. Urban Jr.	North Tonawanda, NY	2 BDE 2/390 DET 2
SFC Harold C. Urrutia	Hope, NJ	1 BDE 3/385 DET 1 CO D&E
1LT Jason W. Vabburen	Schenectady, NY	2 BDE 1/389 (EN OSUT) (-)
MSG David Valentin	Ozone Park, NY	3 BDE 2/98 (MP)
MAJ Peter A. Vanderland Jr.	Remsen, NY	6 BDE 12/98 (C&GS)
SSG David W. Vankeuren	Buffalo, NY	4 BDE 10/98 (QM)

SFC Stevan L. Vankeuren	Clinton Cors, NY	3 BDE 1/98 (EN) (-)
SSG Matthew D. Vanlengen	Syracuse, NY	2 BDE 2/389 DET 1 CO B&C
SPC Kathleen M. Vargas	Altamonte Springs, FL	1 BDE 3/385 DET 1 CO D&E
SSG Jose N. Vasquez Jr.	Long Island City, NY	5 BDE 11/98 (HS) (-)
SSG Naomi Vega	Lakewood, NJ	4 BDE 10/98 (QM)
LTC Peter J. Versteeg	Spencerport, NY	HQ 7TH BDE (TS)
SSG Thomas R. Viger	Saco, ME	7 BDE 3/304 (USMA)
SSG Clayton L. Waite	Minetto, NY	2 BDE 2/389 DET 1 CO B&C
SPC Sharay T. Wakefield	Pleasantville, NJ	7 BDE 2/391 (REC) (-)
SFC Richard M. Washik	Jackson, NJ	3 BDE 3/98 (SC)
SSG Chad D. Waterman	Le Roy, NY	7 BDE 3/391 DET 6
SFC Christian G. Watrous	Richmond Dale, OH	2 BDE 1/390 (EN OSUT) (-)
SFC Keith J. Way	Rome, NY	3 BDE 5/98 (CA/PO)
MSG Mark W. Weber	Edgar Springs, MO	2 BDE 2/390 DET 2
SSG Brian D. Wedge	Waterville, ME	7 BDE 3/304 (USMA)
SGM Peter L. Weinrich	Jackson, NJ	HQ 6TH BDE (PD SCH)
CPT Craig A. Weisser	Williston, VT	7 BDE 1/391 DET 2 CO B
SGT Joseph J. Wertz	Palmyra, ME	1 BDE 2/304 DET 1 CO A&D
SSG Gerald D. Westfall	Webster, NY	7 BDE 2/391 DET 1 CO B
CSM Herbert L. Whaley	Windsor, CT	HQ 8TH BDE (SROTC)
SSG Eric P. Wheeler	Rochester, NY	3 BDE 5/98 DET 1
1LT Curtis D. White	Bangor, ME	1 BDE 1/417 (BCT)
SSG Tanikwa S. White	Dover, DE	7 BDE 2/391 (REC) (-)
SFC Robert F. Wieners Jr.	Brockton, MA	3 BDE 5/98 (CA/PO)
SFC James E. Wiggs Jr.	Asbury Park, NJ	4 BDE 9/98 (-)
SGT Marlene S. Williams	Bronx, NY	5 BDE 11/98 DET 4
SFC Timothy A. Wing	Oxford, ME	4 BDE 9/98 DET 5
1LT Wilem S. Wong	New York, NY	HQ 98TH DIV (IT) DET 19
SPC Michael D. Woodard	Presque Isle, ME	7 BDE 1/391 DET 1 CO A
CSM Timothy L. Woodcock	Cromwell, CT	3 BDE 2/98 (MP)
SGT Arman W. Wright	Clifton Park, NY	2 BDE 1/389 (EN OSUT) (-)
SGT Jeffrey A. Wright	Glenville, NY	2 BDE 1/389 (EN OSUT) (-)
CPT Denise M. Wurzbach	Ambler, PA	4 BDE 8/98 (PS)
SSG Michael F. Wynne	Williamsville, NY	2 BDE 1/390 (BCT) (-)
SSG Gregory C. Wyse	Alexandria, VA	3 BDE 6/98 (MI)
SSG Bieber S. Yaw	Trumansburg, NY	5 BDE 11/98 (LPN) DET 1
SSG Douglas C. Young	Livonia, NY	2 BDE 2/390 (BCT) (-)
SFC Lewis E. Young Jr.	Shelton, CT	6 BDE 14/98 (CT) DET 3
SGT Brian J. Younger	Philadelphia, PA	1 BDE 1/417 (BCT)
SGT Brian R. Zaborowski	Silver Spring, MD	3 BDE 6/98 (MI)
1SG Michael E. Zajac	Cicero, NY	2 BDE 2/389 DET 1 CO B&C
SFC Michael P. Zeeman	Pittsgrove, NJ	7 BDE 3/391 (LOG SPT) (-)
CPT Robert J. Zielinski	Macedon, NY	7 BDE 1/391 DET 3 CO C
SSG Robert A. Zollinger	Elma, NY	2 BDE 1/390 (BCT) (-)
SFC Franklin J. Zywicki	Elmira, NY	3 BDE 1/98 (EN) DET 1

Fallen Heroes

On the battlefield, when the sounds have faded, the fog of war has dispersed, and the battle is done, the warrior must honor and respect those who fought the good fight and paid the ultimate price.

The soldier's tools of battle are simple and basically remain unchanged through the years.

The boots carried our comrade many miles. They carried him through times of joy and pain and to his final resting place.

The rifle symbolizes the firepower of the individual soldier, the burden, the savior, and the ultimate weapon to win and survive. The bayonet is fixed; it is in place for the final battle. Today, it symbolically penetrates the sacred soil of the warrior's resting place. No more will this awesome tool be used to take a life, for now it marks the resting place of this dear comrade.

Upon the rifle rests the soldier's helmet, that protector of life, that gear so valuable and yet so cumbersome. Today it is transformed into a memorial, not marble or granite, but a tribute to our fallen.

Who lies here? What Soldier, Sailor, Marine, Airman, or Coastguardsman has fallen? The dog tags on the rifle tell us who our comrade is.

Now we know that our comrade's battle is done. His tools of battle are here. He would never leave them willingly.

Rest our comrade. Let us not forget.

SERGEANT LAWRENCE A. ROUKEY, 1971-2004

MASTER SERGEANT PAUL D. KARPOWICH, 1974-2004

STAFF SERGEANT CHRISTOPHER W. DILL, 1972-2005

LIEUTENANT COLONEL TERRENCE CROWE, 1960-2005

SERGEANT FIRST CLASS ROBERT DERENDA, 1963 - 2005

One American Soldier

The news report said that one American Soldier was killed.
One man, one father, one son, one brother.
One American Soldier.
One Uncle, one neighbor, one teacher, one friend.

One American Soldier, born to one American family.
Forever altered…first, by his presence,
and now, by his absence.
One American Soldier…one colleague, one mentor,
one special child of God.

One American Soldier with a huge capacity for excellence…
for laughter…and in his own way, and own time…
with a huge capacity for love.

One American Soldier who made a difference in so many ways.
One American Soldier here, not by chance,
but by God's choosing.

One American Soldier here on this earth, at this special time
to fulfill his special purpose for this life.

The news report said that one American Soldier was killed.
140,000 American Soldiers in Iraq,
4,000 American Soldiers in Tall Afar.

What are the chances? What are the odds?
Miniscule. Near zero…virtually, one in a million.
But, we've come to understand that is precisely why.

Because this American Soldier WAS one in a million.
Absolutely, one of a kind.

And each of us here can count ourselves lucky that God has
allowed us to be here…at the same time and at the same place as
One American Soldier named "Terry."

Written by Caroline Kibbe, sister of LTC Terrence Crowe

SERGEANT LAWRENCE A. ROUKEY

3d Battalion, 304th Regiment, 7th Brigade
Lewiston, Maine

Sergeant Lawrence A. Roukey was born and raised in the state of Maine. Like most young American boys, he laughed, played sports, and was captivated by the patriotism and valor of the American Soldier. In fact, one of his sister's childhood memories of him is his seizing of her doll house and converting it into a command post for his G.I. Joe action figures. Perhaps it was during these early years that Sergeant Roukey heard his call to duty.

After graduating from high school in 1989, Sergeant Roukey enlisted in the U.S. Army to fulfill his dream of becoming an infantryman.

Sergeant Roukey served his three-year active-duty tour in the Republic of Korea and then decided to return home to Maine. Ever the soldier, he joined the Maine Army National Guard on a three-year commit-

ment and worked at various jobs until he found a good match with the U.S. Postal Service. He worked diligently and treated others with dignity and respect. In turn, he gained the respect of his peers and supervisors alike at the downtown Portland post office.

In 1996, Sergeant Roukey married Ryann Keller. Ryann would later comment that he was a protector who was both loving and generous. He loved his wife, stepdaughter, and son. He was the steadfast guardian of his family's home.

The attacks of 9/11 on the World Trade Center and the Pentagon rekindled the embers of Sergeant Roukey's warrior soul and prompted him to reenlist in the U.S. Army Reserve. This reenlistment brought him to the 3d Battalion, 304th Regiment of the 98th Division.

"It was a cause he believed in," his sister Dottie Roukey said.

Sergeant Roukey was assigned to the Iraqi Survey Group, an elite unit tasked to search for weapons of mass destruction within Iraq. Sergeant Roukey served as a gunner on Mobile Collection Team 6, a position which required unremitting vigilance and sharp reflexes. His teammates described him as fearless, upbeat, jovial, and the life of the party.

Sergeant Roukey was the first postal worker to die in Iraq and the ninth serviceman from Maine.

U.S. Post Office in Portland, Maine.

On the evening of April 26, 2004, Sergeant Roukey found himself providing security for his team outside of a Baghdad warehouse suspected of containing chemical munitions. A bomb suddenly shattered the deceptive twilight calm and claimed the life of Sergeant Roukey. He was thirty-three years old.

It seemed as though his entire hometown of Westbrook attended his funeral. Even the governor, a Maine U.S. senator, and a U.S. representative were there.

"He touched a lot of lives. He comes from a large family. He was baptized in the church. His whole life story is there," remarked Governor John E. Baldacci.

Framed tribute to Sergeant Lawrence Roukey at the Portland Post Office.

MASTER SERGEANT PAUL D. KARPOWICH

2d Battalion, 417th Regiment, 1st Brigade
Pennsauken, New Jersey

His family called him "Captain Army."

Growing up in his hometown of Freeland, Pennsylvania, Master Sergeant Paul D. Karpowich skinned knees and elbows playing combat and other games with his platoon of neighborhood friends. One of them recalled the time when they built a splatball range among the dilapidated remains of an amusement park only to be chased out by the police. From those boyhood games, he developed a sense for the team.

His teachers and coaches considered him an intelligent student and athlete. He played football for Bishop Hafey High School with a passion.

Intensely competitive, he remained humble in the face of victory and defeat.

After graduating high school in 1992, he enlisted in the U.S. Army, where he trained to be an infantryman and a paratrooper, and was eventually assigned to the 82d Airborne Division at Fort Bragg, North Carolina. When he wasn't parachuting with full combat load into such drop zones as Sicily, Salerno, and Bastogne, he was either in the ring boxing with local competition or burning up the asphalt with his motorcycle down Bragg Boulevard.

In 1996, Master Sergeant Karpowich returned home to Pennsylvania. He earned an associate's degree in architecture and found his niche in the design of office furniture with a small company outside of Philadelphia. He quickly rose through

the ranks to regional sales manager and still found time to continue his architecture studies at Temple University.

After joining the U.S. Army Reserve, Master Sergeant Karpowich earned his drill sergeant badge in 2002. He reflected his sentiment for leadership a year later in his Drill Sergeant of the

Year essay when he wrote, "A good leader must earn the respect of his subordinates by leading from the front and motivating them to be all they can be."

True to his grass roots, Master Sergeant Karpowich married his high school sweetheart Amanda Gadola in 2003. Ever the patriot, he handed out miniature American flags to family and friends at the wedding reception.

Master Sergeant Karpowich embraced the FA-TRAC mission completely. He trained together with his Iraqi non-commissioned officer counterparts as a team. When he sensed fear and anxiety creep into the hearts of the troops, he was there to provide words of encouragement. Through sweat, tears, and grime, Master Sergeant Karpowich gave the Iraqis the

hope of freedom.

Master Sergeant Karpowich and the executive officer from his Iraqi Army unit were among the lunchtime crowd in the mess tent at Forward Operating Base Marez on December 21, 2004, when a fatal suicide bombing ripped apart the tent and claimed their lives along with twenty others. Master Sergeant Karpowich was just thirty years old.

The words and actions of soldiers from bygone eras inspired Master Sergeant Karpowich. The one quote he often referenced came from Nathan Hale, American Revolutionary War hero…"I only regret that I have but one life to lose for my country."

STAFF SERGEANT CHRISTOPHER W. DILL

2d Battalion, 390th Regiment, 2d Brigade
Webster, New York

Staff Sergeant Christopher W. Dill was born on July 9, 1972, in Buffalo, New York. He grew up there and graduated from Kenmore East Senior High School. He enlisted in the U.S. Army in August 1990 and trained as a combat engineer. He served in the Gulf War with the 24th Infantry Division. Upon release from active duty in 1994, he returned to Buffalo, became a firefighter with the Buffalo Fire Department, and joined the U.S. Army Reserve.

While assigned to the 2d Battalion, 390th Regiment, 2d Brigade, Staff Sergeant Dill excelled as a noncommissioned officer. Without hesitation, Dill volunteered for and earned his drill sergeant badge, a distinction recognized and revered by many. As a drill sergeant, Staff Sergeant Dill took great pride in providing the best possible training to soldiers. He always took the time to mentor, teach, and encourage others. Staff Sergeant Dill had the moral fortitude to speak with conviction on matters of importance. In this way, he earned respect and gained many friendships. A hard charger, he possessed excellent tactical skills and

applied them to mission accomplishment. He pursued the harder right and embraced new challenges.

At the same time, Staff Sergeant Dill loved being a part of the team at Engine 21, located on Jefferson and Kingsley in Buffalo. Some said that the firehouse was his second home. He took the job of firefighting seriously and diligently prepared himself for it. He proved himself reliable and forged many bonds of trust. By all accounts, he lived the Firefighter's Pledge: He had the wisdom of a leader, the compassion to comfort, and the love to serve unselfishly.

Staff Sergeant Dill was a man of devotion. He married Dawn M. Derion. His wedding day was one of the happiest days of his life, and he remarked to his wife, "If I were to die tomorrow, I'd be the happiest man."

Not one to sit out the fight, Staff Sergeant Dill volunteered for the FA-TRAC mission. In

Iraq, he was an advisor on the Advisory Support Team assigned to the 6th Battalion, 5th Division of the new Iraqi Army. He taught and drilled the Iraqi soldiers on the fundamentals of soldier-

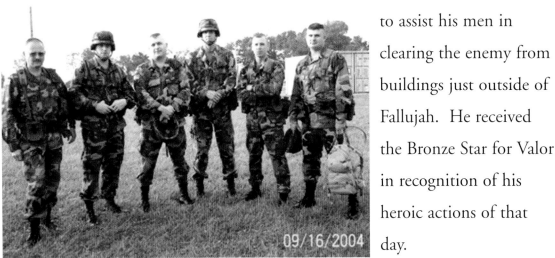

to assist his men in clearing the enemy from buildings just outside of Fallujah. He received the Bronze Star for Valor in recognition of his heroic actions of that day.

ing and small-unit leadership. True to his character as an American Soldier, Staff Sergeant Dill walked the same patrols and faced the same firefights with the men he trained. On November 29, 2004, Staff Sergeant Dill dismounted from his armored vehicle and under heavy enemy fire went

On April 4, 2005, Staff Sergeant Dill and his men engaged in three hours of unrelenting combat with well-entrenched insurgents in Balad Ruz, a small city about 45 miles northeast of Baghdad. He fought and advised right up to the moment a bullet caught him in the side.

In reflecting on the life of his son, William Dill perhaps summed it up best: "I think his message would be that it was a noble mission. He enjoyed it. And when it was over, he was going to be doing what he loved most, being a firefighter."

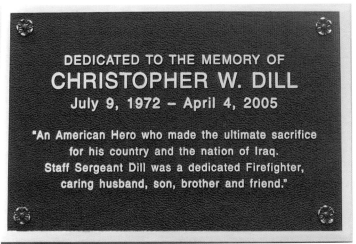

Dedication of the Vertical Skills Building at Fort Dix, New Jersey.

LIEUTENANT COLONEL TERRENCE CROWE

HHC, 8th Brigade
West Hartford, Connecticut

Many soldiers go to war, but not all make an impact while they are there. Most prefer to simply do their time and return, but that was not Lieutenant Colonel Terrence Crowe. He was driven—the type of soldier who was feared by the enemy for his ferocity, commitment, and unwillingness to quit, and was admired by his peers for his toughness and courage.

Lieutenant Colonel Crowe grew up in Grand Island, NY, not far from Buffalo and Niagara Falls, and attended Niagara University, earning a bachelor's degree in economics. Upon graduation in 1982, Crowe was commissioned a second lieutenant in the active Army and attended the infantry officer basic course at Fort Benning,

Georgia. He was then assigned to the 2d Armored Division (Forward) in Garlstedt, Germany, as a rifle platoon leader and later as a company executive officer.

Lieutenant Colonel Crowe's military career carried him from the low-lying lands of northern Germany to the hill-and-lake country of Fort Hood, Texas, and back to Germany again as an observer-controller at the Combined Maneuver Training Center, Hohenfels. He then returned to the Buffalo region and served as a recruiting company commander for the western New York region.

Crowe left active duty in 1992, but continued to serve in the National Guard and eventually joined the 98th Division (IT). As a civilian, he worked as a carpenter with a construction company in North Tonawanda, NY, before taking a position as an assistant professor of military science at Canisius College in Buffalo. As a Reserve Officer Training Corps instructor, he was considered dynamic, direct, detailed, and passionate about doing things in the best way possible.

In the fall of 2004, Lieutenant Colonel

Crowe's passion for what he called "doing the right thing" carried him to the sands of Iraq. By then a twenty-year veteran, Crowe could have retired and avoided service in a war zone, but he insisted on serving. Originally assigned to instruct the company commander's course for Iraqi military officers, a position that would have kept him away from the front lines, Lieutenant Colonel Crowe persistently pursued a job advising the Iraqi Army in the field.

"He felt his place was in the field where he could do the most good," said Major George Adams, a colleague of Crowe's.

Lieutenant Colonel Crowe's persistence eventually paid off and he was assigned as an advisor in northern Iraq, where his presence and drive to succeed had a distinct impact on operations. According to Major Michael Ansay, Crowe's team was responsible for leading the way with capturing insurgents, recovering weapons and explosives, and the collection of intelligence information. Regarding an area handover between Lieutenant Colonel Crowe's team and his own, Ansay said, "I was amazed at all the intelligence his team handed off to me and all the great work they completed there."

On June 7, 2005, Lieutenant Colonel Crowe was leading a foot patrol with his Iraqi unit and an advisor from the U.S. Army's 3d Armored Cavalry Regiment in the northern city of Tall Afar when they were attacked by insurgents. Under heavy attack from an improvised explosive device, rocket-propelled grenades, hand grenades, and machine gun fire, Lieutenant Colonel Crowe was struck several times by automatic weapons fire but continued to fight until he could fight no longer. He died as he lived—leading from the front.

SERGEANT FIRST CLASS ROBERT DERENDA

3d Battalion, 398th Regiment, 1st Brigade, 100th Division (IT)
Paducah, Kentucky

They were known as "the Paducah Dozen" at Camp Atterbury, Indiana. In fact, Sergeant First Class Robert V. Derenda called the unit administrator of his former unit in Amherst, New York, and volunteered the entire company from Paducah, Kentucky, for the FA-TRAC mission. Indeed, heads would have turned had this unit from the 100th Division (IT) mobilized in its entirety.

Yet audacity was very much a part of Sergeant First Class Derenda's character. When he realized an objective, he pursued it with an all-consuming intensity. There was a spellbinding focus to this soldier which some commented as being almost hypnotic. Whether it was splitting wood in a neighbor's backyard or teaching a private to read a topographical map at Fort Leonard Wood, Missouri, Sergeant First Class Derenda engaged in the task

at hand with complete devotion. He worked best at an unrelenting pace whether at work or during annual training with the Army Reserve.

Growing up in his hometown of Cheektowaga, New York, Sergeant First Class Derenda enjoyed the company of good friends, the team spirit of his track team at St. Francis High School, and the artifice of a well-told story. In winter, he pursued his passion of downhill skiing and was a familiar figure at nearby slopes of Tamarack and Kissing Bridge. He combined his desire to serve with his love of the outdoors by qualifying for a position on the ski patrol which he held with a religious dedication.

Sergeant First Class Derenda's leadership first gained notice during his time at the Citadel, the Military College of South Carolina. In his sophomore year, he inspected and corrected members of the freshman class for appearance and wear of the uniform, a responsibility usually given to upperclassmen. Sergeant First Class Derenda earned his first undergraduate degree in psychology at the State University of New York (SUNY) at Buffalo.

Perhaps the call to greater service was ringing in his ear when he enlisted in the U.S. Army in 1986. He honed his skill as an infantryman with tours in Korea

and Panama. He returned to Buffalo in 1991 to pursue a second degree in chemical engineering at SUNY Buffalo. Though completely immersed with entropic equations, reaction kinetics, and unit operation design, Sergeant First Class Derenda kept true to his Army commitment by joining the 2d Brigade, 98th Division (IT) and earning his drill sergeant badge. Considered impossible by others, Sergeant First Class Derenda even found time to work part time at an auto parts store.

Assigned to the Al Kasik Military Training Base, Sergeant First Class Derenda worked with the 4th and 8th Brigades of the new Iraqi Army's 3d Division. He remarked to his sister that he had to be there in Iraq to help make the world safer for his two nephews.

On August 5, 2005, the swerve of an errant civilian fuel truck on the highway outside of Rabiah brought the life of Sergeant First Class Derenda to a tragic end. Two Army Reserve divi-

sions and two cities felt the loss of a great noncommissioned officer and patriot. Because of his deep love of country and for the soldierly values he lived, Sergeant First Class Derenda's family decided to have him laid to rest among America's heroes at Arlington.

THE AMERICAN SOLDIER'S SACRIFICE AND THE FUTURE OF THE WORLD

At the time of this writing, more than 2,300 American soldiers have died in the fight to establish freedom in Iraq. Undoubtedly, it is a great cost which all thoughtful Americans now feel and shoulder. The fight continues, and the path to Iraqi freedom, like all other human struggles, is fraught with anguish, sorrow, and disappointments. Still, it bears the promise of a tremendous peace and renewal among nations. The smoldering resentment and discontent in the Middle East need to be extinguished, and it will take a continued global effort to resolve it.

The media has focused on the soldiers, statesmen, academicians, and nongovernmental organizations. All have their role to play in the successful outcome. We all share a stake in the crafting of stable political systems and armed forces. We are gradually learning the values, traditions, and attitudes of this region of the world. Perhaps it is the soldier upon which so much of this effort rests, no matter how lowly or complex the tasks.

The soldier who smiles at a gaggle of children playing in the street while out on patrol or the noncommissioned officer who shares a better way of motivating soldiers may be the mortar which binds our efforts into a workable resolution. And in that moment of truth, when all of the training and values come together in an instant, a soldier stands his ground, returns fire, and regrettably bears the brunt of mortal wounds from that bitter fight. Fellow soldiers gather around and pray. Iraqi soldiers who fought by the American soldier's side and witnessed his courage and commitment bow their heads in respect. The impact of his actions reverberates from the battlefield to the staff room, upward to the halls of executive power, and to Americans at home.

More than 2,300 statements have been made on American resolve in this war, and time will bear the truth and noble selflessness of these actions. Straining against this loss, we know this sacrifice is necessary in exchange for a world in which the rights of men and women will be recognized and respected.

Editing Staff

Lieutenant Colonel Timothy J. Hansen
Editor-in-Chief

Lieutenant Colonel Hansen served as an Army Reserve officer in a variety of command and staff positions within  the 98th Division (IT). He wrote several articles and produced films depicting the Warrior Ethos of the drill sergeants and Army school instructors of the 98th Division.

In 2004, he served as a logistics officer at the Office of Military Cooperation-Afghanistan and worked on the reorganization and fielding of the Afghan National Army under Operation Enduring Freedom. He traveled extensively within that country on numerous missions. After returning to the United States, Lieutenant Colonel Hansen mobilized as the division public affairs officer to cover the deployment of the 98th Division to Iraq. He coordinated with local and national media to promote the division's first overseas mobilization since WWII.

In the private sector, Lieutenant Colonel Hansen worked in manufacturing as a production supervisor. He lives with his wife Eran and five children, Rosemary, John, Michael, Mary Frances, and Moira in Rochester, New York.

Sergeant Major Jocene D. Preston
Graphic Design Editor

Sergeant Major Preston built a career of exceptional service in the U.S. Army Reserve. Sergeant Major Preston graduated with highest honors from the Rochester Institute of Technology earning a degree in graphic design. Continuing in her pursuit of excellence, she was an honor graduate from the U.S. Army Sergeants Major  Academy and went on to serve as the command sergeant major of the 8th Battalion, 4th Brigade at Red Bank, New Jersey.

Currently assigned as the 98th Division G1 sergeant major, Sergeant Major Preston played a key role in the mobilization of the 98th Division for its FA-TRAC mission. At Camp Atterbury, Indiana, she established a solid working rapport with all key support elements at that post and managed all personnel actions for FA-TRAC soldiers. Utilizing graphic design skills from her civilian career as creative director for a local publishing company, Sergeant Major Preston coordinated the production of the story of the 98th Division in the Global War on Terrorism.

In reflecting on the originator of this project, Sergeant Major Preston respectfully commented, "I stand in awe of Major General Robinson's vision of a lasting tribute to our soldiers. His enthusiasm, advice and support made it a reality."

Sergeant Major Preston takes much pride in her three children, Dustin, Devin, and Megan and of the boundless support from her partner Gregg Henderson.

SFC Crissy, SGM Preston and LTC Hansen;
Photo by CSM Milt Newsome.

First Lieutenant Christopher Henderson

Graphic Design

First Lieutenant Henderson heightened the look of each chapter with his notable graphic design skills. His sense for line and shape added to the book's distinct elegance. LT Henderson took time from the demands of his daytime job at a Manhattan advertising agency and commuted from his home in New Jersey to work on the book at Headquarters in Rochester, New York.

A veteran of FA-TRAC, Lieutenant Henderson understood the tone and themes of the many accounts of the 98th in Iraq. In spite of the book's pressing requirements, he still made time for his wife and two children and even made it to his son's Cub Scout meetings.

Command Sergeant Major Milt Newsome

Photography

Command Sergeant Major Newsome applied the steady aim of his marksmanship skills to shooting with his digital camera. His photos caught the lighter and heavier moments of our soldiers during the FA-TRAC mission.

A veteran of the 82d Airborne Division, numerous deployments, and previous combat missions, Command Sergeant Major Newsome has a deep understanding of the 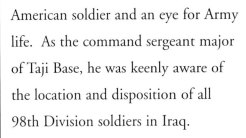 American soldier and an eye for Army life. As the command sergeant major of Taji Base, he was keenly aware of the location and disposition of all 98th Division soldiers in Iraq.

Command Sergeant Major Newsome in turn became a "human" historical archive of the accomplishments and contributions of the division to the fledgling Iraqi Army. While keeping a demanding manager schedule at Xerox, he took time after work to sort through his voluminous photo collection to put together the visual side of the division's story in Iraq.

Sergeant First Class Ryan Crissy

Technical Editor

Every edit team needs an all source expert keenly attuned to the nuances of language. Armed with the Chicago Manual of Style and years of experience in the editing field, Sergeant First Class Crissy ensured proper usage, the appropriate voice and content clarity. Sergeant First Class Crissy has served in the U.S. Army and U.S. Army Reserve for more than eleven years.

After graduating from college with a degree in English Literature, he served six years active duty as an intelligence sergeant with the 66th MI Group in Germany and the 10th Mountain Division in New York, and is currently assigned as an instructor with B Company, 1st Battalion, 391st Regiment, 7th Brigade. He has been deployed four times during his career—twice to the Balkans, once to Central America, and most recently to Iraq.

As a civilian, he has worked as a newspaper reporter and writer and is currently employed as an editor for an academic publisher. He lives in southern New York with his wife and daughter.

Book chronicles four tough years for area soldiers

By Jim Memmott • Rochester Democrat and Chronicle

January 25, 2006

The plan at first was to put together a yearbook, a collection of pictures and stories that would serve as a reference and record of the recent activities of the 98th Division (Institutional Training), U.S. Army Reserve.

But "yearbook" is too limited a word to describe what Lt. Col. Timothy Hansen and Sgt. Maj. Jocene Preston have almost completed. They have chronicled the varied activities of the division since the terrorist attacks of Sept. 11, 2001.

In the process, they have put together an account that documents risks and dangers and successes.

"The stories here had to be told," says Hansen, of Brighton. "We can't keep this light under a bushel."

Putting the 11-chapter book together wasn't easy. Pictures were collected; soldiers were interviewed; timelines were checked and checked again.

But the effort was worth it, Hansen and Preston say, as it not only provided a record of the division's missions, it allowed them to step back and see how much the division has accomplished in four years.

No publication date has been set, but they hope each member of the division will receive a free copy of the book, to be called An Encounter with History, by March.

"It will be something for my kids to take down and show their children," says Sgt. Marlene Taylor, a member of the division who served in Iraq. "They can say, 'This is what

your grandmother did.'"

The division's involvement in the war on terror began on Sept. 11, 2001, as then-deputy commander, Brig. Gen. Gregory Hunt, was at the Pentagon when it was hit by a hijacked jetliner.

Hunt, who was at a meeting, was able to get out. And he helped others reach safety. Now a major general, he's commanding general of the 100th Division, U.S. Army Reserve, in Louisville, KY. Hunt's story is in the book, as are many other stories.

Since Sept. 11, members of the 98th, which is headquartered on North Goodman Street in Irondequoit, have served missions in Afghanistan, Cuba, Iraq and Africa.

Their civilian lives often on hold, they have left families and friends to give service to their country, risking their lives in the process.

Five members of the division, which has units throughout the

Northeast, have died in Iraq during the past two years. Four were killed by enemy fire, a fifth died when his truck overturned and exploded. Three of these men were from Erie County, one was from Pennsylvania and the other from Maine.

More than 700 members of the 98th were sent to Iraq in 2004. The division normally trains U.S. soldiers. Its assignment in Iraq was to train that country's new police and military forces.

Getting used to danger

Taylor, 42, of Waterloo, Seneca County, went to Iraq in September 2004 and returned in September 2005. "If it wasn't for my family, I would have stayed longer," says Taylor, who has a daughter, 20, and son, 16, as well as a stepson who is now in the Active Guard Reserve. He also served in Iraq. A native of Geneva, Taylor enlisted in the Army in 1982, served 4 years and then joined the reserves.

She went to Iraq as a video technician, but her duties expanded after getting there. Essentially, she helped put together computer systems for the Iraqi units, and she installed radio systems. In addition, she taught the Iraqis how to use these communications links. Taylor's units were always in danger.

"No place is safe over there," she says. "You have to be on your guard, but you get used to it."

Despite the danger, Taylor found the work and the experience fulfilling.

"There was a feeling you are needed," she says.

For one thing, she and others were able to help Iraqi civilians, especially the children.

"People in the U.S. would send us care packages," Taylor says. "We would take them and give them to the Iraqi kids — kids who were roaming around in a war zone, no shoes on their feet."

Making strides

Maj. Matt Jones of Eden in Erie County was in Iraq from October 2004 to September 2005. He had been in the Marines from 1988 to 1996, serving in the first Gulf War and in Somalia.

After the Marines, he went to law school and served as a prosecutor in Vermont. While in the Vermont Guard, he served in Afghanistan. After he and his family moved to the Buffalo area, he joined the 98th Division.

In Iraq, Jones spent time in Fallujah, helping train Iraqi army members. It was dangerous on-the-job training.

"We trained them to deal with IEDs (improvised explosive devices) by dealing with IEDs. We taught them first aid by doing first aid."

Jones and the other reservists were always at risk.

"I figure 10 percent of the (Iraqis) wanted to kill you, 50 percent wanted you to live, 40 percent wanted to wait and see," he says.

The Iraqi army trainees were also at risk, he says. The insurgents would try to kill them and their families, doing anything they could to slow down the army's progress.

Nonetheless, while Jones was there, the Iraqi army unit he was helping train grew from 250 soldiers to more than 700 soldiers.

"They made huge strides," he says.

Jones is especially proud that he and the other reservists were accepted, not only by the Iraqi soldiers, but by the U.S. Army and Marine units there.

Don't sweat

Like Jones, Master Sgt. Alfred Tugaoen, 39, was in Iraq for almost a year, going in September 2004 and coming back in August 2005.

Stationed in Baghdad but often going elsewhere in the country, Tugaoen was charged with getting supplies to both the coalition forces and the Iraqi army and police force.

"We provided everything from tanks down to bullets and beans," he says.

Providing those supplies was dangerous, especially as the insurgent forces made more and more use of car bombs and IEDs.

To elude the enemy, Tugaoen and his troops had to keep changing the way they did things.

"You had to be fluid," he says. "If you're not, the insurgents will figure it out."

While he was there, Tugaoen saw Iraq change. He saw more cars in the streets, more satellite televisions in homes. He came away with admiration for the Iraqis who risked their lives by joining the army or serving as interpreters.

Tugaoen, who lives in Rochester, says that the hardest part of his time in Iraq was being away from his family. He and his wife, Aly, have two children, a daughter, Noelani, 3, and a son, Kekoa, 2. Tugaoen says the Iraq experience changed him.

"I have a book I used to read, *Don't Sweat the Small Stuff*," he says. "I haven't touched it since I got back because I don't sweat the small stuff anymore. I have a bigger perspective."

Acknowledgements

The voice of this book comes from the soldiers, staff and families of the 98th Division (Institutional Training). It bears their stamp of authenticity. They are the greatness of this division and of this country.

Notes of gratitude are in order for the following: to Mrs. Cynthia Fien and Mr. Don Montgomery of the G4 for their assistance in the procurement of the Apple laptop and media software and for their patience in the use of G4 computers for the production of this book; to the division PAO for use of its office space; finally, to all who contributed their expertise, words and photographs.

All articles, unless otherwise noted, were written by LTC Timothy J. Hansen.